Summer Triangle

Summer Triangle

a novel

Elizabeth Webster

atmosphere press

For Jordan, I love you beyond words.

(And I love words a lot.)

Part One

May

The Summer Triangle is not a constellation, but an asterism – an amalgamation of constellations easily recognizable to the naked eye. Composed of the stars Vega, Altair, and Deneb, the triangle has always heralded summer for the northern celestial hemisphere. It has been a guidepost for the lost, helping them to find their way; and a benchmark for the restless, reminding them each year of the fleeting sweetness of the summer season.

The stars of the Summer Triangle are among the most brilliant in our universe, but never shine so brightly as when they are together.

Chapter 1

In the soft, blue light of dusk, she reached for him. Grazing his bicep with her knuckles. Curling her toes around his heel. When she flattened her hand against his spine, he stiffened. She, too, went still.

It was like crossing a canyon, navigating the cold, mussed sheets between them. It took forgetting on her part. She had to ignore their shared reality: that he'd always been the one to initiate their intimacy. That, at some point in the last year, he'd stopped.

"Can't," he said, the word still heavy with sleep's sediment. He cleared his throat. "I want to, but I have to prep for a morning meeting."

In the darkness, her heart raced. She swallowed, retracting her limbs and coiling them into her body. She had no idea if this was normal. This arid space between them. This parched earth. Her cheeks burned, even though there was no one there to witness her embarrassment. They were all alone together.

"It's okay. I get it," she said. "I'm going for a run."

"Natalie."

But she'd already gathered her things and shut the bathroom door, her name fading into the ether like distant smoke.

She couldn't change her clothes in front of him. Not now.

When she walked back into the room, knotting her hair into a high ponytail, she found him on his phone. His fingers were flying. He might still be resting in their bed, but he was already long gone.

"Harris," she whispered. He grunted, waiting, but she could only sigh.

Watching him, her body vibrated with a force she couldn't name. She gnawed at her lower lip and took long strides to the door. At the screech of its hinge, she turned back. His face shone like a beacon, illuminated by his phone's harsh, blue light.

Suddenly, she itched everywhere. Natalie had to run.

She'd always found it easier to love a house than a man. Lust faded. Open-mouthed kisses, tongues tussling, would dry to brittle pecks. Roving hands would someday slow, clinging instead to an embrace as warm and known as a threadbare blanket. Skin would loosen. Grey hairs would pop. Someday, if they were lucky, they'd fall back on their friendship.

Someday, if we're lucky.

As she charged up the hill toward her house, Natalie swatted these thoughts away with the gnats around her face. She spotted her home and her breath hitched.

After all these years, she was still into it.

Natalie always came upon her home like it was the first time. She still craned her neck to catch a glimpse of its stony façade behind a towering oak tree. Nearing the end of her run, Natalie hunched her shoulders. Her breath caught, ragged and hot. When she wanted to stop, to rest and breathe, Natalie spotted a familiar rooftop dormer winking at her. The house raised her up and kept her going, just as it had done when they'd first met over a decade ago.

Her belly had been swollen with a nameless child, but she could see his story unfurl in this place. It would become her sanctuary, her castle of stone and ivory columns. If she squinted now, Natalie could see a whisper of lamplight, incandescent from the downstairs study. The rest of the house slept undisturbed, collecting shadows.

She still could hardly believe she'd come home.

Natalie hadn't always been an early riser. As a child, tossing aside sheets had been like tensing for a blow. She would tiptoe downstairs, nimble as a dancer, never knowing what kind of chaos awaited her. Wrinkled beer cans. Wine glasses stamped with lipstick. With a deep, nearly-adult sigh, she would clean up after them, trailing a black trash bag like a comet's blazing tail. She never worked quietly. She didn't have to. Natalie had learned long ago that her parents' sleep was different than hers; theirs was a thick, heavy thing that encircled them like a caul. Nevertheless, her spine wouldn't relax until they both woke up, wincing, as though the day's waiting hours were nothing more than a load to be borne.

It wasn't until college, when an early class forced her to rouse warily once again, that the sunrise caught her by surprise. As darkness gave way to dawn, stone buildings had glowed with painterly light. Gardens had twinkled, pebbled with dew. She'd walked down tidy pathways, sheltering beneath trees that shook rain in the brisk breeze.

Natalie had decided then to never miss a morning. They were yet another thing that could be made beautiful again, now that they belonged to her.

Still, as she sipped fragrant air, surrounded by blushing peonies and hanging wisteria, Natalie sighed. Even here, she could hear her parents screaming. His flattened hand cracking hard against her cheek. Her sweet voice and foul mouth ricocheting through thin walls. She might have belonged to other people now, someone's wife and someone's mother, but Natalie often wondered how long it would take for their fingers to uncurl from the nape of her neck.

She exhaled deeply then, as if she could blow them away.

As Natalie opened the front door, the alarm chimed. She wiped the sweat from her brow and poked her head into the study on her left. Harris, a phone tucked between his ear and shoulder, stood with his back to her. Natalie smiled halfway. The sight of him now – his mesh shorts and white undershirt and unkempt hair – was all hers. But her stomach dropped, too, watching him.

He'd heard her return, but he hadn't acknowledged her. She hurried away.

Natalie tiptoed past her boys' rooms, kicked off her shoes, and stripped fast. As she flung her sweatshirt into the hamper, Natalie stopped short. She ignored the picture by her closet most days of the year. Yet now, on the cusp of summer, Natalie stole a second look.

Conjured by an assured hand, the watercolor showed two girls asleep in profile on the beach. The artist required something of its viewer. One had to lean in, to squint, to see the peak of pigment (green and blue) smudged between the girls' eyelids. They were not asleep, nor were they awake. They were still. While waves curdled in the ocean and sea oats bucked around them, they gave the piece its peace.

Natalie, having studied the painting countless times, believed them to be waiting.

Briefly, Natalie indulged herself, willing a regression back to a time when summer had meant a small cottage in Rehoboth. She could still feel her bare feet curling on a garden pathway laden with cracked shells, flutters carousing in her belly at summer's beginning. Their cottage was small. Its kitchen was rundown. Its bathrooms were cramped. But all Natalie could see in her mind's eye were its yellow walls dotted with her mother's watercolors. She remembered its wooden beams, buttressing a ceiling that loomed cathedral-like to a child her size. While her father grumbled about the bridge traffic and the coastal highway traffic and the tourists (of which they most certainly were but never would've admitted), her mother, Annabel, would circle the house, frenzied with early-summer giddiness, and open every window to *better breathe in the sea air.*

"A reporter called. The band is going on a reunion tour." Harris's voice startled her. She blushed like someone who'd been caught.

"Really. Well, I'm not sure how they can 'reunite' with someone missing."

"In any case, I deleted the message. Just wanted to let you know."

"We need to get rid of our landline. I'm so over these journalists."

"Okay, we can do that," he said, pausing for a beat. "I don't know how many times I've offered to take you back there.

She followed his gaze back to the artwork and forced a shrug. "It's a beach. If we've been to one beach, we've been to them all."

"It's you. It's your history. Our children should know it better."

He took her arms in his hands, using his thumbs to caress the soft skin inside her elbows. When Natalie jerked away, Harris sighed.

"Spoken like a grandson of the Mayflower," Natalie whispered. "You have no idea how lucky you are to be proud of where you come from."

After she pulled the bathroom door shut and braced her shoulders against it, Natalie could hear Harris breathing on the other side. Tears burned where they pooled in her eyes.

Not for the first time, Natalie wondered why she couldn't let him book a room. Harris was right. Or, at least, the handful of therapists that she'd seen and subsequently dumped had all agreed with him. They'd all spoken of closure. There had been vague, saccharine references to sand in her toes. Her most metaphysical therapist had talked often about the "healing" powers of saltwater and sea air. As though childhood trauma was eczema. As though every open wound can be mended by simply circling back to the point of puncture.

While she turned on the shower, Natalie willed herself to splice together snapshots of happier memories. Maybe Natalie needed to edit, to curate a more sentimental home movie.

Certainly, Natalie had collected treasured moments. She'd sprinted with shorts sagging full of seashells. She'd swum in cold water, too impatient to wait for it to warm. She'd floated in the calm space beyond the crashing waves. More than anything, Natalie had cultivated one of the great relationships of her life there. Eliana had been more of a draw than tide pools after thunderstorms, than wriggling sand crabs in the palm, than beachcombing for loose change. Eliana was the only bit of that place that Natalie had pocketed. And, unlike the murky mid-Atlantic Ocean, Natalie had never left Eliana behind.

Because try as she might, when she closed her eyes intending to picture her time there, Natalie only saw their beach cottage. A small house on a quiet street that they had given lungs.

There were too many moments that she preferred to forget. A smashed painting. A spanking that had burned for days. He'd thrown her computer against the wall, back when computers were heavy missiles that could leave wallpapered bedrooms pocked with craters. And there had been countless ear-splitting parties. As she waited for the music to die, Natalie had curled into his velvet-lined guitar case, comforted by his smell even as she hid from him.

The memories all blurred together, their colors bleeding. They faded deep into her grey matter. Until, sharply and unexpectedly, they sparked. Natalie pressed her forehead to the tile, allowed the water to bead on the small of her back, and remembered.

One day, Eliana had shaken her awake from a nap. At high tide, the waves were climbing fast, slithering over packed sand and yesterday's footprints. Eliana was giggling, shrieking that they had to move or they would get wet. Natalie hadn't responded. In the shade of the umbrella, Natalie had thought it was dark. She'd awakened with her heart pounding, her mouth dry. She'd thought that she was running late, that he would be waiting for her. Her teeth chattered. Her hands curled to claws. She couldn't move. At some point, Eliana had dropped to her knees and held Natalie's hands, massaging her tight, curved fingers.

"Just get through it," Eliana whispered. "Just get out."

Natalie blushed deeply when she realized that her friend *knew*. That Eliana had always known about the abuse. At that moment, in that head rush of humiliation, Natalie made herself The Promise: as soon as she got out, she would never go back. Never again.

Natalie was still young enough then that 'never' was a simple construct, and all of its infinite underpinnings could be swept aside for something as clean as a dead-end. She didn't know then that someday well-meaning professionals, their offices papered over with gilded degrees, would instruct her to return. To let go of a promise that she had never vocalized in order to get on with her life. She was fourteen, then. She only knew that there were four more years until adulthood. It would be as simple as surviving a rip tide.

When Natalie was a child, Annabel had been the one who taught her how to swim parallel to the shore should Natalie ever be swept out to sea. Each stroke a trick of the mind. Each flutter-kick an illusion of control: that it would all be over soon.

And when you feel the ocean's grip loosening around you, turn toward the shore. Come back to me. I'll be waiting there for you.

Natalie descended the stairs, rushing toward voices that rose and fell like a tidal swell. She found Aaron and Everett eating breakfast at the island, while Harris poured coffee into a travel mug. Everett pouted, his Mickey Mouse plate untouched.

Embracing him from behind, Natalie rested her chin on his head. "What's wrong, Bug? You don't like your breakfast?"

"He had an accident," Aaron offered, his eyes twinkling. "He put his sheets in the hamper and tried to cover it up. Like the time he was sniffing scented markers and his nose turned blue. Dude, it's always going to stay blue."

"I don't like you, Aaron," Everett said, his lips wobbling.

"Everett, your brother had accidents too when he was your age," Natalie said, bending to touch her forehead to his. "We all make mistakes. They just take a different shape as we grow."

"Like what?" Aaron asked.

"Like last week's math test," Harris countered. "And me – a minute ago when I picked up your mom's phone instead of my own. Natalie, you need to get a new case."

"Why? I like black. Everything else looks vaguely teenage to me."

"Because the last time I accidentally took your phone to work, I was inundated all day with questions about textiles imported from Mexico."

"Yes. It would've been helpful if you hadn't actually tried to answer them."

Natalie tried to wink at Harris, but he stared at his phone. Looking away from him, Natalie smiled through gritted teeth. She yanked her own phone from her pocket and locked her wet eyes on its bright face. Without a word, she strode from the kitchen. Natalie sank onto the couch in the office, straightening her spine and affecting a frown.

She took the time to arrange herself.

Natalie had promised herself five minutes. She'd only meant to give away five minutes to other people's Instagram squares and reels and stories. But she was no passive actor to the algorithm's whims this morning. Instead, her fingertips moved fast: to avoid her own feed and to ignore her friends' stories and to search for his name. Natalie didn't follow him, but his page was public. She flicked through the images under his tiny face.

His world bloomed; his squares were saturated with bright colors. She narrowed her eyes, as though peering through a peephole. The lip of a surfboard over pewter-toned water. Steam breathing from a coffee mug at a café table. Countless paintings, some thick with oil paint and others loose with watercolor. His white teeth framed by his full lips—

"Why are you hiding in here?"

Natalie flinched. "Sorry – work couldn't wait."

"Okay. Look. I was thinking. We should go to dinner," Harris said. "Tomorrow night."

"A date on a Thursday evening? That's living dangerously."

"I think we should, you know, touch base. Alone."

Natalie arched an eyebrow. "Sounds good to me. I'll see about a sitter."

"We don't need a sitter," Aaron called out from the mudroom, his feet squeaking against a beadboard locker. "I'm twelve – I can handle it!"

"You're still a tween," Natalie said. "It's not happening."

"Twelve going on sixteen," Harris muttered.

For a brief pocket of time, saturated with the cut-glass lilt of birdsong through an open window, their eyes met. His brown eyes could be counted upon. She knew them better than she knew her own face. But the depth of that hold, his humor-filled eyes boring into hers, felt unaccountably rare. Involuntarily, her fingers tightened into fists, clutching at something.

"What?" Harris asked, missing nothing. "What is it?"

She glanced away, fumbling. "I wish the boys were kinder to each other."

Harris rolled his eyes. "They're fine. Nothing's ever good enough for you, Natalie."

She startled, as an infant will jerk awake from sleep. "What did you say?"

Harris pecked a kiss on her cheek. "Remember the sitter, Nat. We're running late."

Her arm reached out to skim his broad back, but Harris

gave no indication of having felt her touch. Aaron tumbled into the front hall, a torrent of gangly arms and legs rushing for an exit. Natalie blocked his path, kissed his head, and smoothed a stray hair that wanted to curl. Aaron rolled his eyes, but somehow remained right there.

And there it was, raw and unreachable, on display in those wide brown eyes: that amorphous vulnerability that he hadn't shared with her, that he might never share with her. She could only dig around, as archaeologists will patiently brush dirt from bone and wait for the earth to yield. She could only trust that someday Aaron would tell her what was bothering him.

"Running late," Harris said, sighing.

She leaned in when Aaron reached for her, bowing low into his embrace. Harris held her in a side hug, his hip buffeting hers. And as quickly as they had come together, they pulled apart. She watched them rush down the porch steps, casting long shadows in the morning sun.

In the homes that Natalie designed, there were practical spaces right by the threshold. There were hooks for catching keys, baskets for shoes, and stands for umbrellas. There was always a quiet space, on the precipice between home and everything else, to cast a burden down. In Natalie's own home, she simply touched the wall where she knew the support beam to be. It was there, beneath layers of insulation, drywall, and sparkling ecru paint that she anchored herself to a still point. The keystone of her kingdom.

Suddenly, her eyelashes fluttered open. Natalie could see the day's bullet points blinking in the middle distance. She slid her phone into her back pocket.

First and foremost, Natalie would call the sitter.

Chapter 2

"Well, if you're this stressed about it, why not have it catered?"

Eliana rolled her eyes. "Because it's a playdate, Josh. I'm hosting a playdate for a bunch of three-year-old girls on a Tuesday. Even a Los Angeles caterer would laugh at me."

"I'm sure that it's been done," Josh said. "You're making an edible garden out of mashed-up Oreos. When we were kids, a dirt pie was actually made out of dirt, and we still ate it. I turned out fine."

"When we were kids, my mother opened the door to let us play and we didn't come home until dinner. But they're called free-range children now. And we'd be arrested for it."

"The twins are in preschool, Eliana. Can't they leave their friends there?"

"No. They've already been excluded from two birthday parties because I took your laissez-faire approach to parenting. If I make friends, they have friends. It's that simple."

"They're twins," Josh said, raking his fingers through his hair. "They were born with a buddy. Can't they just exclude everyone else?"

"Your hand is steadier than mine. Are you going to help me pipe a yogurt flower onto this pretzel stick or not?"

Josh sighed. "Give it here."

Eliana suppressed a grin as she watched him work. He was no different on their marble island than he'd been studying against a cement wall in college. His brow furrowed. His tongue poked out from the corner of his mouth. He hummed a Grateful Dead song. Impulsively, she kissed the rough underside of his chin.

"Methinks the lady likes my work," he said.

"Do you think I'm pathetic? Caring so much about so little?"

Josh stopped working. His pale eyes locked onto hers. They were a matched set: black hair, light eyes, dark skin, and lanky limbs. When she met him, she had said they could never date. What would people think? That they were siblings. Cousins. Narcissists. It was Josh who had said that maybe they mirrored each other for a reason. Maybe they'd been *designed* alike. He'd said this while swigging cheap beer in some forgotten classmate's basement, right before he had fit his mouth over hers. He had come up for air, blushing.

Maybe, he'd said, *the universe made it easy for us to find each other.*

She'd rolled her eyes and suppressed a grin. It was a line. The hook of a song. Bad poetry. But it was all theirs, and from that point forward, she had wanted it to be true.

They looked like a matched set, except for one subtle difference: Josh was white. On standardized tests, he'd always known which box to check, whereas Eliana existed in a foggy hinterland. She felt the pull between two poles that he would never know, each as potent as the primacy of her two parents. Per her father's instructions, however, she checked "Caucasian" every time, cowering to his will beneath bright, fluorescent lighting.

"What could be bigger than those two little girls?"

Eliana exhaled. "You always know what to say."

"I don't know about that. I've choked during a lot of pitches. But I did stay up late to erect a beauty salon for a certain cherubic duo's playdate, so I'd say I'm whipped as well."

"Looks like you'd do anything for your girls."

"I *would* do anything, including inviting them to join me to spend the summer in the south of France. From my end, it sounds like a slam-dunk of an ask. And yet."

"I'm sure I'll cave eventually," Eliana said, stiffening.

"I don't understand why you don't want to come."

"Because last summer in Morocco was tough on me."

"It was tough on you to lounge by the pool, eat exotic food, and go off on excursions?"

"Living in a hotel with two small children isn't easy," Eliana said, folding her arms across her chest. "We barely saw you. When we did see you, you were surrounded by other people. The girls didn't eat the food. The trip killed their nap schedule."

"Their nap schedule? Would you listen to yourself?"

"When you're a mom of twin toddlers, a nap is all you have. Besides, I've never felt comfortable at dinners with the cast and crew. People are always asking me how we met."

"Most people love to talk about how they met."

Eliana rolled her eyes. "They're trying to determine whether we were a couple before you became a successful producer. They want to know that I stood by you during the ramen years."

"I think you're projecting some insecurities onto them."

"Maybe. Alternatively, maybe they can't imagine a genuine relationship because they're so accustomed to using people for their own gain."

Josh whistled. He set the piping bag back down on the island. He circled it slowly, stood behind Eliana, and wrapped his arms around her long, lean frame.

Eliana spoke hoarsely. "I'm not sure how much longer I can be this nomad with you. It's harder with the children. *We* can't follow you as easily as *I* once did."

"If you don't want to go, you don't have to go," Josh said, as he pressed his mouth against the crown of her head. "But we have to remember that we're blessed."

Eliana furrowed her brow. "You think I'm being ungrateful."

"I just think we both have to remember it: through some twist of fate, some mixture of fate and work and privilege, we've gotten lucky—"

"And where does that leave me, exactly? Locked into a smile for life?"

Josh held up a hand. "I didn't mean—"

"I heard what you said. If we have everything, I can't want for anything," Eliana snapped, already pivoting away from him. "But I disagree. Because it's not enough."

She kicked up the covers. Curled her toes. Moaned aloud. While writhing in sheets drenched with perspiration, her hands coiled to fists. Her eyelids cracked open right when she broke into a run, horizontally. She fled.

Allegra then sat straight up in bed, her chest heaving and her legs cramping.

From the blinding edge of blackout curtains, golden light pulsed into her bedroom. Her eyes, pupils dilating and blinking wildly, parsed every shadow. As her teeth began to chatter, she cast the covers aside. She raced around the room and checked the locks on each window. She rushed to case the perimeter of her entire apartment. She checked under the beds. She turned over stacked boxes. When she yanked open closet doors, she held her breath each time, readying herself to be startled.

Minutes later, she finally stood still.

"Just a dream," Allegra muttered, as she climbed onto the kitchen island.

There, she settled in to make coffee and a cigarette for breakfast.

Natalie arrived at the job site ten minutes late. The flooring company Natalie had hired blocked the driveway with two large vans. She winced as she peeled off the gravel to park in the grass. Her heels poked holes in the lawn while she sprinted to the front door of a massive Georgian-style brick mansion. On the front porch, Natalie took only a minute to smooth stray hairs around her face before opening the door.

"You're late."

A husky voice echoed from the library. Natalie pivoted, as though summoned.

"You always say that, but today you're right about it. I'm sorry, Birdie. At least the flooring company was on time. What do you think?" Natalie asked. Her green eyes met Birdie Wellington's wry smile.

"Very nice. Wide planks. Ash. It's exactly as we discussed."

"Excellent. It should be stained tomorrow. The other workers are clearing out the old tile in the sunroom – my apologies for the noise."

"It's all right on schedule," Birdie said, while she played with her pearls. "I did, however, wish to discuss the rest of the renovation with you."

"Okay. Which part?"

"This room. I'd like it to be more masculine."

Natalie arched an eyebrow as her eyes swept over the library. Sunlight splattered across walls paneled in mahogany, pooling on shelves filled with vintage books. On the side table next to a leather couch, a replica of an eighteenth-century skipjack rested beside a wooden mallard duck. On the weighty desk behind her, a row of pipes that had belonged to Birdie's late husband stood sentry. The air between them still held the cloying sweetness of his tobacco.

"I'm not sure I understand. I can't imagine a room more classically masculine than this one."

"Perhaps I need to be clearer, then. I'd like it to look more modern. I'd like clean lines and minimal shapes. Blonde wood. You've heard of Scandinavian design?"

Natalie blinked. "Yes."

"And yet you seem caught off guard?"

"This is just such a departure from our initial meeting, where you said that you wanted the library left untouched. You stressed classicism and symmetry. Paint colors from Colonial Williamsburg. Delftware," Natalie said, killing a sigh. "And wicker. So much wicker."

"You won't do it."

"Of course, I'll do it. It's your home. I only want to keep it cohesive with our design."

"I don't see the problem. You're a designer. *Design* a way to make it fluid."

Natalie tried to smile. "It might be helpful if you would tell me who I'm designing the room for?"

"I beg your pardon?"

"Will it be an office for one of your sons home from college? You mentioned someone young? If I were to talk to that person, I might be able to refine exactly what—"

"I think we're done here."

"Excuse me?"

"The contractors are nearly finished implementing your designs, so your services are no longer needed. If there's any publicity following the completion of this renovation, we'll certainly give you credit."

"We?"

"Me and the designer whom I will be hiring to finish the remaining rooms."

"You're firing me?" Natalie asked, her voice suddenly shrill.

Birdie smiled. "Firing is an ugly word for those lacking in imagination. You and I have history now, Natalie. We're *friends*. We simply lack a meeting of the minds on this issue."

"I see."

"You know my home better than I do at this point. I trust that you can see yourself out?"

Without awaiting a response, Birdie yanked both French doors open to exit the room. Natalie hurriedly gathered her things. She exited through the kitchen and circled around the house, tripping and falling like a rookie burglar.

"Rick?"

Rick, a master stonemason, strode over to where Natalie stood beneath an ivy trellis.

"I have to leave early."

"Well, that's fine by me. We're all set here. Is there a problem?"

"Birdie let me go," she said, clutching her stomach.

His eyes narrowed. "Want me to follow you out in protest? You don't deserve that."

"No, I just need to go home. I'll be fine."

"Take as long as you need with the exit details, and I'm here if you need me."

"Thank you. I appreciate that."

"And hey, Nat – how come you never told me about your dad?"

Natalie blanched. "My *dad*?"

"We're buds, and you *know* I'm a music junkie," Rick said, the corners of his eyes crinkling. "His songs were the soundtrack of my high school years. I had no idea that *you* were *his*. I worshiped him. Man, his voice and his style and the way he could riff—"

"I have to go now."

"Nat, hold up – wait!"

But she was running, stumbling in her effort to flee. Her fingers were bound in tulip-tight fists. Natalie fought the sensation of falling, even while running fast. When she tripped slightly over a stick, she cut her ankle but barely felt it. By the time she reached her car, Natalie was coated in perspiration. She went through the motions of fixing herself: unlocking the car, fumbling in the glove compartment for a first aid kit, and cleaning her narrow wound with Bactine. It was the sterile scent that undid her, yanking her back in time like she'd been pulled under water.

"Hold still. You'll feel better soon."

"Do I have to go to the hospital?"

"No, no hospitals," her mother said, as Natalie's hot tears fell with the cool Bactine on her neck. Her father had stamped cigarettes out on her skin. The sticky wounds had bubbled to blisters fast. *"Next time, when Daddy comes at me, please let him come. Don't come between us, okay?"*

"Okay," she said, but a halting whisper escaped her pursed lips. *"Not okay."*

"Oh, Natalie, you know Daddy loves you very much. He's so sorry he hurt you. I think he might even write you a song."

As though trying to clear water from her ears, Natalie shook her head. She tried to rouse herself and root herself to where she was. Her disappearing act was called *dissociation*, the sensation of being both present and far away. Natalie had learned the word from therapy in her first attempt to fix herself. She'd been detaching this way since she was a child. She just hadn't had a name for it. Still, it had been cold comfort when the gentleman with the thick mustache had called it a *textbook response*. He had said that he would heal her.

She had bolted before he had a chance, likely another learned psychological response.

Today, in that same stretch of numbed *derealization*, Natalie somehow returned home. She sat for a long time on her front porch, watching the oak tree craft shadow-patterns on the bluestone driveway. She was home with nothing to do and nowhere to be, all before lunch. Right then, Natalie could've done anything. Right then, she didn't need to work, to be a wife or a mother. Her only obligation for a few hours was to herself. For a time, she was free.

She blinked wildly at the thought. It was paralyzing.

Chapter 3

Eliana's hands shook as she carried the tray from the kitchen. Above the thrumming of her heart, Eliana could hear their voices, high and chirpy, wafting toward her with their expensive perfume. There was too much space between her and the rest of them. Because the ceilings were so high and the floors were so barren, the acoustics were too good. They were talking about her, and she could hear every word.

"... always trying so hard."

"I think these larger homes sacrifice so much in character. It's too much square footage."

"My problem is that it's *so cold* – as if everyone is trying to live in an art gallery."

Eliana hid to the side of the expansive opening of her living room. As her smile wavered, she waited for them to finish. Across the hall, she noticed a delicate watercolor of a beach scene. Eliana passed the painting every morning as she ushered her girls out the door. She passed it so often she'd forgotten to notice it. But now, her eyes locked on the two girls staring out at the slate-grey Atlantic water, nearly hidden in the dunes and fog. Her spine eased. Her breath came steady once more.

"Don't be rude," Miriam hissed. "We're guests in her home. We can unpack why you both might be so jealous of her later. Remember, ladies: it's a playdate, and it isn't ours."

Eliana took the thick silence that followed as her cue. She

plastered a smile onto her face and walked into the room before she could talk herself out of it.

Miriam smiled. "Eliana, we were talking about how much we love your home."

"That's so sweet of you! My childhood friend, Natalie Blackburn, basically designed the whole house. I don't know how she did it – it feels exactly like us, but I didn't pick out a thing."

"Your childhood friend ..." Melissa murmured, her voice falling away. "Tell me, Eliana: what are you?"

"What *am* I?" Eliana asked. Her throat grew parched as she took a seat.

"I think she's trying to ask where you're *from*," Jen added.

"And you thought you were the translator, Eliana," Miriam said, rolling her eyes.

"I grew up all over the place, but I'm American."

"American," Melissa repeated.

"Yes. Just like you," Eliana said, her lips puckering.

"She's asking because you have that whole exotic look," Jen said. "As does your family. Well. Except for Lola. But still, you're all gorgeous."

"Lola doesn't look like you or Josh. She's so fair. How is that?" Melissa asked.

"Recessive genes, I guess," Eliana said.

"Twins are everywhere these days," Jen said. "Are yours natural?"

"As opposed to what? Shrink-wrapped?" Miriam countered before turning toward Melissa. "Look, Melissa: she found you some herbal tea."

"Oh, fantastic," Melissa said, as she reached for a cup. "I don't mean to be a headache. Those lattes you made smelled amazing, but I'm off caffeine. And I'm sorry to have to forgo the dirt cups as well. If it's not organic, Tessie can't have it. We're a very non-GMO family."

As Eliana lowered the tray to the ottoman, she cast a side-long glance at the dirty cups, untouched by the fireplace. Shriveled gummy worms sat in pools of melted yogurt and crushed Oreo. Eliana would've laughed, but her throat ached. Again, she tried to smile.

Miriam cleared her throat. "The irony is that Melissa will go back to coffee whenever she gets pregnant again, primarily because the doctor will tell her to cut down. Our girl has a contrarian streak to her."

"Yes, well, that ship has sailed. I have two kids, one of each, so I'll be headed back to work as soon as we can find a new nanny. What about you, Eliana? Do you miss your old job?"

Eliana tucked a wayward hair behind her ear. "Sometimes, but I'm much happier than I ever thought I would be watching the girls grow up this way."

Miriam nodded. "Me too. But then, my best friend couldn't wait to get back to work. You can't know how you'll feel about motherhood until you're in its trenches."

"As long as you can look back without regrets," Jen said. "That's the important thing."

Eliana paused. "I think that's kind of impossible, though. I was teaching Silvia about choices at a bakery: a cookie or a cupcake. She burst into tears. It was like the idea that there was this other thing that would be left behind – it was too much for her. It's the same for me. There will always be the life you could've lived, and its shadow taunts you sometimes."

"I'm surprised that the wife of Josh Rollins – throwing out names like 'Natalie Blackburn' – would have anything to complain about," Melissa said, slurping her tea.

"That's not what she meant," Miriam said.

"That's not what I meant at all," Eliana said quickly. "I'm very grateful for my life. It's more than anything I could've imagined, but it's impossible to try to have everything at one time. Realizing one dream means losing another. That's all."

Melissa smiled tightly, her lips thinning along wet teeth.

"There's nothing quite like the wisdom of a woman who doesn't have to work."

"Melissa!"

Miriam nearly shouted her name. Beside her, Eliana sank back into the couch. Jen grinned while her eyes darted between the other women, at once an enthralled audience. Melissa merely folded her arms across her chest. She waited.

Suddenly, a girl unleashed a high-pitched screech. Melissa's teacup crashed to the floor, smashing into sharp confetti pieces of chinoiserie porcelain. The women immediately raced out of the room and into the hallway. They crashed into each other as they stopped short at the foot of the stairs. Eliana's hand flew to her mouth.

They stood still, gaping at the vision they found.

Melissa's daughter, Tessie, shook with tears at the top of the stairs. Tessie's long blonde curls were gone. Her head was now encircled with matted tufts of wet hair, an uneven bowl cut. Behind her, Eliana's daughter, Silvia, dangled one ringlet from her fist. Her other daughter, Lola, held the scissors.

"It's only hair," Miriam said, touching Melissa's arm. "It'll grow back."

"Only hair?!" Melissa turned on her heel, narrowing her eyes at the lot of them. "What did I tell you when we pulled into the driveway of this ridiculous pile, Miriam? A big house is a shell for a small soul."

Josh collapsed into laughter over a box of cold Chinese food and promptly dropped his chopsticks onto the kitchen island. "What does that even mean?"

"It sounds like Rumi. Do you think it's Rumi?"

"I think it's a weak fortune cookie."

Eliana sighed. Her eyes drifted outside, to the cloudless

blue sky and the palm trees and the peach roses in full bloom. Clear pool water rippled, barely touched by a breeze.

"Eliana, I feel like you're missing the humor in all of this. You wanted them to play 'hair salon,' and our girls did."

Eliana narrowed her eyes. "How could you have left the scissors there?"

"An innocent mistake," Josh said, his hands splayed. "Personally, I find packaging a modern-day scourge."

"You should have seen Silvia with Tessie's hair in her little fist – it looked like a dead animal. Like she'd actually killed something. And then there's Lola – in case there was any doubt as to their complicity, still holding the scissors. I was mortified."

Josh doubled over in laughter again, wiping tears from his eyes. "I hope they never actually try to break the law. They'll have to confess upfront."

"And poor Tessie looked like a monk. I've fallen all over myself apologizing. Text messages. Voicemails. I'm having flowers delivered. She won't respond."

Josh shrugged. "What's the worst that could happen? Melissa never speaks to you again? I've met her. It's no great loss."

"She's so friendly with everyone at the Academy, whereas I've gotten off on the wrong foot there now before I've even begun."

"They're *three*, Ellie. And look, I was ready to write them off when they wouldn't taste my yogurt flowers, you weren't looking forward to the playdate anyway, and the girls are napping peacefully right now. All is right in our world, so why are you so upset?"

Eliana paused. "I felt like I was being dissected. My race. Our children. They practically interrogated me about when I would go back to work."

"I'm sorry they treated you like that. But just because they asked a question doesn't entitle them to an answer. You used to know that."

Eliana gnawed at her lower lip while she palmed the baby monitor. She raised the volume incrementally and heard someone snoring, someone breathing. Were there a problem, a bad dream or a fevered awakening, Eliana could reach them in seconds. In no time at all, she could be with them, right there, her heartbeat to either of theirs. She could rock them back to sleep, her breath and theirs finding their own delicate percussion until one exhalation couldn't be unspooled from the others.

"I never feel badly about my life until I talk to other people."

"Then maybe those people shouldn't be your people."

"I'm not like you. I always think of the right thing to say long after the person's gone."

Right then, Josh leaned over his take-out detritus, cupped her face in his hands, and kissed her. He pressed his forehead to hers.

"I love that you don't need the last word, Eliana. I've always loved that about you."

"You have to catch your flight," she whispered.

"I do have to catch my flight. Still, thanks for the lunch date."

"I know how you love it when I cook for you."

He tossed back his head and laughed. His laughter had a texture to it, as sleek and warm as polished mahogany. Eliana grinned in spite of her foul mood. She followed him into the hallway. As he gathered up his luggage, her gaze latched again onto the painting on the wall.

It could've so easily been a peaceful seaside scene had the sky been blue, had the sea been calm. The two little girls could've been bold and free had they faced the artist directly, had they been given the chance to move. Instead, they were nearly apparitions, as ephemeral as fog. Eliana loved the painting because it asked questions without providing answers. Was the fog blanketing them or suffocating them? Had the storm passed or was it still out there, roiling just beyond the horizon line? She'd been there, and she couldn't even remember. Eliana had had no idea that she was being watched, that she should have been making a memory.

"I want to go back to Rehoboth."

Josh stopped. The whites of his eyes flashed.

"What?"

"The girls and I could spend the summer in Delaware. You could meet us there."

"I'm filming a movie in the south of France, and you want to go to Delaware?"

"I know it's an unusual choice."

"It's the first time anyone in recorded history has made that choice."

"Josh, I spent every summer of my childhood there and we've never taken the girls. I haven't been back since that last summer before we graduated college."

Josh sighed while he rubbed his palm across his face. "She'll never meet you there, Eliana. She's said as much a thousand times."

"That's not what this is about."

"That's *exactly* what this is about. You're lonely."

"I'm not trying to fill a void," Eliana snapped, her cheeks flushing with rich color. "I want our girls to know my history. I want them to understand where they come from."

"Without me."

"That's not what I meant."

Josh cast a glance out the window. "You hardly even speak to her anymore."

"This isn't about *her*—"

"Yes, it is, and I'm not going to reconfigure an entire production schedule around Natalie Blackburn's summer plans."

"Around me, you mean. You're unwilling to be inconvenienced by me. To hop the flight. To suffer the jet lag. I spend every summer following you to an exotic location. Getting our papers in order. Booking our shots. Packing our bags. I want to make the choice this time."

"And I want to spend the summer with my family," Josh

said firmly, as the muscles in his jaw worked. "How can she possibly be your best friend if you rarely communicate anymore?"

"She's not someone I see every day—"

"Or even every year."

"But she knows me better than I know myself. If anything were to happen, she'd be here."

"Maybe."

"Definitely. Remember how she dropped everything when the twins were born? I was in early labor with a mask on during the pandemic, and she was the first one I wanted to speak to afterward. Because she would've been there with me had it been allowed. As soon as they opened air travel again, she moved in for three weeks."

Josh sighed, pinching the bridge of his nose. "Okay, so she's been there for the milestones, but what about real life? Those women may have put a foot wrong today, but that's what people do. They say the wrong thing and they screw up and they offer a clumsy apology, or they chicken out. But at least they're more real than Natalie—"

"*They're* more real than my best friend? Are you insane?"

"No, I'm the one here. Every single day. I should matter more than your memories, and you're choosing her over me."

"That's not true! Don't you understand? You're my family, but she is, too."

"Natalie might be your family, but she sure as hell isn't mine."

Eliana flinched when the door slammed shut. Her lips broke open. He'd never left her before a flight without a kiss goodbye. She heard a car door slam and an engine roar to life.

With a sigh, Eliana looked toward the painting once more. There, above the horizon line, she noticed low-slung clouds streaked with a greenish tinge. Whitecaps clamored beneath, as though the sea was baring its teeth. There was movement, energy, unrest.

The storm was definitely coming, Eliana thought suddenly. All this time, it had been hovering just out of view.

Allegra ducked into her apartment building, shaking off the rain. She barely noticed that she was dry now, warm now, no longer wet. She waved off the gentleman who tried to hold the elevator for her and pushed open the door to the stairwell instead. Allegra took only a minute to grimace at the height of her climb. She lived on the fourteenth floor, but she couldn't lose this call. She took the steps two at a time. By the sixth floor, he'd paused to take a breath, and she stopped on the landing. She would fill every space he gave her with words.

"My only point is that August has always been our agreement, and I want August."

He chuckled. "Why are you so emotional? So quick to anger? You should work on your temperament. It's not maternal in the slightest."

"I'm not angry," Allegra said, forcing her voice to soften even as her hands shook. "We had an agreement, Etienne. I see the children for their full summer holiday. Your entire country shuts down in August. You have no excuse for keeping them from me."

"They are starting a new school and must return in time for orientation."

She began to grind her teeth. "Which brings me to my second point: I was not consulted as to their change of schools."

"Why would you be? I have full custody of them."

"They're still my children."

"And if you were a different kind of woman, if you had been a different kind of mother, perhaps they would still be yours."

At this, Allegra tore up the stairs, sprinting and muting him. She had heard this all before. Her lawyer advised her to take the long view, to avoid being baited at all costs. Her agent reminded her it was verbal abuse. Her few remaining friends tactfully pointed out an endless cycle of behavior. Everyone reminded her to focus on her children. As if she could ever, would ever, focus on anyone else. She was on the landing of the twelfth floor, sitting and sweating, when he finally stopped talking. She cut the bullshit. "Etienne, I *will* get the lawyers involved again. I want August."

"The same lawyers whom you paid so well to cower last time? How hopeful of you."

"Orientation starts a week earlier," she said, her eyes filling with tears. "Maybe we could compromise? They could return to Luxembourg two weeks early."

"There is a family gathering the first week of August."

"Well, you don't have our children that week."

There was a deep silence, as dark and still as a quarry, on the other end. Allegra pressed the phone to her ear, half-hoping – as she always did – that she'd lost him.

"I saw a picture of you in the magazines recently, smoking," he murmured. "You know that I cannot abide by smoking. Particularly by the woman meant to care for our children."

"I know. I'm trying to quit," Allegra said, blinking back tears. "But the press is seeking out negative images of me as a direct result of your smear campaign. You have to stop, Etienne. It's affecting my ability to work."

He laughed. "Work? You're a model. There was always going to be a shelf life. It isn't my fault if you've become unemployable."

"It *is* your fault if you're leaking false information to make me look bad. As you said, I'm the mother of your children—"

"And you want me to help you sustain the income necessary to take me to court?"

In the empty stairwell, Allegra went still. "That's what this is about," she whispered.

"Finally, we understand each other," Etienne said. "A compromise, then: you will return them two weeks early."

He hung up without waiting for her response. Tears spilled

from her eyes. The last two flights of stairs were torturous. She pulled herself up with her arms, her fingers, as the sobs she would not shed weighed heavily in her chest. When she reached her floor, she whimpered. Allegra turned the key into her apartment and sighed. She'd forgotten about her impending move. Her living room teemed with boxes stacked like tiny skyscrapers. Her hours of hard work, of wrapping breakables in newspaper and folding clothes, threatened to choke her now. She would be the only one who saw the emptiness of this lonely apartment, still so full of stuff.

She raised her chin even as she sank to her knees. She would do better. She would make a better life for them all. The house had had significant water damage, but she'd had it fixed. The yard was coated in crabgrass, but they could still play in it. Her table was already there, waiting for their first meal in their new home. Someday, her children would sit around it.

For now, though, it was her last night in the apartment where she'd rocked her babies to sleep. She fumbled in her purse, retrieved a pack of Marlboro Lights, and extracted the prettiest cigarette of the bunch. The rest, she tossed in the trash. She lit the cigarette, opened a window, and blew a smoke circle into the rain. In time, the lashing rain camouflaged the tears that streamed down her face. The spring rain fell as tepid as bathwater, warming her shivering limbs, making her clean.

Chapter 4

"I'm sorry. Forgive me for leaving that way. I'm an idiot."

Eliana smiled halfway. "You don't have to apologize. It was an impulsive request. I'm sorry for making you feel like I'm prioritizing my friendship over our marriage."

Her chest expanded as soon as she heard his long exhale.

"Ellie, I grew up with Natalie, too. I know she had a rough childhood—"

"You don't know the half of it. Really."

"I know her dad was an alcoholic. I know he had a bad temper and a terrible reputation. And if there's more, maybe it's time you trust me enough to tell me."

"They aren't my secrets to tell, Josh."

"We aren't kids anymore. It's not disloyalty to give your husband some context."

Eliana hesitated, her breath hitching. "There was ... physical abuse. There was chaos and trauma and addiction. All of that coupled with your standard rockstar narcissism."

"My God. All that time, she was ..." he said, his voice thickening. Seconds later, he cleared his throat. "But still. A hard childhood doesn't entitle her to an adult friendship where someone else does all the heavy lifting. I don't think she'll join you in Delaware if that's what's in her past – I wouldn't go back, either. But I do agree that it's your turn. You've spent the past five summers following me from one remote location to another. And I didn't even think about everything that's gone on with your dad – how close you would be to him in Delaware."

Eliana frowned. She hadn't thought much of her dad, either. She'd simply been overcome with yearning when she'd stared at the image of two little girls nearly lost to the dunes. She had seen herself as she was then, wanting nothing more than her best friend and her family close. There was only a longing to bequeath that rootedness to her girls. Eliana had wanted a memory for her daughters that resembled one of her own.

Her cheeks flushed with the realization that she hadn't thought of her father at all.

"You were right, though. I do miss Natalie. Maybe too much."

"And I know she misses you back," Josh said. "Wish she showed it better, though."

"I doubt she'll come. This is more for me. I feel like I've lost myself, and I thought something familiar might shake me awake."

"Say no more," Josh said. "We'll book a house tonight."

"We should sleep on this. It's a big decision."

"It isn't. It's a closer flight to France than if you were to remain in L.A. I have meetings I can take in New York. Besides, what's the point of acquiring a windfall at a young age if you can't occasionally, you know, spend it?"

Eliana smirked. "I can hear you twitching."

"I don't know what you mean."

"You still drive your Honda Accord."

"It gets good gas mileage."

"You broke out into hives when we closed on our house."

"Anyone would have. Our house should've come with a helicopter pad and a fleet of stallions for what we paid for it."

"I bet you're inwardly cursing them out on the tarmac right now."

"Well, that's true. I'm sitting here in a tricked-out Escalade waiting to hop onto a private plane and wondering why these smug bastards couldn't fly commercial."

Eliana laughed. Suddenly, the baby monitor flashed red on a nearby table and her arm jerked for it. She watched Lola, a flash of bright white silhouetted on night vision, stir in her bed. Lola rolled onto her side, her curls splayed like a halo across her pillow.

"But I wasn't angry about the cost," Josh said. "As it turns out, the only problem with marrying your high school sweetheart is that you skip some steps."

"Beg your pardon?"

"I've never known what it feels like to return to an empty hotel room. I've never eaten late-night meals with the crew without you by my side. I've certainly never had to use a translation app. You've always been my lucky charm. My talisman. My constant."

Eliana blushed in her empty living room. It was her habit, when he talked this way, to hide her face behind her hair. Her father had never spoken to her mother like this. When they first dated, she'd felt like Josh was speaking to her in a language she didn't know. She had never known that words could take the place of touch. They could comfort, champion, and make all sorts of love. To love Josh Rollins was to learn a whole new lexicon.

"You make me sound like your crutch."

"Not a crutch. My home. My home is where you are."

She smiled. "And my home is where you are."

"So that's why I lost my temper. I got scared."

"Josh, you don't need me."

"See now, that's where you're wrong."

"Oh, to hell with it. Let's go to France."

Josh barked laughter before sobering. "What are you waiting for? Go call Natalie."

Natalie sat on her patio, her gaze idling on her periwinkle hy-drangeas. As a determined yellowjacket dipped from petal to petal, climbing across the remaining pumpkin-shaped buds, Natalie and Everett ate bowls of Fruity Pebbles in silence. Everett stared at her.

"But, Mommy, you don't like kid cereals?"

"Everett, if you can't eat cereal on a Thursday evening, when can you eat it?"

"For breakfast? On Saturday?"

Despite the tightness coiling in her throat, Natalie laughed. "That, too."

Right then, the patio door burst open. Harris elbowed his way onto the patio, with an arm wound tightly around Aaron, to support him.

"Where have you been?" Harris half-shouted. "I've been calling. I was worried."

Natalie blinked. "Sorry – I must've left my phone in the car. What happened?"

"I think I rolled my ankle at basketball practice," Aaron said.

"One of those jerk kids knocked him down," Harris said, gently easing Everett into a chair. "These 'teammates' are something else."

"Oh, my goodness, Aaron, can you bear weight on it?" Natalie asked.

"A little. I'm really fine – wait, are those my Fruity Pebbles?"

"They are. You're welcome to it, but I've already ordered a pizza and it's en route."

With matching furrowed brows, Harris and Aaron exchanged a glance.

"Why are you guys wearing pajamas?" Aaron asked slowly.

"Why not?" Natalie asked, as she stood and dropped a kiss on his forehead. "I'm going to get you some ice for that ankle."

Harris followed her inside the house. Natalie fluttered around the kitchen, hurriedly examining the contents of their freezer and grabbing a dishtowel.

"I feel like our ice packs are too big. Would peas work?"

"Nat, are you feeling okay?"

"About as well as can be expected," she said while wrapping a bag of frozen peas in a dishtowel. "Considering."

"What? What happened?"

Natalie, peach-toned but for a sprinkling of tan freckles across her nose, could never just blush a little. To her chagrin, she always turned beet-red at the exact point that her hands began to quake, tiny tremors that rolled through her body like waves. She wore the most minimal embarrassment like a blinking neon sign. Natalie rolled her eyes, annoyed suddenly at her churning stomach and everything bound to it, and took a seat at the kitchen island.

"I was fired."

Harris's eyes widened. "You? For what?"

"Birdie wanted to go in a different direction. We'd discussed a very traditional aesthetic, and she wants something modern now. She probably meant to say *someone* modern."

"That doesn't sound like termination for cause. Let me look over your agreement."

Natalie raised her hand. "I want to wind this down. I don't want to work with someone who doesn't want to work with me, and she said she'll give me credit where I'm due."

"You have to know that this isn't about you," he said, taking her cold, clammy hand in his. "You've done excellent work for a decade. This is a bad day."

"You mean a bad summer."

"Come again?"

"Our timetable had us working on her estate until at least the beginning of August. I'm going to have to get creative to fill that void. I have to figure out a way to land a new client before word gets around that I was sacked," she said, before gasping. "Oh no! I forgot to call the sitter. Of all the days, of course I forget to call her when I could most use a date night."

Harris blinked rapidly, while a flat-line smile crossed his face. "Don't worry about it. We're on a waitlist with that one as it is. Another time."

Natalie sighed. "I should get my phone from the car. I totally forgot about it. I'm already acting like an unemployed person."

"Hey there, that's my wife you're talking about," Harris called out.

Her words were lost to the weak acoustics of their small mudroom. As she opened the door to the garage, Natalie vowed to not return a single missed call. She would give herself the day to wallow. Tomorrow, Natalie would begin the tedium of canceling orders, returning shipments, and parsing contractual language with her subcontractors. Tomorrow, she would smile through it all, doing her best to save face.

Tomorrow, she would try to fix it.

Tonight, however, Natalie curled into a ball in the driver's seat as her index finger slapped against her phone. Names and numbers began to blur, a ceaseless stream of unmet needs, until one familiar name stood out from the rest. Her heart leaped and her eyes filled.

With her phone in hand, Natalie made her way to the front porch. She took a seat in a rocking chair and tucked her legs beneath her. In the midst of her pain, there was fresh beauty all around. Across her lush green lawn, against the first coral tones of the sun's descent, dogwoods wore petals as white as bridal lace. She pressed the phone to her ear, smiling already.

"It's you!" Eliana exclaimed.

She could hear Eliana, bubbling and vibrating with spillover energy, being Eliana.

"It's me."

"You never call me back this soon! Is everything okay?"

"Just a regular Thursday. You act like I never get back to you!"

"I mean, I do believe you'd pick up were I being held hostage."

"I appreciate your faith in me. Well, if I'm the person who takes too long to call back, you're the one who calls with a very specific reason in mind. You're like a guy that way."

Eliana paused. She opened her mouth to speak, but there were no words to formulate the question she knew she shouldn't ask. The question that came bundled with an immediate response. Instead, Eliana stalled.

"My girls cut another little girl's hair on a playdate and, naturally, it was all Josh's fault," she began.

Five minutes later, Natalie giggled behind her hand. Eliana spoke breathlessly, one word tumbling over the other. All the while, Natalie found herself enjoying this fine, gilded stretch of time. The slight chill of early evening. The pungent air saturated with the soapy smell of climbing roses. The long day's soft landing.

"So, what are you waiting for? Say something."

Natalie sighed as she yanked a rubber band from her wrist and knotted her hair into a low bun. "This too shall pass."

Eliana rolled her eyes as she set about making a platter with crackers and hummus for her girls. "There's that time-tested advice that I was hankering for."

"I can tell you what I wish someone had told me: you don't have to be friends. Even if the little people in your life are friends, you can be polite and move on. Think of it as an ongoing Thanksgiving dinner."

"That sounds like ... purgatory," Eliana muttered. "Do you remember when we were in college and we had those long, wine-soaked talks late at night on art and politics and religion?"

"Sure."

"It's not like that anymore. Not with anybody."

"No," Natalie said. "No, it isn't."

"I miss those days sometimes."

"Me too, though I would probably need to go to bed earlier."

They laughed, their soft laughter like a weighty woolen blanket that stretched far enough to cover them both. In the silence that followed, Eliana walked to her window and watched a ladybug crisscross a potted palmetto. The waxy frond moved only infinitesimally, catching a rare breeze as the ladybug shimmied down the length of it. Her mother would've raced to it and cradled it in her palm for luck. Eliana, never one to wish on eyelashes or blow dandelions to the wind, merely watched it until it flew away.

"I was fired today."

Eliana gasped. "What? That's impossible!"

"I feel like I have whiplash."

"I'm certain you did nothing wrong," Eliana said, her eyes narrowing. "Did you hear me? You did *nothing* wrong."

"You're sweet, but you can't know that."

"Sure, I can. There are countless rich people who lack impulse control and act erratically and treat people they've hired like garbage. I know this because they've invited me to sit at their table. They're like toddlers with expense accounts. These are my people now."

"They're not your people, Ellie," Natalie said, smiling loosely. "I'm your people."

Eliana heard faint footsteps and turned to see Lola standing in the kitchen, sucking her thumb. When Eliana gave her a smile, Lola came running. Together, they sank into the vast, comfortable couch, boasting a high back and a grey linen upholstery that Natalie had chosen.

"Yes, you are," Eliana agreed, as she took a breath. "So, you're free, then?"

"For the foreseeable future, yes. Wait – what do you mean?"

"The girls and I are staying close for the summer."

"You're not going to France with Josh?" Natalie asked, before drawing out a pause. "Why on earth wouldn't you go to the south of France? Is everything okay?"

"We're all fine, though I'm a bit worn down from the bohemian lifestyle."

"Well, I can certainly understand that. My summer is wide

open, so I'd love to plan a visit. Are you staying home in L.A.?"

"No. We'll be coming closer to you."

"Really? That's fantastic! Where?"

"Delaware."

Natalie stopped rocking at once, though she felt that she was still moving. She gripped the ends of her chair tightly. She couldn't hear the birds, still warbling close in the oak tree, over the ringing in her ears. Her stomach flipped. She fought a sudden urge to weep.

"Why?"

Eliana blinked. "My father – you know, he isn't doing so well. We can visit him in Virginia more easily, and I want to give the girls a summer like the ones we used to have."

Natalie nodded vigorously, even as she hugged her stomach. She thought to Aaron and Everett, as a tidal wave of her own memories – bleak and fine and wild and loud – hovered too close, a tsunami of dark water deep enough to drown them all. It was out of the question to even conceive of giving her family the memories that she once had. She would not regress, self-destructing in real-time with her husband and children at her heels.

"We're going to rent a house right on the beach. Will you come visit, Nat?"

"Eliana."

"Don't say 'no,' " Eliana said, nearly pleading.

"Eliana, you were the best part of my summers at the beach. But even though our memories of that time are similar, they're not the same. They'll never be the same."

It was the most she'd ever said on the matter, maybe the most she would ever say.

"You can't make new ones? With me?"

"Not there. I can't go back."

Eliana nodded, her throat dry. "I'm sorry I asked. It was unfair of me."

"Don't be," Natalie said gently. "As it turns out, you were

the only person I needed to speak with today. You always make it all better for me."

"I miss you, Nat."

"I miss you, too, Ellie."

"We'll come to you this summer."

"I'd like that very much."

"Speak soon?"

"I promise."

"Love you."

"Love you."

Years ago, they'd stopped saying goodbye when they hung up the phone. A decade apart had taught them a new etiquette, whittled down to a warmth that always lingered like firelight between them. There was no need for goodbye when a conversation had no end.

Instead, Eliana pulled Lola to her chest. Lola giggled wildly as Eliana tickled her. Eliana smiled back without her eyes, waiting for her jagged-edged disappointment to subside.

For her part, Natalie set her phone aside as though burned by it. Logically, she knew that nothing had changed. Here was the cloudless, dusky sky, saturated now with a pale violet color. Here were the honeybees, roaming across fleshy rose petals. Here was the oak tree, towering in a formal bow, reaching toward her. Here was the pizza guy, whose name always escaped her, careening into their driveway. It was all exactly the same. She was still Harris's wife. She was still Aaron and Everett's mother. She was still fired.

And yet, she sat crowded on an empty porch. Her nostrils flared, searching the air, as she smelled the magnolia oil that her mother had dabbed behind her ears. She heard a distant, haunting G-minor chord, a rich, painterly sound like the wailing melody strummed from her father's guitar. In the rustling oak trees, Natalie might've heard their shared laughter. As goosebumps ricocheted across her skin, her shoulders slumped.

She'd worked so hard to build a life without them. Yet, as

she waved to the approaching pizza guy and cracked a tight smile across her face, Natalie realized that she hadn't outrun them after all. All this time, her parents had kept her pace.

Chapter 5

She tossed and turned in her cold bed, burrowing deeply into a thin blanket that she had resolved to give away tomorrow. Scattered thoughts streamed across her mind's eye like a meteor shower. Allegra stole a glance at her clock. 12:03. With a sigh, she realized that there would be no sleep here this evening. She sat up, intending to get a glass of water and a good book, when her phone vibrated.

"Allegra."

Her upper lip curled as he said her name. She wasn't sure when exactly her body had started reacting to him. Her frame recoiling. Her hands perspiring. She only knew that her body had known the truth about him long before her mind eventually latched onto the idea.

"Etienne," she said evenly. "It's late. What do you want?"

"I wanted to inform you that I've decided that you may have our children through the first week of August."

"Etienne!" she said, nearly shouting his name even as she willed herself to find her breath. "We spoke only a few hours ago. You said I could have them for three weeks in August, which is still one week less than our agreement. Why are you doing this?"

"There is a family gathering the second week of August, and I want my children to be there. They have titles. There are expectations of them. You wouldn't understand, my love. You haven't got much family. Moreover, you're American. Your country lacks history."

"We have plenty of history. We just prefer a self-made man."

There was silence on the other end. She could hear his teeth grinding. If she closed her eyes, Allegra would've seen his nostrils flaring. Her lawyers had warned her against baiting him, but there was a brief, delicious satisfaction in knocking him down a peg on the eve of the day when she would unload their former apartment.

Allegra liked talking back to him now that she was out of his reach.

"Why are you doing this, Etienne? Using our children as chess pieces?"

"Because I can, *amour.*"

Her hand shook when she reached for her cigarettes. Nothing. She'd thrown them away. Allegra groaned before spitting out more words: "I told you never to call me that again."

"Yes, I remember, but as it turns out, I don't need to touch you to lead you. A shepherd doesn't use a hand to guide his sheep. He only needs a staff."

She blanched. "And you use our *children*. What kind of man are you?"

"I'm your children's father, Allegra."

Tears blurred her vision. She wiped her eyes, her nose, and her mouth with the back of her hand. "I'm warning you, Etienne. I have lawyers, too. I will not hesitate to call them."

"Do what you must," Etienne said. "But don't forget: they nearly bled you dry last time. That's not what I want for the mother of my children. For my wife."

At that, Allegra stood. "Ex-wife."

"Semantics. Come back to me, and you can have everything."

Her eyes narrowed. "Our children are not yours to give back to me."

"They belong to me, like you belong to me. And it is my duty to keep reminding you of this, of the vows you took and forsook, until you remember."

He hung up on her. He always did. Allegra sank immediately to the floor, crumbling into a heap where she'd stood, as she always did. Through a vale of tears, Allegra tried to remind herself that tomorrow was the beginning of a new life. There would be a house, a yard, and a soft stretch of shoreline all waiting for them. It was one place he hadn't touched, stripped clean of all the memories he'd dirtied for her. It might not be everything, but it was something.

Allegra decided then that, on her last night in what had been their home, she would sleep far from the room where he'd slept beside her. With tears streaming down her face, she stalked into the living room. Allegra sank onto the couch, rolled onto her side, and lost more sleep.

Awakening with a gasp, Natalie sat up straight in bed.

"What time is it?"

Harris groaned, rubbed his fists into his eyes, and looked at the clock. "Four in the morning. You can't possibly intend to go for a run this early. I won't let you."

"I have to go," she whispered, before pressing a kiss to his cheek.

"Go? Go where?"

"It's 10 AM in Italy, so I might still catch them before lunch."

"Them?"

"The antique dealers who found an eighteenth-century Venetian standing globe for me. It was meant to be a gift for Birdie—"

"You give gifts to your clients?"

"Always."

His forehead crinkled. "I wasn't aware of this."

"The dealers were going to ship it today," Natalie said hurriedly. "If I explain the situation, maybe they'll give me some sort of refund. Doubtful, but I have to try."

"I'm sorry you have to do this, Nat."

"Not as sorry as you'll be if you have to make room for that globe in your study. Go back to sleep."

Even as she rushed for the door, Natalie glanced back at him as she always did. He'd already tunneled beneath the covers, the duvet pulled above his nose, his broad back turned away from her. Harris often grumbled about the extra throw pillows and blankets, but she later found him asleep having made a kind of nest of them. He slept well here. Their bed, with its goose-down pillows and stiff mattress, had been designed to his tastes. Just as she'd hoped, Harris rode one REM cycle to another there like he was catching waves.

Natalie crept into the study. She spotted her phone charging on the settee by the window. She hurried to it, yanked it from its wire, and caught a sucker punch to the gut. Her eyes blurred. Her heart hammered. She forgot how to breathe.

It wasn't her phone. It was *his* phone.

She saw the image the same way she took in Cubist artwork: finding form from shapes and shadows, finding a body in the layering of circle and square, in the patchwork of light and darkness. And so, Natalie at first struggled to lock eyes with the woman staring back at her. She saw her long neck first. Her full breasts. Her narrow ankle. Her ears stuck out, and it was the meanness boiling in Natalie's fist-sized heart that held tight to this imperfection. Because the rest of this anonymous woman was taut, tan, filtered perfection.

Her mind roamed wildly, replete with half-thoughts that made little sense. *He would never. It can't be. Not Harris. Her mistake. Who is she? How dare he?*

And yet the only known truth, glistening like street-pennies in moonlight, was that this anonymous beauty meant the image for her husband. There was no mistaking the text message.

*Can't wait 4 this weekend, Harry! C u soon. Luv u.
Xoxo.*

She'd thought he hated to be called Harry. She'd thought
he was going to a conference in San Francisco this weekend.
She'd thought her husband was all hers.

Natalie sank into the office chair, directly onto her actual
phone. She squirmed and twisted and reached for it. Her screen
was filled with missed calls and text messages. All work-relat-
ed. All school-mom-friend-related. All boring and predictable
and as aligned with her phone as her fingerprint was to her
thumb. Her hands shook. She wanted to weep but found her
eyes bone-dry. There was only a hollowness deep within that
threatened to overtake her, spilling throughout her body as
iodine would fill the veins.

Swim to the shore. I will be waiting for you.

Natalie smelled magnolia and knew suddenly, unequivo-
cally, that she would not drown. She anchored her entire being
to this awareness. She would not be carried out to sea by the
tide. She would cut against it.

Twenty-five hundred miles away, Eliana wearily rolled over
when her phone rang. She expected to see Josh's name blazing
in the blue light, but instead, she saw Natalie's. She looked at
the clock, did some quick addition, and sat straight up in bed.

"Natalie?"

"Sorry to call so late. I wanted to hear your voice."

"What's wrong?"

"Nothing. Everything. Just ... I may need you."

"I'm right here," Eliana whispered. "I'm always here for
you. Are you okay?"

"I'm okay," she said, and then lower: "Not okay."

"Natalie, what happened? Please tell me what's wrong."

"I can't," she said, her voice cracking. "I don't have the words
yet."

In nearly three decades of friendship, Natalie had never

hung up on Eliana, but she did then. She ached to the bone, so tired that her teeth pulsed. She had only enough energy to make the call. Afterward, there was only the barest spark left to scrawl a note and tear off her bathrobe. The only action left to take was to walk out the door.

By seven o'clock in the morning, Natalie sat on the deck of their boat, numbly taking in their slice of the Potomac River. She wore her pajamas. She held a stale gas-station cookie in her hand. She chewed the cookie slowly while squinting hard against the rising sun. Harris had named their boat *Milady*. Natalie had cringed to have his pet name for her displayed for all to see, painted in bold navy on sparkling white fiberglass.

"Milady?" Harris asked.

As she admired the massive red rock towering above her, Natalie smiled. "Why do you keep calling me that?"

"Because, when I'm on my knee, 'ma'am' doesn't cut it."

Natalie turned to find him bent down, his full grin scarcely contained in his face. He was framed by a vast expanse of copper-colored canyon walls and scraggly pine forests. On his palm was a blue velvet box. A diamond ring flashed in the desert sun.

"I hear that this place hasn't been wet for a while, and I wanted to take you as far from the ocean as I could to prove to you that I can set you free," Harris said hoarsely. "Marriage to me won't be a confinement. We can liberate each other. Champion each other. Make each other better. Natalie, will you—"

"Yes!"

And then he rushed to her, embraced her, and swung her in circles in the shadow of a butte. Somewhere, in the short interlude of a long kiss, Harris managed to slide the ring on her finger. He was hers. She was his. Later, there would be vows and a party and cake, but as far as Natalie was concerned, that was the moment they became a family. He kissed her frantically. Her mouth. Her neck. Her shoulder. And finally, her stomach. He cupped the curve of it in his palm, as though connecting the little life within her to the moment, too. In time, he danced with her, though there was no music. They swayed and watched the sunset descend across Sedona. She had thought then that, in a place so visibly marked by hundreds of millions of years of erosion and evolution, a promise of forever might last.

She smelled the indole river muck again long before her vibrating phone jolted her from her reverie. A grey cloud passed overhead, firmly displacing the desert sun that had hovered so close. With a sigh, Natalie took her phone in hand.

"I haven't been able to sleep," Eliana said. "Please tell me what's going on."

Natalie bit her lip. "Harris is cheating on me."

"Are you serious?"

"I have his phone in my back pocket, which includes a not-safe-for-work screenshot and text message. Of course, she's younger and prettier and can't spell – all as expected."

"I can't believe it," Eliana breathed.

"I thought nothing could feel worse than being fired. As it turns out, it's not only my professional life that's in ruins."

"Let me come to you, Natalie. Right now," Eliana said. Her voice had never been so clear, so calm. Natalie hardly recognized the icy edge to it.

"I think Harris and I should be alone when we discuss this," Natalie said while pinching the bridge of her nose. "I have to do the *exact* right thing, Eliana. I have to figure out what I'm going to say, and all I can focus on is how many damn barnacles I've scraped off this boat for this man. I never even *wanted* a boat, but I would've done anything for him. It's not a productive line of thought."

"You're not a robot. You're allowed to sit with your shock. How do you *feel*?"

Natalie exhaled and then licked sprinkles from her fingertips. "Achy all over. Like my entire life has become the preamble to a migraine. What do I do now?"

"The bare minimum. You go home. You make your kids' breakfast. You get them to school. And then you talk to your husband. He's still your husband. Even if there's been—"

"Infidelity? Deception? A whole separate relationship?"

Eliana exhaled. "Even if there's been all of that, you know him best. You know how to talk to him. All you have to do this morning is talk to him and demand that he tell you the truth."

The truth. As those two words reverberated in her ears, she set the cookie aside. How many times had Harris made the same demand of her? He'd asked thousands of casual questions, each one as innocuous and as surprisingly painful as a paper cut, in an endless effort to dig deeper. He'd wanted to know her history, her secrets, and her unspoken dreams. And when he'd talked that way, she'd rolled over, or she'd turned away, or she'd left the room. Not too long ago – maybe weeks, maybe months – he'd stopped asking.

"What if he's leaving me?" Natalie whispered the question.

"What if you decide to leave him?" Eliana asked, her voice rising an octave. "He's not the only one who could lose someone here."

Natalie swallowed hard. "I don't even remember my life without him."

"But I do," Eliana said. "Go home and talk to him, and then call me back. I'll be here."

"Love you."

"Love you."

As soon as their call ended, Natalie laid flat on the floor of the boat's hull. She tried to steady her breath. When she closed her eyes, she could surrender to the boat's rocking and pretend that she'd floated away. But the untethered sensation would not last. Every few seconds, Natalie's eyes blinked open again and darted to the berth's dock posts. She had to ensure the dock lines were still tight, each rope carefully knotted by her husband's hands.

Chapter 6

"What do you mean 'there's nothing you can do'? You must be able to do something," Allegra snapped. "I can't believe I have to convince my attorney to work for me."

"We've discussed this. You lived a lot of life with Etienne in Luxembourg. The state of New York ultimately determined that it wasn't the 'home state' in this instance and did not have jurisdiction over your case. Our only recourse is to seek full custody in Luxembourg."

"But he's violating the terms of our divorce agreement!"

"As I stated earlier, we'll coordinate with local counsel in Luxembourg to bring suit against him this autumn."

"I don't see why we need to wait that long," Allegra said, as she sidestepped the two movers carrying her couch out of the apartment.

"These things take time. Luxembourg's civil code doesn't provide for joint custody, so we need to build a strong case as to why you should be solely responsible for the children."

"I'm their mother."

"Yes, but the court will always focus on the child's welfare," Jack said quietly, like an adult soothing a child's tantrum. "Etienne is a wealthy man from a powerful family. The children have joint citizenship and have lived in the country since they were toddlers. It's their home. We'll argue that they should live with you, but it's a mountain of a case to make."

With a deep sigh, Allegra stepped into her bedroom and

shut the door behind her. It was finally empty. Bright sunlight varnished the pale plaster walls in splatters of gold. Sparse whispers of shadows collected like spiderwebs behind the ceiling's dark beams. Allegra sank to her feet, tucked her knees underneath her, and absently traced the floor's herringbone pattern with her fingertips. She held her breath.

"Are you there?"

"I'm going to lose. He always wins, and I always lose."

"You can't think that way," Jack said, as his voice intensified. "You are not in a passive position simply because you're the one reacting. And your measured reaction is the one thing you can still control. You have to keep the faith, Allegra."

Allegra blinked away tears. "But it's been so many years away from them."

"I know."

"And it's all so expensive: the flights, the homes, the lawyers – no offense."

"I understand your concern, and this is an incredibly expensive matter to litigate. It's why I would strongly suggest that you continue to take jobs this summer."

"No," she said. "*No*. I promised the kids I would be around. I can't make them a snack when they come home from school, but I can do this."

"With respect, you'll feel more emotionally secure going into a difficult court case if you're more financially secure. And with their nanny accompanying them—"

"What nanny?"

Jack paused. "Allegra, we've discussed this. In the amended divorce agreement, we agreed to allow their primary caregiver to travel with them this summer."

Allegra's grey eyes roved frantically over the beamed ceilings and the crown moldings, as though looking for a place to land. She blinked rapidly. She tried to breathe.

"I know, but I thought their nanny was just helping them with the transatlantic flight and their baggage and their transport and then she would, you know, go away."

"No," Jack said slowly, drawing out the word as though deflating it. "Their nanny is intended to serve as a consistent presence as they adapt to their new surroundings."

"I thought I was their 'consistent presence.' It's why I spend such an exorbitant amount to maintain a residence in Luxembourg."

"And all of your efforts will be noted when we go to trial. Until that time, it reflects well on you to be as agreeable as possible. It will be easier on you if, for the time being, you accept what you cannot change."

"Are you really repeating the serenity prayer to me?"

"I was only trying—"

"Let's acknowledge reality for a moment: Etienne won't be with us this summer, so he's sending his proxy instead. It's not the 'illusion of control' if he's actually always in control."

At this, Allegra started to weep. She choked on thick, weighty sobs. Tears carved brittle pathways down her cheeks. She took a long moment to gather herself.

"Are you still there?" she asked in a voice that shook.

"Yes, of course."

"I'm sorry. I'd hoped to have them all to myself this summer. Away from him."

"You'll always be their mother. Whatever tactic he uses to control the situation, he can't diminish your love for them or their love for you."

"That's kind of you to say, but what do I do now?"

"Go to your new home and enjoy this time with your children. If you can put up with being married to Etienne for years, you can certainly tolerate an elderly nanny for a few months. And, in autumn, we'll review our options."

As soon as they hung up the phone, Allegra pulled her handbag over her shoulder and slid on her sunglasses on her nose. She crossed the entirety of her prewar apartment in a handful of long strides, bypassing the movers as they eased her desk out of the door. When it was her turn to leave, Allegra didn't look back.

If she were to ever break free of him, Allegra knew she had to move forward. She would face her uncertain future incrementally, in a procession of tiny, manageable moments. Stepping into the elevator. Riding it in solitude. Easing into the lobby. Rushing across its marble expanse. Stepping into the revolving door, into the pulsating crowd, into the bright sunlight.

Away from him.

Natalie pulled into the garage and killed her engine. A psychedelic diamond, etched in silver-streaked light, hovered at the periphery of her vision. She knew well the blurry purgatory of waiting for a migraine headache. Slowly, she rested her forehead against the steering wheel.

When Harris flung the door open, Natalie blanched. She could feel him staring at her. With a deep sigh, Natalie gathered her things and opened the car door.

Harris stood in the doorway. He wore stale sweatpants. His hair was spiked and curled haphazardly. His cheeks were shadowed in dark stubble.

"I got your note," Harris said, his voice raspy. "I thought you'd gone for a run, but then the car was gone. Where did you go?"

"Where are the kids?"

"Just put Aaron on the bus. Everett is eating cereal."

"That's good. You'll need to take Everett to school."

"I can do that. Are you okay? Is this about being fired? Are you sick?"

Her eyes narrowed. Not for the first time this morning, Natalie wondered how she would ever share space with him again; and, alternatively, how she would ever live without him.

Natalie rifled through her handbag, extracted his phone, and put it in his palm. She painstakingly wrapped his fingers around it.

"You're right, Harris," she murmured. "I need to get a new case for my phone."

She'd taken two steps into the house when she heard him gasp, sucking air through his teeth. She ignored him. While he stood stock-still in the garage, Natalie rushed to Everett at the kitchen island, wrapping him in a big hug.

"Mommy, you must really like those pajamas," Everett whispered.

Natalie's abrupt ripple of laughter caught her by surprise. She tucked his head under her chin, pressing kisses on his soft, brown hair, as though trying to commit this brief bit of their morning routine to memory. Natalie took a deep breath. Everett smelled of Cheerios and satsuma hand soap and Dreft detergent. She exhaled with tears in her eyes.

Already, she had begun to grieve.

Natalie waited for him, showered and dressed in their bed. As she pulled the coverlet to her chest, she thought idly about what she would've done differently if the room were hers. A pillow-top mattress. Fluffy pillows. Mounds of faux-fur blankets. A linen duvet, pale lavender. Because her entire adult life had been shared, Natalie couldn't remember what it was like to sleep alone. She tried valiantly to sketch the contours of a life that didn't belong to her.

Even though Harris hadn't said anything, Natalie suddenly sensed his presence. She turned his way. He stood in the doorway, partially obscured in shadow.

"Natalie," he croaked. "I'm so sorry. I never meant for you to find out this way."

The left side of her head had begun to pound. Her vision blurred. Natalie thought quickly to Eliana's words: all she had to do was talk to her husband. She would not break apart into a thousand pieces, shattering like glass. She would gather information. She would work the problem. She would remain whole.

"How long has this been going on?"

"About six months now."

Natalie winced and looked down at her hands, clasped tightly in her lap. "Who is she?"

"Her name is Sophia. She is … she was my yoga instructor."

Her stomach churned. Her heart hammered. She'd already spent too many hours conjuring this phantom woman in her head, but nothing could have prepared her for the serrated edges of this dialogue. A name. A job title. A shared history.

"How exactly were you planning to tell me?"

"I had hoped to take you out to dinner—"

"Thursday," she breathed.

"I wanted to have a conversation. It was never my intention to hurt you."

"And where do you stand with her now?"

With a halting sigh, Harris continued. "We've been looking at real estate."

And there it was: the only answer to the only question that mattered. This woman was not his mistake. Whatever apology he offered would be for Natalie's broken heart, for his own bad timing, rather than the irrevocable wrongness of Harris's coupling with another woman. Natalie shuddered, overcome with teeth-chattering tremors, to think that Natalie wouldn't only share her future with Harris, but with *her* as well. She fought the urge to retch.

For a few long minutes, neither one of them spoke. Natalie tried to manage her fast-beating heart and her hard-pounding head. Harris covered his face with his hands. Then, without warning, Natalie remembered how to body surf. Arms forward. Legs lunging. Head bent. Waiting for the approach of the wave and the pull of the tide and the propulsion of surf. Natalie remembered that catching the wave hadn't been like floating at all, but what she imagined flight would feel like. A casting-off of gravity. A comet streak of magic. An ascent.

"Okay, then. Here's what I propose we do."

Harris raised his head quickly, blinking. "You have a proposal?"

"Eliana asked if we would go to the beach with her this summer. I could take the boys alone with me, and we can look at this summer as our trial run. You can take them home, too. We'll need to work out the details, but this would be a way to ease them into our ... our separation."

"Which beach?"

"Rehoboth."

Harris narrowed his eyes. "I've offered to take you back there since we were first married. You've never gone with me, but you'll go with her—"

"It's a little late to be indignant, isn't it?"

He quieted at once. When Natalie noticed the muscle ticking in his jaw, she thought about how easily she could hate him. His sanctimoniousness. His arrogance. His pride. The way he slurped his coffee and refused to eat mushrooms. She'd been privy to his every shortcoming. Natalie had met divorced women who kept running tallies of their ex-husbands' imperfections, and she'd never cared to witness their grudges. Still, as Natalie circled the well and stared into the reflection of someone she didn't recognize, she realized how easily she could fall into that dark water.

"It's a good idea," Harris said. "I'll miss the boys, but it would give us the space to make plans. After all, even if you and I aren't together anymore, we're still a family."

Her eyes filled with tears. "Yes. I've heard other people say that."

He reached for her hand, but she yanked it away.

"You'll never know how sorry I am, Natalie."

Her eyes locked with his while she considered this. He certainly looked sorry. The dark shadows under his eyes, the chapped ridges to his lips, and the grimace on his face all suggested guilt. If he hadn't just broken her heart, Natalie would have pitied him. But he had, and she felt this raw heartbreak as acute chest pain, an electric pulse radiating into her gut. Natalie wondered if she'd ever again take a breath that didn't feel bruised.

Impulsively, like someone tearing out a hangnail, Natalie asked the one question that Eliana had later texted her to warn her against asking.

"Why her?"

Harris's eyes fell. He paused. Sitting at the foot of their bed, he'd never been so far away. When he did finally speak, his voice was hoarse and his words were ragged.

"Because I've never been able to relax until her."

It was the very worst thing he could have said. Natalie wanted to offer him a succinct kiss-off, to spit a four-letter word at him that she rarely usually used, but she thought to her children and rolled away from him instead. Harris stayed with her for a long time. The room darkened with every passing cloud before gleaming with sunlight again, wavering in shades of grey. Natalie tried to ignore him, his deep, slow breathing, as she stared out the window.

She often looked at the old oak tree anchoring their front yard, but Natalie seldom took the time to really see it. Its starry-shaped leaves. Its hard, scaly bark. The acorns it scattered, the shade that it offered, the verdant beauty that, with any luck, would outlast them both. Each year, the tree collected another ring, expanding in stillness. It grew on, oblivious to the tragedies and triumphs of the humans scuttling at its roots. She marveled that, while she stood ankle-deep in the sludge of her own private hell, nature could go on and beauty would endure. Spring blossoms still scattered in the wind.

Natalie drifted toward sleep, surrendering to its sweet relief. Here, she floated untethered.

With a jerk, her eyelids fluttered open. Too fast, she sat up.

There was only her breath, only her heartbeat. She reached out to touch a patch of wrinkled coverlet at the foot of the bed, but it had already gone cold. He was gone.

Part Two

June

The Summer Triangle glows as a patchwork trifecta of the constellations: Lyra (the Harp), Aquila (the Eagle), and Cygnus (the Swan.) According to Greek mythology, Orpheus once dropped his harp into a river. Before it could be lost forever, Zeus directed his eagle to fetch him the harp. Zeus then ordered the lyre and the eagle into the sky, entrapping them there. In time, Zeus turned Orpheus into a swan and banished him, too, to twinkle among the stars.

Because there could be no music, no beauty, and no power unless they were his to have.

Chapter 7

"That's the last of it," Harris said. He snapped the trunk of their Tahoe shut.

While Harris circled the car, Natalie moved out of his way. Their last two weeks had mirrored their first two weeks together. She was hyper-aware of his presence, always attuned to the space he took up in a room. Natalie found herself laughing too loudly. She smiled as widely as she had in the beginning, though it hurt her face to do so now. She was an actor in an unending production; she played opposite her children even as she found an audience in their small faces. It was a gift that she was determined to give their two kids: to see their parents happy, even kind, right up until the end.

Natalie had tried not to give the future too much thought, though her hands shook as she served her kids their dinner. Her heart beat in wild palpitations. Her entire physiological system stood on high alert as she collected memories like rations. She couldn't sleep much. She couldn't eat much. When Harris embraced her, always in front of the children, Natalie tried not to hold on too tightly. He had never tried to kiss her again. Already, she felt like his co-parent, rather than his wife.

Harris tossed two last duffel bags into the car. He caught her eye. She looked away.

"Kiddos!" Natalie called out. "We're ready! Come and say goodbye to Daddy!"

Aaron and Everett had been rocking together on the front

porch, already greedily tucking into their respective electronics. They knew that cars, trains, and airplanes were the last bastions of endless screen time, and they reveled in the blue light glowing against their faces.

After they set aside their tablets, Everett came running. He flew heavily into Harris's waiting arms, knocking him off-balance. Aaron trudged along at his heels.

"I'll miss you, Daddy," Everett whispered as he kissed the side of Harris's face.

"You'll forget about me as soon as you see the beach," Harris said, but he squeezed Everett and buried his face in his neck. He made no move to set him down.

"Why can't you come again?" Aaron asked, squinting at the sun.

"I can't get away from work for the summer, buddy."

"You can't get away from work *at all*?"

With a sigh, Harris shifted Everett to his back and pulled Aaron into his arms. "Aaron, we've discussed this. Aunt Eliana and Mommy need to see each other sometimes, and you lucky dudes get to spend most of the summer at the beach with the twins. I have a busy summer, just like Uncle Josh, but we're still going to see each other lots."

"But we'll miss you," Everett whispered.

Behind her sunglasses, Natalie brushed wetness away from her eyes. She wondered again if this harebrained scheme of hers was a good idea; was it a lazy stretch of time where they could adapt to a new situation or simply a childish tactic to delay the inevitable? At the very least, Natalie told herself, the beach house would be a home unmarked by their father. They had never been there, so there would be no transition yet to a life without him. It was the transient, foreign beauty of the rental home: a house without memory, free of the grey din of reality.

"Remember what I promised you both," Harris said.

"A family vacation," Everett said. "Just you, me, Aaron, and Mommy."

"At the end of the summer, the four of us are going away to Tennessee," Aaron repeated.

"That's right," Harris said. "We're all going to take our own trip. Until that time, you'll come back home for your summer camps and for weekends. We'll see each other a lot."

Natalie winced to think of the looming week that had been set aside. They would vacation together in a small cabin on Lake Douglas. If she closed her eyes, Natalie could hear the low drone of boats skimming across the lake's smooth surface. What she couldn't envision is what they would tell the children. She had no idea how to soothe an open wound that she herself had made.

"So, when we're with you, we'll miss Mom. And when we're with Mom, we'll miss you," Aaron said evenly. "You didn't even ask us what we wanted our summer to be."

Harris frowned. "It's only two weeks until—"

Aaron climbed into the car and slammed the door. Harris lifted Everett into his car seat. When Harris kissed Everett and whispered goodbye, Natalie felt her throat tighten.

In time, Harris came to stand beside her.

"Well, that didn't go as well as we hoped it would," he muttered.

"It's the beginning of the end," Natalie said. "Maybe he feels it, too."

Harris reddened. "Natalie, I'm sorry for—"

"Oh, come off it already. Where is she?"

Harris sipped a breath. Natalie turned her back to the car, strategically hiding the deep, rosy flush rising up her neck. She hid her pinched lips and her narrowed eyes. It had been exhausting to be so patient for the past two weeks, to avoid tripwire in her own home.

"Don't be ridiculous."

"How am I being ridiculous, exactly? It seems perfectly reasonable to me that you both would be relieved to see us go. The lying and scheming and sneaking around must be getting old by now. Unless, of course, the forbidden fruit is all you have."

"I know you're angry—"

"It's still my house."

"Of course it is."

"Good. Then, I have two ground rules going forward. The first is that she cannot meet our children until we decide together that it's the right time."

His lips thinned, but he nodded his head. "Okay. That's fine by me."

"The second is this: keep her *out* of my house."

Harris paused for a long moment. Natalie watched as he chewed on words, holding them tightly within the curl of his tongue before releasing them.

"I've never invited her into our home. Not once."

Natalie expelled a hot rush of air. The affair immediately became less invasive somehow. To know that another woman hadn't walked in her space, hadn't eaten at her table, hadn't climbed into their bed. Her tight shoulders drooped.

"Good."

"And I will agree to your terms. I think they're more than fair."

She tried to smile. "When you talk that way, it's like I recognize you again."

"But," he began, jutting out his chin, "Sophia is important to me. And if she's important to me, she'll become important to our children. Someday, they *will* meet."

Her smile snapped apart. "But not today."

Allegra bustled the length of the small cottage, frenetically tidying. She arranged tulips in a vase. She'd seen them at a roadside farmer's market this morning. Allegra had stopped at once, filling a straw basket with purple dahlias, ripe tomatoes, and fragrant melons. As she dropped a penny in the vase, Allegra flushed with the sense that she'd never been as happy as she was right then: living in a tiny house in a tiny seaside town, only a few blocks from the ocean.

Allegra heard a car door slam. She burst out the front door.

Delphine and Jules rushed towards her.

She fell to her knees.

They sunk into her arms.

Their three faces smeared with tears. They hiccupped in laughter. On the scratchiest crabgrass, her two towheaded children fell against Allegra as though they'd cast their weightiest burdens down. And finally, Allegra exhaled.

"*Maman*, I missed you," Jules whispered into her ear.

"I missed you more," Delphine said into her other ear.

Allegra cupped each of their two small faces in her hands, smoothed back their hair, and kissed away the tears pebbling their eyelashes. They spoke English for her through thick accents, never French, as though it were a secret language that belonged only to them.

"I love you both so much," Allegra whispered. "My heart is so full to have you here. Welcome home."

A shadow fell upon them. Allegra covered her brow with her hand, squinting to acknowledge her children's nanny, Véronique. Allegra would not stand to greet her. She eyed the small, thin woman from head to toe, as though assessing a car for purchase. Her sleek white bun. Her small round glasses. Her hands were paper-fine and subtly manicured.

"*Bonjour*, Véronique. Thank you for traveling with the children."

"You're welcome," she said. "Where shall I have the driver place their bags?"

"The children's rooms are upstairs."

"May we see them?" Delphine asked.

Allegra smiled. "Make yourselves at home."

With shrieks of laughter, Delphine and Jules bounded wildly

into the little house. Allegra closed her eyes for only a moment, savoring the loud pounding and screaming echoing through the open windows. Her arms already ached from the void left behind.

"And my room?" Véronique prompted.

Allegra rose to her feet. "Downstairs. It's not much, but it gets lovely light. It'll be nice for the children to have you here. Thank you for coming."

"It is kind of you to be so hospitable. I know that we have only met in passing, but I do hope that you will come to see me as an asset this summer."

"Me too."

Because the driver had already gone inside with her children's bags tucked under his arms, Allegra walked to the rear of the car and began unloading Véronique's bags herself.

"Oh, you don't need to do that, *vraiment*," Véronique said, as her long fingers fussed with her hair. "I can wait for the driver. It is his job, after all."

"Véronique, in my home, I'll always lend a hand. You don't work for me. You work with me. When you're not watching the children, I hope you can enjoy your vacation here, too."

The older woman stiffened. "Thank you. I suppose this will take some time."

"For us both," Allegra said, offering a grim smile.

"But, *Mademoiselle* Allegra? I do *not* work for you. I work for *Monsieur* Etienne."

Allegra's teeth clenched, but she held open the door for Véronique. "I'm aware of the arrangement."

"Good. I want to make certain of our roles at the outset so that there will not be any misunderstandings later. Now, I think I shall go freshen up. By my watch, the children will need their afternoon snack in fifteen minutes."

"That's fine by me."

"Excellent," Véronique said with a curt nod of her head. She turned to leave.

"But, Véronique?" Allegra called out. She waited until the other woman had turned back to meet her eye. "I'm their mother, and I'll be making their snack."

Very slowly, Véronique nodded. Seconds later, the guest room door clapped shut. Allegra leaned back against the wall and closed her eyes. Above her head, her children were jumping on their beds, running sprints between rooms, and taunting each other with a rapid-fire lingual duel of French and English. Allegra grinned at their high-pitched, musical roughhousing. She rushed right past the kitchen, raced up the stairs, and joined them.

Chapter 8

On the drive from their nook of the Potomac River to the Atlantic Ocean, Natalie witnessed her boys endure a full riot of emotion, as a shifting prism will cull different colors from the sunlight. They squirmed through the traffic, inching toward Annapolis. Aaron swatted at Everett. Everett, relying on his only effective defense, tried to bite him. Natalie tried not to scream. She wondered how she would make this daunting drive, and so many of the other unknowable, inevitable tasks still to come, all on her own. Her mind spiraled while her two sons utilized their most time-tested tricks to make each other cry.

At the Bay Bridge's ascent, however, they all fell into silence. The sky had never been so blue, so expansive, so close. Countless white sailboats skimmed over the Chesapeake Bay. Barges lumbered heavily in the distance. The bay unfurled like a pale grey ribbon, incandescent in the sunlight. In their descent, they drove parallel to birds, sharing the humid air with pelicans and seagulls. Aaron and Everett pressed their noses to the windowpane. Glancing back toward them in the rearview mirror, Natalie realized that they'd never seen this toe-curling, vertigo-inducing view. She'd never let them come. With that spark of recognition, Natalie rolled down all of their windows. Together, they breathed deeply, relishing the rush of bay-stroked air.

It's the preamble, Natalie thought, as she accelerated onto the peninsula. Pointedly turning her head away from the exit toward St. Michaels, she opted to avoid eye contact with the town where she'd lived alone with her mother in colder months. She would not land there yet.

East. East is better.

Because despite the dysfunction that she'd known as a child, she'd also known what it was to sit in the backseat of her parents' sedan and scan the changing landscape for any sign of the sea. She'd known the dragging weight of every slow minute until they reached the shore. The long trip had always sweetened their arrival. When Natalie noticed then that Aaron had ditched his device to stare out the window, she grinned in recognition.

Maybe she wouldn't mind bequeathing some of her memories, after all.

In time, the scenery of the Eastern shore took on a familiar rhythm: flat, emerald-green fields and roadside stands made space for small towns capped with church spires. The rolling dance of town and farmland gave way to clusters of tall, star-grazing pines and the watershed's spindly canals. Her boys drifted to sleep while Natalie grew more awake. Her eyes roved across fields of cornstalks and sunflowers, lingering for long moments on white farmhouses with picket fences and porch swings. She took in every garden bed, every climbing rose. As a little girl, these historic homes belonging to other people had only been signposts, a way to mark minutes until they arrived. Now, these cottages were evidence of lives lived at a slower rhythm, of survival etched out on verdant land.

So little there had changed. It was still enough to point east and know the path forward.

Hours later, Natalie merged from Route 16 onto Route 1, heading south toward the Delaware beaches. Synapses fired in her brain. When she eased the car toward Rehoboth, her pulse quickened. But right when Natalie began to grind her teeth at the first glimpse of familiar cottages framed by hydrangeas and beach roses, her GPS guided her south instead.

When she drove in the opposite direction of her family's cottage, Natalie exhaled. She wound the car around Silver Lake. She gazed at the green foliage reflected in the lake's calm water, at the whitewashed docks dotted with gazebos. A man and girl guided their kayaks under the small bridge, cleaving the water with their oars. Canadian geese passed beneath the bridge, entirely unfazed by the swarm of people above biking and running and pushing strollers.

Natalie held her breath as she turned onto East Lake Drive, a narrow road at the end of Queen Street. Her eyes widened while she took in the neat line of mansions, each more exquisitely detailed and imposing than the next, all straddling the thin strip of land between lake and beach. She turned down the driveway of a grey clapboard home that took her breath away. With her years of experience as an interior designer, Natalie could ordinarily assess a property quickly. But there was too much beauty here to move too fast. She cut the engine, cupped her chin in her hands, and took it all in. Its widow's walk as white as teeth. Its gingerbread detailing. Its floor-to-ceiling windows. Its stonework and archways and window boxes overflowing with geraniums. The house had a long dock that stretched into the lake, with a small gazebo providing respite at the end. She rolled down the windows again, heard the ocean's roar, and closed her eyes.

"Wait a sec, this is where we're staying?" Aaron asked.

"Yes," Natalie said.

"Where's the ocean?" Everett asked.

"Think of the lake as the front yard, and the ocean as the back."

From the backseat, her boys whooped unintelligibly, bubbling over with laughter. Her car rocked as they bounced. As they scrambled to unbuckle their seatbelts, Natalie turned back, removed her sunglasses, and met their eyes.

"I want to hear 'thank you' all summer long. So many 'thank yous' that you learn a new language for Aunt Eliana and then you say 'thank you' all over again."

"We get it, Mom," Aaron said. "Grandparent manners."

"We're good boys," Everett said with a grin. He brushed a stray curl away from the red mark on his forehead that Aaron had put there. Natalie couldn't help but smile back.

As soon as she had extracted Everett from his car seat, they tumbled out of the car. They roughhoused, skittishly looking toward the lake and then the ocean. With a grin pinned to her face, Eliana stepped out onto the front porch.

"You made it!" she yelled, clapping her hands.

Natalie helped Everett up the circular stairway, shaking her head in wonder. Aaron scooted past her, taking the steps two at a time, and immediately kissed Eliana's cheek.

"Thank you for the beach house, Aunt Eliana."

"Aaron, I think we're officially the same height now," Eliana said with wide eyes. "I can't believe it. It's almost as if you're about to have a thirteenth birthday."

When she embraced him, Aaron obliged, squirming only slightly.

"Go on and let Silvia and Lola show you around. You know how those girls like to give a tour, or any basic directive."

"Will do," Aaron called over his shoulder as he raced into the house.

"Hi, Auntie Ellie," Everett said, flushing with rosy color. "I've missed you."

"I've missed you too, Master Everett," Eliana said. "Looks like you've gotten big, too."

"The doctor says I'm bigger than Aaron was. And that he should be nice to me."

Eliana laughed. "He should get on your good side while there's still time."

"Is this place our house?"

"Yes, it sure is. For the whole summer."

Everett squealed, briefly offered his cheek to Eliana, and then rushed on into the house.

"You are unbelievable," Natalie said, shaking her head as she opened her arms wide and folded Eliana into them. "I was picturing a cottage, and you went ahead and rented a palace?"

"Do you remember this street from when we were little?"

"Are you kidding? I remember getting ice cream cones, walking to the very edge of the boardwalk, and craning our necks to spy on the people in these houses. And now, here we are."

"It felt like a full-circle moment."

"It's amazing. Like waking up inside of a dream and deciding to stay there."

Eliana smiled. "Come on in, Nat. Make yourself at home."

After Eliana held the door open for her, Natalie stepped slowly through the massive double doors, and her breath caught. Two stairways rose upward from a marble foyer. She moved through the archway as languorously as one walking through water and stepped into the great room. A dome of pale, blue-stained glass crowned a double-story wall of windows. Marble countertops glimmered with stainless steel appliances from a fully stocked chef's kitchen. Large, deep couches anchored the great room. Modern art and potted foliage punctuated it with color.

"This place is unreal. You have to let me contribute in some way."

"No. The three of you are our guests."

"Ellie, this would be extravagant for a week, let alone for an entire summer."

"Think of it as a gift, then."

"Is this because of my separation? Because, financially, I'll be okay. I don't need pity."

"I would never pity you. Now, come with me – you have to see the view."

With a furrowed brow, Natalie followed her onto the back porch. Their children had acquired a pink soccer ball, and the little ones chased Aaron in the sand. In the distance, the Atlantic Ocean loomed as smooth as slate, without a single whitecap cracking its surface.

"You know, after they listed Josh's earnings last year in Forbes, you and Harris were among the only people who didn't ask us for money."

Natalie flinched. "People have asked for money?"

"Yes, they've come out of the woodwork calling us their friends. Making demands."

"I never would've imagined that."

"And I never would've imagined your marriage ending," Eliana said. "You need a safe place to land this summer, and it's okay to rely on other people. To catch your breath. And what's the point of all of this money if we can't use it to lift up the people we love?"

Tears sparked in Natalie's eyes. As she wiped them away, Eliana squeezed her hand.

"How do you feel?" Eliana asked.

Natalie sighed. "Like a paper boat out on the ocean."

"The big goodbye was that bad, huh?"

"He was fine. I was the one who lost control. I couldn't hold it together any longer. Our marriage – our family – it's all falling apart."

When Natalie whimpered again, Eliana narrowed her eyes, as if she were staring down some shadow hulking in the middle distance. She raised her chin and straightened her spine.

"That's it. I was going to save this for this evening, but it's time."

With that, Eliana slipped into the house. Natalie looked down at the golden sand where a trio of toddlers was burying Aaron up to his neck. Aaron laughed so hard that the packed sand around his belly cracked. Natalie realized with a jolt that she couldn't remember the last time Aaron had laughed this way: deep from his belly, his shoulders shaking.

Eliana returned with a bottle of Veuve Clicquot Brut and two champagne flutes. Wiggling her eyebrows, Eliana opened the bottle with a satisfying pop of unleashed pressure.

"We're day-drinking now?" Natalie asked, though a faint smile crossed her face.

"That we are."

"Eliana, you know me. I'm not going to be the lady in Vegas with the divorce cake, though more power to them. I'm just not ready to celebrate the end of my marriage."

"This has nothing to do with your marriage," Natalie murmured, as she poured bubbling champagne into the flutes. "This has nothing to do with him. This is about *you*."

She raised a glass. Mirroring her, Natalie raised her glass as well.

"A toast: to the next grand adventure of your life. Because you know better than anyone that we are not what happens to us, we are what we make happen for ourselves."

Natalie lowered her glass before taking a sip. "You really think I'm that strong?"

"I do. And if I can't remind you of that, this place certainly can."

They clinked glasses, took a long sip, and stared beyond their children to the ocean. They watched the waves rise and fall, each wave a rippling, frothing explosion that climbed the sand before quickly retreating back to the sea. Natalie closed her eyes and took a deep breath. It was all exactly as she remembered. She knew the feeling of her toes in that warm sand before she ever sunk a foot into it. She knew the bracing chill of the Atlantic in June. She knew the ease with which her body would accept the saltwater, craving it and coveting it, until the salt tightened her slick skin while she baked in the sun.

"Hey, Mom!" Aaron shouted. "What are you waiting for? Let's get wet!"

What are you waiting for? His words echoed like a chant.

Natalie nearly taunted herself: why *had* she waited so long to return? This landscape had never wronged her. The ocean, at once calm and fierce and strong and playful, had been her salvation. Always, it had reminded her of the vast beauty and mystery waiting beyond the suffocating walls of that small cottage.

And maybe her life could someday be more than this fresh pain, too.

As if on cue, Natalie and Eliana set their champagne flutes down to follow a sand-coated Aaron to the ocean. The children led their mothers, pulling hard with what weight they had, to meet the climbing tide. Natalie shielded her eyes to watch Aaron tear off his t-shirt and charge into the ocean. When Aaron looked back at her, Natalie smiled and nodded.

She could give him permission, as she gave herself permission, to slog onward to the sea.

When Natalie rolled over and stretched, she blinked awake with mild alarm. She reached for Harris, but he wasn't there. A dull headache throbbed beneath her temples. Her lips smacked together, still parched. Slowly, Natalie began to remember yesterday. A quick goodbye. A long drive. A remarkable house anchored between a lake and an ocean. An early bedtime for the kids. A pitcher of margaritas that they'd shared on the deck, as they watched dusk slide into a blue-black night. An endless swath of stars and sky and sea.

Natalie stretched her arms high. She couldn't remember the last time she had taken up so much space in a bed. Just then, she remembered Eliana's parting instruction and reached into the side table's drawer. She extracted a small remote, bit her lower lip, and pressed a button.

Silently, the blackout curtains lining one wall of her room

glided apart. As her eyes grew large, Natalie crawled to the foot of her bed. There it was: a full, unobscured view of the sun rising over the ocean. Without a single window open, Natalie could feel the wind kicking up. Whitecaps scarred the ocean's surface. Grey clouds curdled in the sky. Still warm in her bed, Natalie shivered.

In time, Natalie climbed out of her covers and padded down the hallway. She'd almost reached the stairs when she heard Everett's faint weeping. She rushed into his room.

"Everett! What's the matter with you, Bug?"

"I forgot where I was," he said, still sobbing. "I forgot which room you were in."

"Oh no," she whispered while sitting on his bed. "Can I tell you a secret? I forgot where I was, too. It's a scary feeling until you remember. Is anything else making you feel sad?"

"I miss Daddy."

"Me too," she whispered, her chest tightening. "Wait a minute. Daddy used to wake you up early to get donuts, right?"

"Right. 'Cause Aaron sleeps too late."

"Well, how about we get dressed and surprise everyone with donuts? Just you and me."

"Right now?"

"As your big brother would say: what are we waiting for?"

Before her eyelids had cracked open, Allegra was smiling. She stretched her long arms high above her head and kicked a wiggling foot out from beneath her duvet. Milky, muted light pooled beneath her open windows. Allegra sat up against her pillow, pulled her knees to her chest, and listened for her children. They were quiet, likely tired from their travels. Her fingers itched to make them breakfast, to gaze at their sleepy faces over a mug of coffee.

What am I waiting for? she thought loudly.

With a surge of energy, Allegra bounded out of bed. She raced down the narrow hallway. She could picture exactly how awkwardly her smile would photograph, goofy and crooked and full, but she couldn't control it. Hurriedly, she pushed open the door to Jules's room. He was gone. She stepped across the hallway and opened Delphine's door. She was gone as well. Swallowing hard, Allegra tried to ignore her hammering heart.

Allegra rushed down the stairs to find the house empty. Her lips fell apart. She loped into the kitchen. There was a note on the table. The penmanship was perfect; every loop and slant of the cursive was like a manufactured font.

> *Mademoiselle Allegra,*
> *The children woke early from their sleep and would love to see the beach, so I am taking them. You will sleep better this way. We will be home soon.*
> *Sleep well,*
> *Véronique*

The paper fluttered toward the floor like an autumn leaf. Before it had reached the linoleum, the front door slammed shut. Allegra's fingertip shook when she pressed the button to turn on her car. She peeled out of the driveway, her tires screeching, and drove a few blocks east, bracing her eyes against the rising sun.

Chapter 9

With a box of donuts from the Fractured Prune balanced against her hip, Natalie trailed Everett along the water's edge. He stopped every few feet to collect a seashell and drop it into his bucket. She held their flip-flops in her other hand. A cool breeze blew westward from the ocean, licking up against her face. She hadn't yet gone for a run or even enjoyed a cup of coffee, yet Natalie found herself unable to stop smiling.

"What's this one?" Everett asked as he raised a shiny seashell for her inspection.

"Clam."

"And this?"

"Oyster."

"What about this?"

"Slipper shell."

He raised his eyebrows. "Really?"

"Really," she said, her tight chest loosening with laughter.

Natalie couldn't remember the last time she'd so brazenly lost track of time on a Saturday morning. Normally, she awoke in a panic, wondering if she'd remembered to toss a jersey in the dryer before Aaron's first game or if she could manage a cup of coffee before Everett's swim lesson. And there were so many chores. There was a garden to tend, a car to be serviced, and a meal to prepare. Ankle-deep in cold water, she realized she couldn't remember the last time that she and Harris had walked through an entire Saturday together, side-by-side. Every weekend in recent memory had been a relay race. They passed the children back and forth, always watching, always doting. And through every bullet point that could be deleted as the hours passed, they worked stoically, retreating to their devices when the children finally rested.

They hadn't been on a date in nine months.

Natalie looked west then, away from the ocean. Her eyes settled instead along the arcades and shops along the boardwalk, as naked in daylight as a clown scrubbed free of face paint. Everywhere glass bulbs and neon signs sat dull and lifeless. Natalie sighed.

For as long as she'd summered in Rehoboth, Natalie had loved the boardwalk at night. Its blinking kaleidoscope of color. Its cacophony of carnival music and tempered screams. Natalie had found a kind of peace in this unremittingly loud and bright place. It had taught her that darkness could be engaging. Just as some children seek out rollercoasters to fall and know they will be caught, Natalie had known that this boardwalk was awake with her on those long nights when sleep would not come.

She wasn't so alone, then. Because they had been out there, awake with her.

Natalie now caught a glimpse of the Ferris wheel, still and sculptural. She saw Thrasher's French Fries where she and Eliana had doused fries with vinegar before claiming a bench, staring at the sea, and talking for hours. They had ridden bikes here. They had lost money and won prizes here. Even the funnel cake stand remained where—

"What are you doing here?"

Hands quaking. Heartbeat pounding. "I got a funnel cake for Eliana."

"You're late."

Voice shaking. Chest tightening. "I'm not. Not for another hour."

"I'm your father. If I say you're late, you're late."

"Yes, sir."

"Now, go home before you make me get mean."

"Yes, sir."

He had never shouted. He had been calm and clean and sober. But he had grabbed her arm. She had jerked away, mewling like a kitten. His eyes had darkened. She had known that look and would never forget it. With a sleight of hand, he reached under her arm, grabbed hold of the plate of funnel cake, and shook it out over her head.

Powdered sugar had fallen like snow. She'd closed her eyes and licked her lips, wishing as she so often did for another life. The cake had bounced off her forehead before falling to the wooden planks beneath her feet. A crowd had gathered. Her cheeks had flushed. She had taken off running. She hadn't run away. She'd run straight home, exactly as he had ordered. Her tears and half-formed thoughts had cascaded together, falling like rainwater from a gutter.

What did I do so wrong? Why is he so mad?

"Mommy!" Everett hissed, yanking on her sleeve. Natalie shook herself awake.

"What is it, Everett?"

"Why is she so mad?"

Natalie followed the trajectory of his pointed finger. At some point, a woman had materialized amidst the few colorful umbrellas already anchored in the sand. She rushed toward them. She didn't blend in: tall, rail-thin, and swaddled in black. Her scarlet hair fell past her waist. Everett hid behind Natalie while the woman walked right past them.

An elderly woman stood in the shallow water. She held hands with two children. Natalie couldn't see her face, but she could hear her laughter as the children jumped into each crashing wave. When the red-haired woman tapped her forcefully on the shoulder, abruptly, the laughter stopped. The elderly woman turned around slowly. Natalie watched her face drain of color.

"What do you think you're doing?" Allegra spat out the question.

She hadn't even bothered to roll up her leggings before joining them in the ocean. Saltwater soaked her legs. She knew that people were staring, but she was accustomed to being the center of attention, ignoring the glances of the mob and getting the job done anyway. When Véronique blushed, Allegra nearly rolled her eyes.

"Did you not see my note, *mademoiselle*?" Véronique asked.

"I did. You couldn't wait to ask for permission, so you thought to ask for my forgiveness instead?"

"I beg your pardon?"

"You took my children out of my house without asking me!" Allegra shouted.

"*Maman*, why are you yelling?" Delphine whispered, tugging on Allegra's sleeve.

"*Maman*, people are staring," Jules whispered.

Allegra jerked her head back to the shore. Sure enough, a small crowd had gathered to watch them. By the water, a small boy hid behind his mother. The sight of the other woman nearly made Allegra snarl. Shoulder-length blonde hair. A loose fisherman's sweater and rolled-up, expensively distressed jeans. A box of donuts in one hand. She reeked of suburbia, though she clearly lacked the tact to look away.

"*Monsieur* Etienne demands that I let him sleep late on Saturday mornings," Véronique said, her fingers worrying her necklace. "The children have not adjusted to the time change yet. I thought only to let you sleep as well."

At the sound of his name, Allegra narrowed her eyes. Her fingers balled into fists.

"Etienne doesn't live here."

"But, *mademoiselle*, I work for *Monsieur* Etienne."

"And you live in my house. My house; my rules. You will never again take my children anywhere without asking me first. Have I made myself clear?"

"Perfectly clear," Véronique said, though her voice was hard and flinty.

From the corner of her eye, Allegra watched the suburban mom guide her son inland. The other woman bent to ruffle his brown hair and kiss his forehead. She whispered something that made him laugh. She was distracting him.

Let her keep her judgment, Allegra thought. *No one is trying to take her boy away.*

Allegra held out her hands to her children. They paused for a moment, staring back at her with their own wide-set grey eyes, before clasping her fingers.

"We should go home now," Allegra said. "People have started to stare."

Véronique pursed her lips. "*Oui, mademoiselle*. People are always watching.

"Donuts!" Aaron shouted.

Leaping from his stool at the kitchen island, Aaron raced towards them to grab the box.

"I made eggs," Eliana said. "Want some?"

"Absolutely. Sorry for taking so long," Natalie said, before stealing hugs from Lola and Silvia while they ate their breakfast. Everett scrambled onto a stool at the island. He smiled broadly at his plate, piled high with eggs and toast and berries.

"Thank you, Auntie Eliana."

"You're welcome, kiddo," Eliana said. "And Nat, I will not accept any apology for lingering. That's the whole point of the vacation."

Natalie smiled. "Point taken. Aaron wasn't worried, was he?"

"Hard to tell. He's been on that thing the entire time you've been gone."

Eliana jerked her head in Aaron's direction. He stood in front of an open window, not looking outside at the sun now peeking through porous clouds. Instead, he scarfed down his donut with one hand. With the other, he flicked his finger over his phone. His brow furrowed.

"Aaron, is that Daddy you're texting with?"

"Nope," Aaron mumbled, his mouth half-full. "Already talked to Dad this morning."

"Okay then, it's time to put your phone away."

"But Mo-om, my friends!"

"You won't feel any closer to them because they posted a picture of their breakfast."

Aaron rolled his eyes, but he set his phone down and stepped outside. She watched as he took a seat in an Adirondack chair to finish his donut there.

"That looks like a lot," Eliana said. "I'm alarmed to think of all of the parenting that I still have to do."

With a grin, Natalie poured herself a mug of coffee. She nodded to Lola, Silvia, and Everett who were giggling at the island and mumbling verboten potty words under their breath.

"Fortunately, it doesn't happen all at once. And when I'm exasperated with my tween, I still have Everett who needs to learn to not chase a ball into traffic or swallow a grape whole. You know, basic survival training."

Eliana chuckled. "How was your first walk on the beach?"

"Draining."

"What? What happened?"

"Nothing really, except that there was this horrible woman screaming at her mother."

She looked out to the beach: the few whitecaps, woven into the dark water like ivory thread, had dispersed. The wind had settled. Natalie willed her own quick pulse to do the same.

"That's odd," Eliana said. "It's a little early for a confrontation. I'm willing to let everybody win before I've had coffee. To each her own, I guess."

"I actually stood my ground and just stared at her. I wanted her to know that I would witness everything. Her children seemed really upset."

"Your hands are shaking."

With a grimace, Natalie set her fork down gently. Silvia slid down her stool, yelling, "Can't catch me!" before she tore off into the darkest recesses of the mammoth home. Everett and Lola gave chase immediately. Their echoes rattled the walls. Natalie cast a glance outside to where Aaron sat. As she watched him watching the water, Natalie felt her spine loosen.

"Remember: your parents are gone now."

Natalie exhaled a ragged sigh. "I know, but I can't seem to let them go."

"You will," Eliana said, cupping her hand over Natalie's fingertips. "Someday, you'll realize that you're either here with us or you're with them. And you'll choose to stay with us."

Nodding, Natalie pulled a long, deep breath. After stealing a last sip of coffee, Natalie gave Eliana a parting wink and stepped outside.

"Aaron, want to toss the ball around before you hit the ocean? I'm the one who taught your Aunt Eliana to play lacrosse, you know. I've got skills."

Aaron shot a quick glance toward Natalie. As she stood barefoot on the deck, jiggling a ball in the worn lacrosse stick she'd had since high school, a slow grin crossed his face.

"You did tell me you'd help me with my stick grip."

Natalie nodded. "And now that your hands and mine are finally free, we can play."

On the back lawn, Jules whacked the ball with his cricket bat. Delphine ran to collect it for him, her long blonde curls bouncing against the back of her smocked shirt. Allegra's nose wrinkled as she watched Delphine from the kitchen window. She wore a grosgrain bow, a cashmere sweater, and tailored culottes. Allegra made a mental note to procure for her some sweatpants from the local outlets.

The thought of how Etienne would rage when he heard about it all, discount shopping and ever-so-slightly flawed clothes, made her smile. Biting back a laugh, Allegra carried a tray to the patio.

"Thanks for the cricket set, *Maman*!" Jules shouted.

"Yes, thank you so much!" Delphine parroted.

"Anything for the littlest loves of my life," Allegra said.

They stared at her, their smiles plastered to their small faces for a beat too long. She tried to ignore the nagging, hangnail sense that something was off.

They're just polite, Allegra thought. *The most well-mannered children in the world.*

Still, she poured glasses of lemonade with a parched mouth. It had been six hours since she'd lost her temper on the beach and a full twenty-two hours since she'd last seen them laugh.

"Thank you, *mademoiselle*," Véronique said quietly as she accepted her glass of lemonade.

"You're welcome."

She took a seat across from Véronique at the table. The other woman would not meet her eye. Allegra had baked cookies studded with M&Ms, but neither Véronique nor the children ate them. Jules and Delphine snuck glances at their mother as they played, while Véronique read her book and sipped her drink. The lovely picture they must have made, women and children relaxing in the backyard on a temperate summer day, belied the tense undercurrent running beneath their gathering. Allegra sighed. None of it was ever as it looked to be.

"I'm sorry, Véronique."

Véronique continued to look at her book, but her fingertips went still on the page.

"I beg your pardon, *mademoiselle*?"

"I'm so sorry for losing my temper with you earlier. You didn't deserve that treatment."

Véronique raised her chin, flashing steely blue eyes at Allegra. Her nostrils flared.

"I require a professional working environment at all times."

"I understand that."

"That is good to hear, *Mademoiselle* Allegra."

Allegra paused for a long moment, pulling a long drag of air that contained a potpourri of lilies and salt air and honeysuckle. "But your professional working environment is also my home. I haven't seen my children for any length of time since last summer, aside from monthly visits to Luxembourg. Being apart from them for so long has been unbearable. I may be your employer's wife, but I'm also their mother. And when I woke up to find them gone, I panicked."

Véronique closed her book. "Then I will not take them anywhere again without your prior approval. You will always know where they are. Is that better for you?"

"Yes," Allegra said, her lips quivering. "That is much better for me. Thank you."

Just then, Jules discovered the small squirt gun that Allegra had stashed behind a hydrangea bush. He immediately ran towards Delphine and squirted her right in the face. Delphine burst into tears. Jules raced to Delphine and helped her brush water from her cheeks. Carefully, he smoothed back her hair.

"*Désolée*, Delphine. *Désolée*."

Allegra shook her head. "Five minutes of roughhousing and he's already apologizing to her. I can't believe that half of him came from me."

"Yes, they are quite well-mannered, *mademoiselle*." Her voice fell away.

"I wish they would start their game again. They don't play enough."

"But he is not playing with her," Véronique said. "He is parenting her."

Allegra straightened her spine. It was then that she realized how little had changed with a transatlantic flight and the shedding of time zones. They might be in her home, but her children were still locked away in their own world. If she were to embrace them now, they would submit to her hug, as all polite children offer their slight forms to the grown-ups who demand their affection. But they would remain right out of reach.

They weren't hers or Etienne's, after all. They were old souls masquerading as children, biding their time until the day when they would finally be permitted to chart the course of their own lives. They were already gone, Allegra realized. They just weren't able to leave her yet.

Véronique and the children, ever polite, looked away as Allegra folded her hands across her face and wept.

Chapter 10

"Come on, Everett! You can do it! Just two more steps!"

Natalie tightened her grip on Lola while the toddler thrashed wildly on the edge of the foamy surf. As Aaron boogie-boarded past them, Everett yelled words lost to the wind.

"What did you say, Bug?" Natalie asked.

Everett folded his arms across her chest. "It will *eat* me."

"Everett, look at your brother. He's been going out farther than me and he's fine."

"He's not as tasty as me."

Natalie watched Everett retreat to his sandcastle. In the five days since they had arrived, Everett had been resistant to even getting his feet wet. He preferred soft, warm sand. He only tolerated the packed sand by the water's edge, eyeing the ocean like it could bare teeth. He sought out seashells and driftwood. He chased seagulls. He napped under the umbrella. However much he'd taken to the rhythm of life by the ocean, Everett would not take his mother's hand, float on the water's wavering surface, and let it carry him.

Silvia joined Everett by his sandcastle. Eliana, still on the phone, caught Natalie's eye and shrugged with her. Sandwiching her phone between her cheek and neck, Eliana applied more sunscreen to Everett's nose and lowered a baseball cap onto his head. Natalie watched as Eliana tossed back her head, laughing loudly into the phone, and turned her back on them all. Natalie sighed, trying valiantly to ignore last summer's memory: Harris laughing with Everett, carrying him on his shoulders in the aqua water of the Florida panhandle.

Natalie felt an insistent tugging on her hand.

"Me do that!" Lola yelled as she pointed to Aaron riding another wave to shore. "Please, please! Me can go faster than Aaron!"

"I bet you can, too, but the thing is: you're still three."

Lola groaned before smashing her face into the water. When she raised her head again, Lola was sputtering and giggling and splashing. Natalie couldn't help but laugh. Lola growled when Natalie pulled her out of the water.

Moments later, Natalie shook her head at the towel that Eliana held out of her.

"I forgot how much you remind me of a certain blonde-haired beauty."

Eliana raised her eyebrows, knotting her own dark hair into a topknot. "That one? Josh and I ask ourselves all the time where she came from. We call her our 'little recessive gene.' "

"I'm not talking about the way she looks. I'm talking about her fearlessness."

"Oh, I'll never be as brave as Lola. None of us will. She was scaling countertops at one. She finds choking hazards like a heat missile," Eliana said. They watched Lola raise a shovel like a sword and point it menacingly at Everett's belly button. Eliana tented her hands to her mouth and shouted: "Don't even think about it, Lola!"

While Natalie chuckled, Lola took off towards the dunes. Once there, she sunk her sword into the sand, like she'd claimed the land as her own.

"What do you think: so far, so good?"

"It's been dreamy, but I wish Everett would get his feet wet. I mean that, you know, literally."

"He'll get there. Aaron seems happy, though."

Aaron tucked the boogie board in his armpit and took long strides to carve a path back into the ocean. He glanced back at

Natalie and waved to her before looking out to sea again.

"He does. I love that he's off his phone and outside all day," Natalie said. "And tell me: how is Josh on this, the sixth phone call so far today?"

Eliana reddened. "It's a bit too much, isn't it? We haven't spent the summer without each other since we were teenagers, so we're still figuring it all out."

"Well, I'm in complete favor of your East Coast sojourn – and not only because I'm the primary beneficiary of it. I think it's brilliant to have a summer on your own terms."

"You do?" Eliana asked softly.

"It's what Lola would do."

Eliana chuckled. "That's very true."

"Have you given any thought to visiting your dad?"

"Have you given any thought to calling a divorce attorney?" Eliana asked, though she winced as soon as she clapped back with a question of her own.

Natalie paused. "I guess I'm not quite ready yet."

"I'm sorry. I guess I'm not quite ready yet, either."

"Can you take the helm?" Natalie asked, rising to her feet. "We need some food. I'm going to head out to the grocery store."

"Yes, of course. We're fine here."

"Let my favorite fish know where I am if he ever comes out of the ocean."

"Will do. And Natalie? I really am sorry."

"Me too."

Natalie enjoyed the languid trip to the grocery store by herself, padding through its warren of aisles in her flip-flops. She'd forgotten the sweet reminders of beach life that punctuated even the most banal errands. An entire aisle dedicated to sunscreen. An offering of sand toys near the florist. With a soft grin, Natalie tossed an extra pint of ice cream and a bag of coffee into the cart. She crisscrossed the store haphazardly, without her customary list. Having returned to the deli for a second time, she came upon a box of Berger's cookies and grinned. She'd forgotten how much she and Annabel had loved the fudge-coated treats, how they'd eaten them on the patio as fireflies flickered near the hydrangeas.

She could taste the chocolate on her tongue. And just as suddenly, she smelled magnolia.

Even though she knew her mother would make her wait to taste them, she'd salivated as she'd dropped the cookies into the grocery cart. She could see her mother, Annabel's face hidden by her curtain of flaxen hair, standing beside her.

He was there, too, but Annabel hadn't seen him yet. As soon as she'd spotted him, Natalie had quickly taken the cookies out of the cart and put them back. He had never cared for chocolate. Though her head only reached her mother's hip, Natalie moved to shield her.

She'd seen him coming, but Natalie still fell hard to the floor when he shoved her with such force. Her mother yelped. Without a word, he twisted her mother's shiny, spun-gold hair into his fist and led her out of the store that way.

And just as abused dogs will be led, though their teeth are sharp and their bark is loud, Annabel followed him. Natalie followed them, too, as silent as a shadow.

Natalie quickly put the cookies back. Her pulse quickened. Sweat bled across her brow. She rested her hand on her stomach, trying to remember to breathe. The space, at once too bright and too loud, seemed to spin. She looked at her full cart. She turned on her heel and ran out of the store, abandoning the ghosts that had once more come too close.

"I couldn't do it," Natalie said, before handing Eliana her meatball sub.

Like seagulls to sandwich scraps, their children came running. Aaron was already chewing his sub by the time Everett reached them. Aaron methodically unwrapped the paper covering Everett's sandwich for him, while Natalie helped Lola and Silvia smooth out their beach towel for a picnic. Eliana chewed her sandwich slowly, barely tasting it, while she watched her friend, unable to meet her eye.

"What do you mean?" Eliana asked.

Natalie waited a moment until the children were situated. When they had each claimed a spot on the sand with a sandwich in their lap and a drink by their side, Natalie took a seat beside Eliana. She exhaled a long, shaky breath.

"I think I had an anxiety attack at the grocery store."

"What?" Eliana asked. She dropped her sandwich and took Natalie's hand.

"Did I ever tell you about the time the police were called to the grocery store?"

"No."

"I must've forgotten the whole thing, but being back here, I don't know. I remembered. My father surprised us. He did that a lot. He would show up where we were. I think he wanted to track her or to make clear that we were never really free of him. Most of the time, people looked the other way. But that time – he led her out of the store by her *hair*, Ellie. We were walking home from the store and the police found us on the way. I remember so many questions. They took us to the police station. They gave me juice and animal crackers."

"Oh, Natalie. I had no idea."

"My mom left the cart full of groceries. What choice did she have? And today, I did the *very* same thing. I felt like I couldn't breathe. Like I was about to die," Natalie whispered, while her skittish eyes swept across the stretch of dented sand. "I'm in this exquisite home on a perfect beach and I'm falling apart. I'm a mess."

"You're not a mess. You're a *survivor*. You survived your dad's abuse and your mom's choice to stay with him. And maybe this is the first time you're really dealing with it."

"I don't think I can ever go back to that store. When my heart rate normalized, I went to a farmer's market instead. Do you think we can split up the grocery trips?"

"Nope."

Natalie blinked. "What?"

"We're going back to the house."

"Did you hear what I said?" Natalie said, unable to snuff out the panic from her frantic whispers. "I can't handle a grocery run in this town from one blasted memory and you want me to go back to the source of some of the worst experiences of my life?"

"I do, but I'll go with you."

"Eliana!"

"If you avoid what scares you, your fear expands and your world shrinks. You have to face it. Come on. We'll bring the kids. We'll try to make it fun."

Natalie opened her mouth but found her tongue dry. She watched, unable to move or speak, as Eliana rolled up their beach towels. She glared at her friend. Eliana caught Natalie staring at her and shrugged, her smile wilting.

"At the very least, we have to go back to that house to prove to you that your father doesn't live there anymore."

They ambled down Rehoboth's quaint Main Street, flanked by restaurants and storefronts, like any other family out for a leisurely stroll. Eliana pushed her girls in a double stroller. Aaron helped Everett ride a scooter down the sidewalk. Together, they avoided crashing into passersby. Natalie had lingered in front of The Coffee Mill, and again in front of Browseabout Books.

"We could stop here for a moment," Natalie said. "What's a vacation without a beach read? We haven't made a pilgrimage to the bookstore yet."

Eliana nodded while gently guiding Natalie by her elbow. "That's a good idea. We'll come back tomorrow."

They crossed the street. A few minutes later, Natalie planted her feet in front of the Dogfish Head Brewery. Watching her, Eliana suppressed a smile.

"Do you think the kids are hungry again? Looks like there's some empty tables in there."

"There isn't a crowd because it's three o'clock in the afternoon. We agreed that we would grab dinner afterwards. Stop stalling, Nat."

"I don't think I can do this."

"Sure, you can. And even if you can't, I'm not giving you a choice in the matter."

After passing Dogfish, they turned left onto Grove Street, and Natalie's heart constricted a little more. She tried to ignore her chest, tightening and flaring with pain, as she focused instead on the children. Aaron, so often in trouble for antagonizing Everett, was guiding him expertly over pavement and sidewalks. Meanwhile, idle chatter drifted from the stroller. Lola and Silvia shared a whispered conversation. Natalie heard Silvia's soft phrases overlaid with Lola's loud, pulsing thoughts. She closed her eyes, her lips formulating the muted wish that she could go home. And then her eyes shot back open, her gut churning with the stark realization that there was no home left to go to.

"I used to get anxiety attacks a lot in my old job."

Natalie jerked her neck toward Eliana. "What?"

"Not the whole time – mainly in the beginning. When I first started working as a translator for the UN, I felt so out of my depth. I worried constantly that I would, quite literally, miss something in translation. A word that had no English counterpart. An idiomatic expression that I would get wrong. Looking back, it was straight-up imposter syndrome. But I was sure that I was the only person who'd ever felt that way."

"I had no idea."

"I never told anyone," Eliana said. "Not even Josh."

"What did you do?"

"I realized that everything golden is right beyond what terrifies us."

Gilded light filtered through to puddle on dry, hot streets. Smoky, warming scents continued wafting toward them from the town's restaurants, but now the oil-fryer fragrance hovered with notes of honeysuckle and rose. Closing her eyes, Natalie realized that it had been years since she had smelled grass cuttings laced with an ocean breeze.

They turned another corner. Her eyes locked on her boys, walking side by side now like asymmetrical bookends, and she stopped walking. Natalie lost her breath.

"Maybe we should go back," Eliana said, as she wrapped an arm around Natalie.

"What? What about 'facing what scares me'? And 'expanding my world'?"

Eliana winced. "I'm sorry. I don't want to force you to do something you're not ready to do. It's your summer vacation, and you've been through a lot. I think it's a bad idea."

A block ahead, Aaron raced alongside Everett. Natalie heard their laughter, closed her eyes, and took long, deep breaths.

"I want to go," she whispered. She resumed her steady pace.

"Are you sure? I feel like I've given too much unsolicited advice today. It's your life, Natalie. Yours. Not mine or anyone else's to—"

"I want to go," she began, louder this time, "but you may have to do the talking."

"That's never been a problem for me.

Natalie nodded. "My heart feels like it's about to burst."

"But your feet are moving fine."

Through dark sunglasses, Allegra watched them come. She planted her feet and braced herself. If she were anyone else in her position, she would've locked the door. But then, if she were anyone else, they wouldn't have come for her.

She sighed. Why did they have to find her today? Today, of all days. Today marked the first day since the reckoning that her children had laughed again. Today had been beyond anything Allegra could have designed in her wildest dreams. She had done her part, of course, with Mickey Mouse pancakes for breakfast and new sand toys for the beach. Still, it was Jules who had asked her to play catch and Delphine who reached for her hand in the waves. Even Véronique, bastion of buttoned-up etiquette herself, had purchased take-out for an impromptu picnic. They'd eaten crab cake sandwiches, while seagulls cawed overhead and waves crashed. Time had unwound at a syrupy pace, measured only by the shifting light inching across the sand.

Allegra flattened her lips into a thin line. She'd grown too smug, caught in the quicksand illusion that they were alone in their own little world. Yet, there could be no hiding with her familiar face. There was only a finite sense of elation when she outpaced the mob nipping at her heels.

She couldn't understand why they had brought children with them.

Allegra sighed a broody puff of air. It would either be a standard ask for an autograph or a new reporter's tactic, the motherly equivalent of keeping a drink filled. A way to loosen her defenses. Shaking her head, Allegra watched them come closer. They were already pointing at her, whispering behind their hands to their children. She was accustomed to being talked about in a low hush by people who would stare but couldn't quite meet her eye. She was accustomed to pictures taken without her consent. She knew what it was to have people come too close, each step toward her a small, clumsy invasion.

Let them come, Allegra thought.

But then, Allegra recognized one of the women: the suburbanite blonde from the beach. She recognized the floppy-haired boy, now riding a scooter. With this awareness, any last attempt at politesse faded. Allegra narrowed her eyes. Her perfect mouth, all polished veneers framed by plump lips, contorted into a snarl.

The house was smaller than she remembered. In her memory, the house boasted cathedral-height ceilings and a sprawling lawn. But it was diminished now, nothing more than a small cottage on an unkempt lot. She noticed other details, too. Peeling paint. Overgrown bushes. A screen-door hung crookedly in its frame. A fence around the backyard bent westward, slouching away from grueling gale-force winds that had beaten it sideways.

When Natalie stared into the two windows of her childhood room, partially shuttered now as though half-asleep, she steeled herself to be considerate. Someone had clearly tried. Grass seed had been scattered in patches around the yard. Zinnias bloomed in the garden bed and potted geraniums framed the cracked stoop. Natalie heard laughter fall like rain from open windows. The musical high notes of children playing, maybe two or three, ricocheted from shaded rooms. The sound of laughter was so incongruous with her childhood memories that her chest expanded, her heart sopping up the sound as though to quench a thirst.

Too soon, however, Natalie spotted a woman dressed entirely in black standing on the stoop. Her tentative smile faded.

"We should go," she hissed to Eliana. "That's the woman who—"

Eliana braced her shoulders. "We've made it here, though. Let me do the talking."

"You don't understand. She's—"

But Eliana had already marched away from her. Aaron and Everett flanked Eliana, who now carried the green scooter against her hip while she made her way to the lady in black. With a deep sigh, Natalie pushed the stroller behind them. She felt weak, even dizzy, as she took sluggish steps toward her childhood home.

"Hi there, my name is Eliana Rollins, and that's my friend, Natalie Blackburn."

"Hello," the woman said. She didn't smile.

"We – Natalie and I – we grew up on this beach. We came here every summer."

"Did you," she said. It wasn't a question.

"Yes, and – funnily enough – your home was actually Natalie's beach house. We were wondering if we could poke our heads in and take a look around? The kids would love to see where their mom grew up. Isn't that right, Aaron?"

Aaron raised his brow. "Sure."

"It would only take a moment," Eliana said, fixing a bright smile on her face. "We wouldn't want to intrude."

"But that's exactly what you would be doing: intruding."

"I'm sorry?" Eliana asked, a rising flush reddening her skin. "We certainly don't mean to bother you. We were taking a walk in the area and feeling nostalgic."

"It may have been her house then, but it's my house now."

Aaron shot rapid-fire glances from his mother to Eliana, to the other woman, and back again. His forehead creased. Biting his lower lip, he pushed Everett behind him and took a step away from Eliana. He retreated closer to his mother.

"I think you misunderstand our intention," Eliana said, speaking slowly.

"And I think it's time for you to leave."

Eliana gaped at Allegra, while Allegra folded her arms across her chest. Aaron took the scooter from Eliana's closed fist and centered Everett on it once more.

"I think we should go too, Aunt Ellie," Aaron said. "We don't need to see Mom's old house. It wouldn't look the same anyway. Nothing ever lasts."

Behind him, Natalie tore her gaze from the other woman, still vibrating with unspoken hostility on a patch of parched grass, and stared after Aaron instead. She watched Aaron place a hand on the small of Everett's back, guiding him away. Not walking toward her but walking *away* from it all. A chill shot up her spine to think that they were following in her footsteps, putting space between themselves and the adults meant to guide them.

As soon as Eliana reached her, her pupils dilating and her lips pursed, they followed the boys away. Back toward the beach. Back toward the lake. Neither one looked again at the small cottage.

"I know her," she whispered.

"Me too," Natalie said. "She was the angry woman from the beach."

"No. *We* know her. You and me. I knew what her voice would sound like before she even opened her mouth to speak."

Natalie paused. "I know. I thought that too: we have a history with her."

Allegra entered her home and yelped, bumping immediately into Véronique.

"Who were they?"

Allegra shrugged. "Random fans? Nosy people? Reporters? Who knows?"

"Reporters? But they had children with them?"

"It could be a tactic. They're a bloodthirsty bunch. They'll do anything for a story."

Véronique shook her head, clucking her tongue against her teeth. "To think that anyone would come for you here, while you're with your family."

"They'll always come for me."

Her own children continued playing upstairs. Allegra closed her eyes to the sound of their boisterous laughter, as though it were a sonorous river that could wash over her.

"But how did they find you? I thought this house was held in *Monsieur* Etienne's trust?"

"No," Allegra said. "It's in my name now."

"Well, I guess it's inevitable. Possibly like the thrill of the hunt, *non*?"

"Possibly. Or, Etienne could have sent them after me," Allegra said, ignoring Véronique's sharp intake of air. "It wouldn't be the first time."

Chapter 11

The days and nights, ablaze as they marched toward the summer solstice, moved with a languorous rhythm. Their families rose with the sun, roused by cartoons and endless cups of hot coffee. They ate breakfast on the deck. For lunch, they picnicked on the beach. In the stickiest hours of the day, they put the little ones down for a nap. The house quieted then, when Natalie, Eliana, and Aaron climbed into the large sectional couch in the great room and read books with the windows open. They drank more coffee. They talked about what to eat for dinner, what to savor for dessert. They took an evening walk on the beach. They held out for as long as they could, lingering until the sand fleas nipped at their ankles and a violet haze blanketed the ocean. With dusk settling at such a late hour, they put the children to bed while lavender color still stained the sky. When the night faded to black, Aaron headed up to sleep. Most evenings, Eliana and Natalie enjoyed a glass of wine on the deck, taking comfort in the gentle roar of the ocean even when they could no longer see beyond its rim of frothing, swirling foam.

It was Saturday morning. Very quietly, Natalie tiptoed through the front door with a box of donuts under her arm. She'd taken it upon herself to maintain Harris's traditions. When Natalie put the donuts on the island, she looked out the kitchen window and smiled to see a familiar brown head.

Seconds later, Natalie pushed open the sliding door.

"Hey there, Birthday Boy."

"I made coffee," Aaron said. He sat on the deck with his back to her. His brown curls moved with the wind.

"And I appreciate that. Moving on to more important matters: Happy birthday to *you*, happy birthday to *you*! Happy birthday, dear—"

With a plated marble donut in hand, Natalie went still. The lone birthday candle flickered wildly in the cold morning wind. She glared at Aaron. He'd shoved something under the blanket covering his lap. He looked away, unwilling to meet her eyes.

"What do you have there?"

Aaron smiled without his eyes. "Is that donut for me?"

"Aaron, your father and I have discussed this with you before. You are not allowed to be on your phone so early in the morning. It's unhealthy for you."

"My phone's still charging in the kitchen."

"What is it, then?"

With a sigh, he yanked a yellow legal pad out from under the blanket. He pursed his lips, glowering, while he exchanged it for the donut. He blew out the candle. As she turned the pages, Natalie forgot to remind him to make a wish.

It was a legal pad unlike any she'd ever seen. Marked with still-life sketches and curlicue doodles. Shaded with pencil and charcoal. Her hand froze on his latest effort: a landscape sketch done entirely in a #2 pencil. He had drawn a near-mirror image of their view of the Atlantic. In his creation, she could see the high tide swelling and swallowing more of the shoreline. Seagulls fluttered in a sky strewn with long, finger-like clouds. A small fishing boat rode the horizon line.

"How did you get such a deep color from a pencil?" she asked, her voice thick.

"I used my tongue to wet the pencil. It's tricky to do it and not break a hole through the paper, but I'm getting better," Aaron said, squirming. "So, what do you think?"

"I think it's breathtaking."

Aaron smiled, licked some icing from his thumb, and stared back out to sea.

"It's for Dad. This way, he can have some of our mornings, too."

Natalie closed her eyes briefly. "He'll love it. It's so thoughtful of you."

"He doesn't know I can do this yet. It's a surprise."

As he hadn't in years, Aaron shed his blanket and climbed into her lap. Natalie took a good, long inhale of his scent, all faint perspiration and Tide detergent and donut, and rested her chin on top of his head. She would hold him as long as he would let her.

"Sweetie, I didn't know you could do that, either."

She felt his smile broaden against her neck. "My art teacher gave me charcoals as a present. He made me promise to practice all summer. I'm doing my best. I'd like to try a watercolor class. See what I can with less control."

Unexpectedly, tears coated her eyes. Natalie could then see a hand moving over the canvas in the sunlight, sketching the circle that would become a face. When she closed her eyes, she could smell the strong odors of oil paint and turpentine softened by a hint of magnolia.

"You know, my mother started with sketches like this when she was a girl."

Aaron looked at her, his forehead folding. "I've only seen her paintings."

"She never stopped sketching. She used to call her sketches the 'bones' of a 'body.' But I always thought they were beautiful all on their own."

Aaron looped his arms around her neck. For a long moment, neither of them spoke. They looked at the ocean and watched the waves roll in and out. Their own breath latched onto its rhythm, moving in lockstep with the surf.

"I'm sorry we didn't get to see the house."

"Me too," Natalie murmured. As soon as she spoke the words, she knew them to be true.

"And I'm sorry, you know, that you don't have your mom and dad anymore."

"I still have them," she whispered. "They come back to me in all sorts of ways."

"Like how?"

"Like today, when I saw your sketches. No one else in our family can do that. It's your gift, but it's a gift my mother would have understood. She would've been awake with you this morning. Sketching right alongside you. You can keep people with you when you love what they loved. So today, you brought her back to me."

He smiled at that. For a brief moment, Natalie looked beyond him to steal a glance at the world through his eyes. The dewdrops on the potted zinnias. The sunlight on the sand. The sandpipers skittering across the sand. All of it was worthy of Aaron's careful attention. In time, she rested her chin on his head and closed her eyes.

Maybe her heart hadn't been broken, exactly. Maybe it had cracked wide open.

But even the dreamiest morning eventually collapses into day.

Natalie groaned as the thought took hold, quelling the urge to climb back into her pajamas. Instead, she examined the contents of her closet. Her borrowed closet was a jewel box that she would never fill with her belongings. Her clothes, carefully chosen and dutifully loved, looked plain in this room with endless shelves and drawers and mirrors. Blowing out her lips, she sank onto an ottoman. Maddeningly, she was thirty-five years old, and she had nothing to wear.

After a handful of minutes had passed, a gentle knock sounded at the door.

"Yes?"

Eliana peeked into her closet. "The little ones are down for their nap, and Aaron and I miss our reading buddy. Did you get lost?"

"No. It's just ... seeing Harris again."

"Oh, him."

"Yes, him," Natalie said, exhaling. "Is it crazy to be nervous to see your own husband?"

"Not exactly, but I don't think a man who walks out on his wife and family deserves a second thought. If it were up to me, he wouldn't have been invited."

Natalie raised an eyebrow. "If it were up to you and Josh, I wouldn't have married him in the first place. Don't gloat, now. It's poor form."

"Maybe that was true a long time ago, but you built a beautiful life with what's-his-face," Eliana said. She took a seat next to Natalie. "I won't wish the years you spent together away."

"But?"

"But. I don't think you should dress up for him. Not anymore."

"I'm not primping for him. It just bothers me that he thinks he knows me so well," Natalie said. "I hate that he knew I would put the kids first, that I wouldn't make a scene. I hate that my favorite sweatshirts were his first. I hate that he knows every outfit I own."

"Well then, what do you want to wear tonight?" Eliana asked, squeezing Natalie's hand.

"Don't know. I guess I want to surprise him. I want to prove to us both that I still can."

Eliana's eyes glittered in light filtered from dewdrop crystals hanging overhead from a chandelier. "That's what I was hoping you'd say. Come on."

Before Natalie could utter another word, Eliana grabbed her by the hand, started jogging, and dragged her down the hall to another master suite. Eliana pushed open the double doors and led Natalie to her own borrowed oversized closet. When Eliana pushed open the door, Natalie gasped. She took small, reverent steps inside.

Every open closet bloomed with dresses. Shoes sat sculpturally on the open shelves. Handbags were arranged by color. Sunglasses were arranged by shape. Natalie's eyes glazed over at the bold-faced names. Valentino. Gucci. Prada. Burberry. Givenchy. Without a word, she brought a soft Liberty scarf to her cheek and sighed.

"Are all of these yours?"

Eliana nodded. "Josh had them shipped. You know I've never been good with clothes, but he has these endless events, so I have a stylist now."

"You do realize that you live like royalty."

"Not royalty," Eliana said as she winked. "Maybe a landed marquess, though."

"Sweetie, I couldn't possibly wear any of this. What if I stained something or tripped or lost a button? Thank you, but we're not even the same size."

"Check the closet closest to the window."

Natalie raised an eyebrow but walked over to the closet as directed. Her fingers thumbed through gorgeous dresses, all at different lengths: mini, midi, maxi. When she looked at a tag, Natalie went still. They were all petite. All her size. All her favorite colors. She glanced back at Eliana, who was examining a necklace and determinedly not meeting her eye.

"All of these dresses are my size."

"Are they? How funny. My stylist must've made a mistake."

"You're 5'9". I'm 5'2". No one makes mistakes like that."

"Okay, fine. Maybe I wanted to buy you a few things."

"Ellie! I'm going to be okay. I can afford my own clothes."

Eliana rolled her eyes. "Just because you're capable of doing everything on your own doesn't mean you should have to. I know you pretty much raised yourself, but most of the rest of us require a tribe. It's only a dress, Nat."

"If it's only a dress, then I should wear something I already own."

Eliana paused. "He really broke your heart, didn't he?"

Through a sudden blur of tears, Natalie looked away to the window. The open window overlooked the lake. She could see the lake, smooth and clear and empty except for a trail of ducks. They glided over the calm water, hardly giving any indication at all of their wild, furious kicking right below the surface.

Natalie swallowed away the lump in her throat and turned back to Eliana with a half-smile. "I'll live."

Eliana cleared her throat. "When I worked as an interpreter, I wanted to blend. It was my job to serve as a messenger, so I wore a lot of black. Earth tones. Hair yanked back in a knot. Not much make-up. When Josh first started promoting his work and it was my job to stand beside him, I pretended like I didn't care. But really, I didn't know what I was doing. I was lost. I was anxious. I was starting all over again. Sound familiar?"

"I can't imagine *you* ever lost. What did you do?"

"I did what I always do: I delegated."

They both burst into laughter.

"I had no respect for my stylist at the beginning," Eliana continued. "I was horrible to Lisa – a total snob. I mean, how does one put shopping on a CV? But she saw something in me that I never saw in myself. She saw what I could be, and the clothes helped me get there. She had a vision for my new life. Lisa was the first person to ever see me in color."

"Oh, Ellie, everyone else sees you in color, too."

"Perhaps, but I wasn't aware of it."

"Not until you found a stylist."

"Amen."

They laughed again, a soft chortling interspersed with sighs.

"Well, if you needed a stylist, I'm going to need a whole glam squad," Natalie muttered.

"No, you don't. You need to know that you can change. And you're not the woman Harris thinks you are. You never were. If he knew you, he could've never hurt you this way. Because he would know that you're too good for this cheap, common pain. Forget him."

"I can't. He's the father of my children. My life with him going forward is going to be a constant act of diplomacy. That's the rub: he's always going to be there. Just not with me."

"Well then, *lucky* you," Eliana said, while she took fast strides to the one closet replete with clothes that wouldn't fit her. She pulled one dress from the bunch, turning it over in the sunlight like it contained its own prism. "I remember a dress like this one. A yellow dress."

Natalie rolled her eyes. "Don't even start. You know I can't stand that song."

"Your dad might've been playing the music, but you were the one dancing to it. His music belonged to *you* that night. Everyone was ignoring him because they were too busy watching you. You were beautiful."

"Were."

"*Are.* You're no different now than you were then. And, if memory serves correctly, you weren't dancing alone."

"Eliana," Natalie said, unwinding her friend's name into a low growl. A note of warning.

"Your life didn't begin with Harris Blackburn," Eliana said, as she draped a yellow dress over Natalie's lap. "It's time for you to remember that."

Eliana sat on the blacktop with the children, biting her lower lip as she sketched a chalk road. While she concentrated on making her road wide enough to accommodate multiple lanes of Everett's matchbox cars, Silvia tackled a parking lot. Eliana couldn't have cared less that she wasn't dressed for chalk drawing on pavement. She knelt down in a fitted Missoni dress covered in whisper-thin zigzags of tangerine and violet; she barely noticed the soft, fragile material, except for the passing thought that Lisa would be proud. She certainly wasn't dressed to blend in this evening.

Nearby, Aaron expertly dribbled the basketball as Lola mimicked his every movement in her smocked lavender dress. Eliana heard a whisper of sound every time the ball sailed through the net. It rarely smacked against the rim. He shot lay-ups and foul shots, occasionally stopping to pass the ball back and forth with Lola. Watching them from the corner of her eye, Eliana was careful to pretend like she hadn't noticed Aaron, not his ease with a basketball nor his tenderness with her daughter. She remembered what it was like to be thirteen and tried hard to not smile at him.

But when he took a shot that seemed impossibly far and absolutely worthy of three points, when it sailed through the air in a perfect arc and swished through the net, Eliana whistled.

"That was a pretty one, Aaron."

He grinned. "Easy peasy."

"You're too young to be so smug."

His smile faded, catching shadows in the bright sunlight. She opened her mouth to speak.

Before she could, a black town car with tinted windows rolled slowly into the driveway. The car came to a stop. Eliana took off running. She opened the back door before the chauffeur could even get to it. Josh exited the car, laughing. Eliana draped her arms around his neck and kissed him. Before too long, their two little girls each grabbed hold of his calves. Shaking his head and smiling widely, the chauffeur circled them, walked to the trunk, and began unloading Josh's bags.

"I missed my girls," Josh whispered, exhaling a long sigh. He nipped lightly at Eliana's ear and whispered. "You look stunning, Ellie."

Eliana blushed, wholly warm now in his arms. "You've seen this dress before."

"The way you wear it, it's new to me."

His words were throaty, his voice was deep, and she wanted to lean into him. But she pulled away, giving their girls space to scramble into his arms. They laughed while he tickled them and pressed kisses to his cheeks.

"Scratchy cheeks, Daddy," Silvia said with a giggle.

"That's Mommy's fault. Mommy picked a beach house far, far away. Daddy took a train, a plane, and a car to get to you."

"A horse?" Silvia asked.

"There's still time, Silvia. I'm sure I can work something out."

Lola stroked his other cheek and sighed. "Me grow fur here, too."

"Never know quite how to respond to you, Lola girl, but I'm happy to see you haven't changed," Josh said, while Eliana laughed with him. "Did you miss me?"

"So much!" Lola said.

"Love you, Daddy," Silvia said, her voice soft.

Just then, Eliana remembered that they weren't alone. Everett had abandoned his chalk drawing. Aaron had stopped playing basketball and stood beside him. They chewed on lips that drooped. Eliana felt her throat tighten. Spotting the boys, Josh set his daughters to the ground.

"What's this? No greeting from my godson? And you too, Everett, get over here and give me a hug. Hustle, boys!"

Both brothers broke into a grin and raced into his open arms. Eliana smiled, fighting the urge to kiss Josh hello all over again. She noticed that they both held on to Josh longer than they ever had. Josh, very reluctantly, was the first to pull away. He smiled widely at them.

"I have presents. Favorite godson and Birthday Boy goes first," he said. He pulled a small box from his back pocket.

"I'm your only godson," Aaron said, but he couldn't stop smiling as he unwrapped the small box and opened it. He gasped. "Are you serious?"

Josh nodded. "You have to take good care of it. It's one of a kind."

"What is it?" Everett asked. "A ring?"

"It's the ring that Ecne Knight wore in the movie! He twists this knob here, and it changes colors and helps him to fly and grow armor on his skin. Thanks so much, Uncle Josh!"

Josh chuckled. "No problem, Birthday Boy."

"I should find a special place for it in my room. You guys can help me," Aaron said.

He raced into the house with the children all on his heels. He seemed as assured of their constant presence, always hovering in his wake, as he would've been of his own stark shadow on the sunbaked driveway. Too young to play with Aaron properly, the toddling trio had nonetheless woven their routine and games and earnest conversation into his day. He was as much theirs as they were his. For a few stolen months, they belonged to each other.

"A family," Eliana said.

"What did you say?" Josh asked, wrapping an arm loosely around her shoulders.

"I didn't realize I'd spoken out loud."

Josh paused. "How is she?"

Eliana shrugged. "She's starting over, figuring out how to live on her own again."

"Promise me you won't learn the same lesson."

"What's that supposed to mean?"

Josh shrugged. "We've never lived apart, either. And here I am, visiting every other weekend. Don't get me wrong – I'm glad you can be there for Natalie, but our life right now scares the hell out of me. It's not that different from them."

"It's a whole different world," Eliana said, as she cupped his face in her hands and kissed him. She came up for air as the chauffeur, waiting politely on the front porch, cleared his throat. Their foreheads touching, they ignored him.

"How can you be so sure, Ellie?"

"Because we always try to fix what's broken. Because we want to be whole, to be together. Because our life will be what we want it to be. Because we're not them."

Chapter 12

Natalie tugged uncertainly at the spike poking out of her earlobe. She hadn't ever owned jewelry that could draw blood. She pushed a clammy hand through her hair and tried to exhale. Eliana had loaned her the spiked earrings, along with a delicate rose-gold charm bracelet that boasted a heart, a miniature Fabergé egg, and a shark's tooth.

"Tonight, of all nights, you can't come across as *all* soft," Eliana had said.

And perhaps she had a point because, since her wedding day, Natalie hadn't ever looked quite as soft as she did right now. She wore a dress by Bottega Veneta that looked like it had been designed for a paper doll. Layers of flowing yellow, textured tulle skimmed her calves. Braided satin straps grazed her shoulders. Half-moon cut-outs hugged her waistline. She had been anxious to try it on, yet the dress fit like it had been cut to her shape. With her hair styled into soft waves, she appeared diaphanous while the afternoon sun licked her silhouette. Natalie stared into the mirror at a woman she didn't recognize.

With tremulous fingers, she dragged pale pink lipstick across her mouth. She faked a smile.

A car door slammed. Laughter ricocheted with birdsong through the open window. She would've laughed at the absurdity of it: being nervous to see the one man she'd spent more time with than any other. If she were to close her eyes, Natalie could easily see the constellation of freckles on his back. The gold flecks in his brown eyes. The auburn hair along his forearms.

But those had only been surface intimacies, belying the deep ocean of betrayal that Natalie still couldn't reconcile with her husband. Her stomach churned with the sinking sensation that she'd never really known him if he could leave her so unmoored. He'd ambushed her with this reckoning before she too had had the chance to get on with it: to belong to someone new, to someplace new, or even, to belong to herself again. He had built himself a new life long before she'd known she couldn't depend on their old one.

Not for the first time, Natalie wondered if she would learn to hate him.

She sighed a ragged breath. A seagull cawed insistently, shaking her from her spiraling thoughts. Natalie squared her shoulders with the hefty realization that her boys would see this. They'd see their mother spitting out their father's name, lips curling and eyes narrowing, her soul blackening with each recounting of all the ways that Harris had wronged her. Or she could show her sons a tidal shift. The wind turning. The waves swelling.

If she played it right, they would see nothing more dramatic than a mariner reading the wind and changing course.

He'd told her two days ago that she could have the house. He'd told her this like he was giving her a gift. She'd hung up without a word, rushed to the bathroom, and dry-heaved. She could have nearly everything so long as he was free of her. However lovely she looked in this borrowed dress, Natalie couldn't shake the feeling of having been thrown away.

Others must be out there – right now, with her – choosing to go on. Maybe moving forward was down to the most minute decisions. Choosing to rise when she wanted to sleep. Choosing to eat when she couldn't taste. Choosing to hold her tongue when she wanted to trash him. Choosing to cry alone in the shower. Her sons might not remember all of this summer, but Natalie was damned if they wouldn't remember her looking beautiful in this yellow dress. Her sons would either know her as a victim or as her own champion. She would begin again for them. And maybe someday for her, too.

"You can do this," Natalie whispered, as she caught her eye, raised her chin, and dared her own image to defy her.

Her parents had raised her to fake a smile. She'd lie so well that they would all believe it. She would blow smoke. She would spin tales. She would fool them *all*.

After all, Natalie was nothing if not a woman who knew how to build a castle in the sand.

"Give me a squeeze, little ones!" Gloria shouted.

As they came running, she laughed and managed to wrap her arms around all four. She peppered their clean, damp heads with kisses. When overcome, Gloria Smyth muddled her careful American accent with her formative, Mexican lilt, each word saturated with weighty, rich color. Eliana, grinning, hung on to her mother's every word.

"What's this, my loves? You even look older. Taller. Stronger. And lucky for you, Aaron and Everett, exactly like your mom," Gloria said.

"Mother," Eliana hissed.

"And how are you, Aaron?" Gloria asked, ignoring her daughter and the trio of toddlers who had since wandered back to their chalk. He fidgeted under her hard gaze.

"I'm good. Same as always."

As though to punctuate this, Aaron ducked out of her embrace and curved an arm to sink the basketball through the net in a fast lay-up.

Josh whistled. "My inner nerd is starting to feel insecure again."

Gloria chuckled. "Your inner nerd has done quite well for himself."

"Still can't sink a foul shot, though," Josh muttered, applauding after Aaron leaped to shoot a three-pointer that never kissed the rim. "You're on fire, kiddo!"

Eliana linked arms with her mother. Together, they crossed the street, passed through the rolling wall of high grass, and stepped onto the narrow dock that jutted out into Silver Lake. They watched a pair of geese pass, casting ripples across the water.

"It's heavenly here," Gloria whispered. "I'm glad you stayed close this summer."

"I'll come visit soon. I promise."

"Whenever you're ready. He's very much changed now."

Eliana opened her mouth to speak, but the slam of a car door silenced her. Eliana looked back, narrowing her eyes. Her forehead pinched at the sight of Harris waving his boys over, kneeling to take them in his arms, and bowing his head as though in prayer. Aaron and Everett burrowed their faces into his neck. For a long moment, only Lola could be heard sword-fighting, having absconded with a handful of sea grass. Seagulls cawed. Geese honked. No one spoke.

Josh crossed his arms against his chest and met Eliana's eye. He shook his head.

"It breaks my heart to watch them this way," Gloria whispered.

Eliana swallowed. "Your heart isn't the one I'm worried about tonight."

Natalie had slipped onto the front porch. As her dress billowed, she was made golden by the high sun, reflecting off the water and making her glow. Her fingertips rested on her lips. She stood motionless and watched her boys hug her husband.

Eliana's breath caught. A rush of nostalgia quickly eclipsed the moment. She could see Natalie vividly as a skinny little girl wearing a dirty yellow bathing suit. Her oily hair. Her burned skin. She had stood at the top of the dunes, all alone, and Eliana had decided to be her friend. She had decided it the same way she'd decided to have a peanut butter and jelly sandwich for lunch, asking her to play with a shrug of the shoulder. She wondered now if the decision had really been hers to make, or if she'd recognized Natalie as she'd recognized Josh. A soulmate. A lifelong love. Family. And her stomach turned now to see her friend standing apart, alone yet again. Eliana turned her back on them all for a moment, back to the lake, gathering herself while her eyes pooled with tears. Her mom touched her shoulder. Eliana searched the lake for the geese once more, but they were gone.

"Mama!" Everett shouted. "You look boo-ful!"

Eliana and Gloria turned back like they had been summoned. Natalie had moved to the top of the stairs. Harris took a step toward her but stopped where he stood. His mouth opened and closed. Aaron looked at Natalie, his face a mask of naked consternation, as though trying to solve a puzzle.

Josh walked past them all, took the stairs two at a time, and wrapped Natalie in an embrace. Eliana smiled broadly, nearly clapping when she watched her husband guide her best friend down the stairs. His voice boomed.

"Nat, you do clean up well."

"Thank you," Natalie whispered, and then more loudly: "Looks like the gang's all back together again."

Natalie took a step towards Harris, faltered, and he quickly made up the difference. He embraced her so fast that she lost her breath. Natalie ached to push him off her. Just as she wanted to forget his smell and his name, she wanted to tell him – in the crudest terms possible – that he would never touch her again. But there was an audience. There would always be an audience. Everett joined their embrace, locking his arms around their legs. Aaron had resumed playing basketball, but Natalie knew full well that her soulful boy was taking it all in.

Someday, it would matter to him that it had mattered to

her to get it right.

She did pull away first, though, peeling her limbs from his.

"You do look beautiful," Harris said, and probably she was the only one to recognize the slight catch in his voice.

"Like a princess," Everett whispered.

Natalie ignored Harris, squatting to meet Everett's eye with a big smile. "Thank you, Bug. You know that I dressed up for you, right? You're my date."

He squealed. Harris forced a smile. He walked to where Josh waited with his own wide, hard grin, his face contorting painfully to support it. Natalie accepted the matchbox car that Everett handed to her and angled her ear toward Harris.

"It's good to see you again, Josh," Harris said, clasping Josh's hand. "Glad you could make it. How's the Hollywood life treating you?"

"You know me: luckiest man alive."

Harris smiled tightly, breaking the handshake. "I did see your profile in *Forbes*."

"That's not what I meant, friend. I have the most incredible wife. Two healthy girls. A long weekend with the loves of my life before I'm back to the grind. So, I'd say that all is well. What about you, Harry? Any developments?"

Aaron and Everett passed the ball back and forth. The smack of basketball meeting pavement pocked the stark silence that followed Josh's question. Natalie closed her eyes. She listened for sounds of water, for the ocean's roar and the lake's whisper. The thrumming between her ears softened with the water's gurgling sound. Natalie had forgotten how safe she'd felt at the edge of the ocean. It was the only place she'd ever known that could make her problems feel insignificant, as fleeting as any passing storm trudging along the coastline.

But she had still spent years trying to forget it.

When she opened her eyes, she found Harris looking at her. He looked away. The muscles in his jaw worked, a subtle flickering of light and shadow. Having stepped away from

Josh, Harris walked toward Aaron.

"So, Birthday Boy: it's your choice. Where are we having for dinner tonight?"

Aaron stopped dribbling the ball. He propped it onto his hip. He scanned the adults, all waiting on him. Perhaps he noticed their dresses, their jewelry, their fresh manicures, their pressed shirts, their shined shoes. He wiggled his eyebrows.

"Thought we might go crack crabs."

Unexpectedly, laughter erupted, as welcome a relief as light rain on hot skin. While they laughed, Aaron grinned and straightened his spine, drawing himself taller.

Only Natalie's smile wavered: to see her boy looking older, to see her husband managing so awkwardly, and to witness the fault lines widening within her family. They were on the precipice of fracture. Natalie prayed to the God she had never accepted, who had been Harris's more than He had ever been hers.

Please, give me one more day, she prayed. *Just one more day with my family.*

"You're certain you can handle this?" Allegra asked the question again.

Véronique sighed. "I have traveled across oceans with these children. I am quite capable of a long-distance drive, thank you."

"But you weren't the one doing the transporting. That was the pilot," Allegra muttered, while she tossed their luggage into the trunk and slammed it shut.

"What was that?"

"Nothing."

"I'll miss you, *Maman,*" Delphine whispered.

Allegra startled, turned on her heel, and immediately wrapped

Delphine in her arms. Jules came up behind her and embraced her from behind. Initially, these ninja hugs of theirs had caught her off guard. Allegra was unused to children gripping her tightly as she cooked, as she piled groceries into a cart, as she planted flowers. It became a dance of theirs: she would jump, they would apologize, she would make a funny face, and they would laugh. Eventually, her body relaxed to them. She realized that her children were simply checking in, making certain that their mother was still with them.

At least, Allegra hoped that was the reason. As much as she couldn't stand Etienne, she hoped that her children weren't as starved for affection as they appeared to be. She hoped he held them. She hoped he smoothed their hair. She hoped he plied them with big, noisy kisses. But from a hollow place deep within, Allegra knew that he did not. After all, Etienne had never held her unless it was the introduction to something more.

Not for the first time, Allegra wondered how she had ever married him. How could she have loved someone so deeply who didn't care to touch her?

"You'll be home when we get back?" Jules asked.

"I will. We'll have lots to talk about at dinner tomorrow night."

"You promise?" Delphine demanded.

"I promise."

"*Allons-y*, children," Véronique said. "It's time to go."

Reluctantly, they pulled apart from each other. The children climbed into Allegra's car. Allegra dropped her keys into Véronique's hand.

"And it will not trouble you too much to be without your car?"

Allegra shrugged. "The job's in Cape May, so I'll take an Uber to Lewes and catch the ferry from there. I'll be fine."

"I'm surprised that you trust me with your car. *Monsieur* Etienne does not."

Allegra tilted her head to the side. "I trust you with my kids. Nothing matters more."

Véronique nodded. For a long moment, they said nothing. A strong wind ruffled the bunch of Black-eyed Susans that Allegra had planted by the slouching mailbox. Allegra gazed at their sooty faces framed by rays of delicate burnt-orange petals. Unexpectedly, her eyes filled with tears. Véronique cleared her throat.

"If I may say so, *mademoiselle*, it is good what you are doing. It is good for you to take this job tomorrow. I know you don't want to go, but I believe it to be the right thing to do."

Allegra looked down at her hands. "It's just catalog work."

"But you are doing it for them," Véronique said softly. "You are doing the hard things all for them. As you said: nothing else matters."

Allegra nodded her head, chewing the inside of her cheek. Véronique reached forward, paused for a brief moment, and patted Allegra on the shoulder. Her gruff touch pulled an impish grin from Allegra. She shook her head with the realization that she was sad to see her children's nanny, an individual whom she had long referred to as "the other woman," go. It wasn't only the children she would miss this time.

Delphine rolled down her window. She waved a dog-eared paperback of Misty of Chincoteague out the window. Her eyes were large. Her voice was breathless.

"Do you think I'll see the horses, *Maman*?"

"*Madame* Véronique is taking you to Assateague, so I'm sure you'll come across lots and lots of equine traffic. Be careful on the pony boat tour."

"We will," Jules said, a glint of determination in his eye.

With more pointed coughing, Véronique started the engine. Allegra smoothed a stray hair from Delphine's forehead one more time and stepped to the side. With her arms crossed, she retreated to the crooked front stoop. She would not go inside yet. She wanted to be seen.

They waved wildly from their open windows. She waved wildly from her cement stoop. She plastered a massive smile on her face, and her bright, white teeth met theirs. As the black Hyundai eased down Newcastle Street and turned left onto Bayard Avenue, Allegra found herself wondering if their grins ached as much as hers did.

But then, they would be seeing wild ponies roam the beach and spending the night at a charming inn in Chincoteague, Virginia. Their smiles were probably real. She was the one who had to work, to play pretend with her own face. She shuffled into her house.

Two hours later, Allegra was carrying her carryall down the stairs and about to order an Uber when her phone began vibrating in her open palm. Her agent's name winked at her from the screen. She frowned.

"Hey, Penn," she said, tucking the phone between her neck and ear. "What's the matter? You don't trust me to make the shoot on time? I'm a handful, I know, but I've never been late."

"It's not that. I don't know how to say this. I'm so sorry."

"Why?"

"The client has decided to go in a different direction."

Allegra sunk into the couch. "What does that mean?"

"It means the client is pursuing other options."

"Is it because of my age or my ex?"

There was a pause, entirely vacuumed of sound. Allegra's brow furrowed as she pressed the phone hard against her ear.

"The client did acknowledge their reticence to hire you due to your tabloid presence."

"They didn't Google me until after the booking?"

"Apparently not," Penn said. "They knew your name had been more visible in recent years. It rang a bell for them. They just didn't know exactly why."

"What a waste," she breathed.

"Of course, they did acknowledge your truly excellent portfolio. They hope for the chance to work with you in the future once things have died down a bit."

"So, they can stand me up again at the last minute?"

"I'm so sorry," Penn said quietly. "I called as soon as I could."

"I know you did."

"And I guess this means another day with the kiddos. Every little bit counts, right?"

"Right," she whispered, her eyes already stinging. "Nothing else matters."

They hung up the phone, each racing to end the call as soon as they could. Allegra growled then, a guttural howl. Her flinty gaze landed on the fireplace. How she hated it with its flesh-toned brick and its dirty firebox, as useless as the gaping mouth of a dead fish. It was meant to be the heartbeat of their home, yet Allegra couldn't even make a fire. She laughed bitterly. Allegra pulled her knees to her chest. She couldn't formulate a thought beyond the visceral sense that the wasted, unproductive fireplace and she were the *same*.

She would hold tight to that grey thought. Allegra would not think then of lost time, of what had been taken from her, and of what she had willfully given away.

Chapter 13

After much haggling (and acknowledging the futility of choosing a favorite crab house on the Eastern shore), they settled on The Blue Crab in Bethany. In no short order, they managed to get a table, claim their seats, and take a collective deep breath.

"I have to go to the bathroom," Everett said.

Natalie and Harris sighed in tandem.

"I'll take him," Harris offered.

"No, I can do it," Natalie said, still looking anywhere but directly at her husband.

She took Everett's hand and led him away. He insisted on using the men's room by himself, so she waited outside the door. She was looking at her feet, eyeing her chipped pedicure, when Harris came to stand beside her.

"I figured it would be less awkward for all of us if I came by to say hello."

"Hello," Natalie replied in a flat monotone.

He paused. "I know that I caused all this, but that doesn't mean it isn't hard for me, too."

"It's hard for you, too," Natalie repeated, having gone numb, still staring at her toes.

"Yes. Is he in the men's room?"

"He is. He wants to be all grown up."

"Should I wait for him, then?"

"Okay. I'll go back to the table."

She turned to leave, but his fingers snaked through hers.

He attempted a grin.

"I'm tempted to force Everett to trade seats with me so I can sit next to the resident champion crab-cracker. I'm going to need help with mine. Again."

At that, Natalie raised her eyes and glared at him. "You screwed your yoga instructor, Harris. Crack your own damn crabs."

She left him without looking back. By the time she returned to the table, Natalie found her hands trembling. She raised an IPA to her lips and drank a third of it. Across the table, Eliana and Josh stared at her, their foreheads creased.

Just as Everett and Harris returned to the table, servers arrived with serving platters piled high with crabs. They were red and hot and speckled with Old Bay seasoning. Natalie inhaled the familiar scent, briefly closing her eyes. Her dad had taken her to crack crabs once or twice each summer. He'd been happy doing this, eating this way, so content that he often brought his guitar and lavished establishments with impromptu performances at the end of meals. He'd taught her to crack open a carapace as infrequently he'd taught her to strum a chord. Natalie couldn't remember ever wanting to learn what he taught her so much as she had coveted the closeness of him teaching her something. Anything.

Natalie couldn't picture him easily anymore, probably because she'd worked so hard to forget him. But she could inhale and remember him here; the memory wasn't entirely unpleasant.

"Disgusting! Dad – you know the yellow stuff is all guts, right? You want the white stuff. Not the yellow stuff!" Aaron exclaimed. "So gross!"

Harris stopped chewing and quickly covered his mouth with a napkin. Natalie snickered at him from the opposite end of the table, her lips twitching. Though she turned her head away, Natalie knew he knew that she was trying not to laugh at him. When she snuck a glance, Harris glared at her. His dark eyes were like beady, black pebbles.

Gloria coughed. "So, tell me, Aaron: have you received any presents yet or are we waiting until later this evening?"

Aaron sat up straighter and grinned. "Uncle Josh got me an Ecne Knight ring – like, from the actual movie. It's upstairs in my room."

Harris, in the midst of a long sip of hazy beer, went still. "Wow. Son, you should take good care of it. I'm sure that'll be worth a pretty penny someday."

"Someday?" Josh asked with a smirk. "It's worth a pretty penny now."

Eliana elbowed him.

"But feel free to play with it, kiddo," Josh amended. "I can get you another one if anything happens to it. I'd rather it be on your finger than in a box, you know?"

Aaron nodded with a grin. "I do."

With a stony smile, Harris clapped his hands together. "Buddy, I was going to save this surprise until later this evening, but the heck with it: I managed to get you a spot in that basketball camp! The one in Virginia? Where your friends are going?"

Aaron's smile faded. Watching him, Natalie frowned.

"Really? Thanks, Dad."

There was a pause. Harris furrowed his brow. "You know what I mean, right? The same camp where Smith and Foster and Parker are going?"

"Do all of your buddies have a surname for a first name, Aaron? It's like they're about to form an LLC together," Josh said, chuckling until he caught Harris glaring at him. "Right. Sorry about that, *Harris*. Wasn't thinking."

Natalie forced a smile. "It will be the same week as Everett's art camp. So that's fun!"

"And you can come, too, Mommy," Everett said, grinning. "Right, Daddy? Mommy can come, too."

A heavy silence shrouded them.

"I think I'm going to go get another drink," Natalie said.

She rose to her feet and walked briskly toward the Oyster House next door. In her wake, Natalie could hear Aaron encouraging Harris to "give it up already and have some of Everett's mac and cheese."

Natalie took a seat at the bar. Her teeth chattered while she drummed her fingernails, wondering why she couldn't stop shivering. Minutes passed. No one came for her. She fingered the soft fabric of her dress, smoothing it against her lap.

"Sidecar for the lady," the bartender said, as he set the drink down in front of her.

"Oh – there must be some mistake – I didn't order this."

"I've been told to give you this and then the best that I have. Anything you want, anything at all, and the tab's been taken care of," the bartender said with a smile.

"But, who?" Her voice trailed away, but the bartender had moved on, wiping down the bar and chatting up more patrons. Natalie swiveled on her stool to scan the room. In the doorway, a head of black hair attached to a familiar build, broad-shouldered and tall, exited in a rush. He disappeared into the day's waning, golden light, and Natalie lost her breath. She took a sip of her sidecar. The drink, ice-cold with cloying, citrus sweetness, tasted like a dream she had only just recalled. She sipped it in six gulps and promptly ordered another.

Natalie had forgotten she'd ever liked this drink, but he had remembered.

Her thumb cramped from endless flicking. Her eyes burned from the blue light. Her neck ached from two hours spent staring downward, eyes boring into the device situated in the palm of her hand, but still, Allegra couldn't stop. She had downed half a bottle of warm Riesling, each sip emboldening her mindless doom-scrolling.

It felt like picking away a fresh scab and stripping the delicate skin to a satiny, pink color, all the while knowing that it would scar. Allegra knew better than this. She knew better than to drink this fast, than to read this vitriol. Each anonymous comment pricked, barbed with spikes. Each new lashing split skin more surgically than the last. She shook her head, reading them, as she wondered if any of these sub-humans had mothers, if anyone had raised these anonymous people to know better. Allegra couldn't stop, and apparently, neither could anyone else.

Immediately after their short phone call, Penn had shot her a text message: *Don't go on the internet today. Wait a week.*

Immediately after receiving the text message, Allegra had logged onto every social media account she owned.

As soon as various fashion bloggers had gotten word that Allegra had been dropped from this latest job, this national campaign for an up-and-coming boutique, they had taken a knife and fork to her. The content creators promptly got to work picking her apart. There was pithy discussion of her replacement. Names were floated, each one younger and fresher and relatively unscathed by the tabloid press compared to her. Some questioned her net worth. Others questioned her actual worth. Not yet thirty-five, they called on her to retire. To open a restaurant. To start a fashion line. To go be with the *children* and *husband* she had abandoned *on the other side of the world.*

Allegra swirled the dry white wine like mouthwash and returned to the most colorful comments, the ones that had resonated with a pitchfork's tinny sound.

Anorexic whore ... Drunk party girl ... Washed-up has-been – go take a shower & go HOME ... Worst mother in the world ... Vapid, two-dimensional paper doll ... Old.

Reluctantly, Allegra wrenched herself from her virtual rubbernecking and looked briefly at the photographs that Véronique had texted her. Photographs of feral, caramel-spotted horses eating scraggly brush. Jules making faces from the backseat. Delphine, her open face enraptured on the boat tour, gesticulating excitedly toward the horses that roamed the beach. Allegra brought this image of her daughter to her lips and kissed the cold screen. She smiled without her eyes.

What would you do if you were your own child?

When the thought flashed within, Allegra stiffened. She looked around the room with narrowed eyes, as though her thoughts could be heard aloud, as though there was someone around to hear them. Her cheeks reddened with embarrassment that had no witness. She blew out her lips. She shook her head. But she could not un-think the thought, either.

"I would end this," she whispered.

And before she could talk herself out of it, Allegra spent the next forty-five minutes killing every social media account she owned. She took an ax to TikTok, to Twitter, to Instagram, to Facebook, and to Snapchat. She doggedly logged out and deleted the mob until she felt a blank space within where her Google alerts had once resided, the nothingness that had resonated before she'd had an internet presence.

When it was done, she took a deep breath, walked into the kitchen, and poured out the wine from her glass. She tidied up the room. She turned on some music, giving herself over to a Mumford & Sons song until she couldn't do much beyond hum along to its soft timbre.

She heated up some warm milk, resting the cup against her cheek. She took it with her. Allegra turned off every light and locked the doors. She retreated to her room, put on the softest loungewear she owned, and scrubbed her face clean. Her paperback had fallen to the floor. When she bent to retrieve it, Allegra squinted at a faint etching on the wall beneath her bed.

She thought she could make out a heart.

Allegra enabled the flashlight on her phone and bent onto her belly. There, on the wall beneath her bed, was a heart that had been carved into the drywall. The words were faint and barely decipherable, having survived a paint job or two. Inside the crooked heart were the words *Mommy + Natalie.* Allegra gasped. She clapped her hand across her mouth and then pressed it to the etching, as though a pulsing warmth could still be found there.

During the short drive back to the beach house, no one said anything. Harris's jaw ticked while he gripped the steering wheel. Aaron bobbed his head to the music screeching from his AirPods. Everett purred in his sleep.

And, in her own pocket of quietude, Natalie ducked into her phone. With three flicks of a finger, she was staring at his Instagram page. Only an hour earlier, he had posted a new image to his permanent feed: a close-up photograph of a sidecar, its amber liquid and coiled orange zest winking in the bar's low light, and a pale, open hand reaching for it.

Natalie gasped.

Harris glanced at her. "What is it?"

"It's nothing."

No regrets, the caption read. *The stars found me tonight.*

The crescent moon reminded Eliana of an open gash. She had been collecting beach towels below their deck, but she stopped for a moment. She let herself take in the fullness of the sky, the rhythm of the ocean. She could look out to the dunes and remember walking with her father, *right there.* They had always taken walks together on the beach. They had never spoken much, but their pace had matched perfectly. Looking back, Eliana guessed that the beach was the only place where they had ever fallen in step with one another, where words and meanings couldn't be misconstrued because there was only silence.

All this time, Eliana had thought she'd come back to this place to help Natalie forget her father. Eliana couldn't have known how vividly she would remember her own.

A sliding door opened with a sigh. Footsteps crossed the length of the deck above her head. Eliana blinked like she was waking from a dream, shook out the last towel, and tucked it under her arm. The door slid open and closed again.

"They're both clean and ready for you to tuck them in," Natalie said.

"I'll be right up," Harris said. "I wanted a minute with this view."

Eliana froze. No one spoke for a long time.

"You looked so lovely tonight. In that dress."

"Thank you."

He paused. Eliana could hear the click of his tongue. "I can't stay here tonight, Natalie."

"What?"

"It's not working – us together like this."

"Harris, it's your son's birthday. You can't leave. If you don't want to stay on the couch in my room like we talked about ..." Natalie's voice trailed away. "If you don't want to stay with me, there's another bedroom downstairs. Use that one."

"It's all of the pretending in front of them. I feel like the kids know that something's off."

"You lied to me for months. I didn't know."

There was another pause. "I'm sorry—"

"Stop saying that. People say 'sorry' for accidental things or putting a foot in their mouths, not for an affair like yours. Not for a hundred tiny lies every single day. You made a choice as to how you wanted your life to go. It didn't happen *to* you. You made it happen."

Harris sighed. "Will you ever stop *punishing* me for this?"

"It's still somewhat *raw*," she said, so calmly, so coldly. "I don't even have my real name back yet."

Below the deck, Eliana had dropped the towels into the sand. Blood rushed in her ears.

"Look, I'm leaving tonight. I'll pick them up in two weeks, maybe take them back to Salisbury for a Shorebirds game. I'll bring them back to you on Sunday evening."

Her voice was laced with acid. "Don't think I don't know that this is all about her. You can't last a night with us. You want to get back to *her*."

"It's not about her. It's not about you. It's about *me* and what I can withstand."

"So, this is how it's going to be, is it? You drop into our lives every two weeks—"

"No. I'm their father. I hope to ultimately have more custody than that."

When Natalie spoke, her whisper was barely audible and wrapped up in the rising wind. "I *hate* you, Harris. And I don't think I ever loved you at all. Not really."

The door slid shut. Eliana didn't realize she was shaking until she heard her own teeth chattering. The door opened again. There were more footsteps. She heard heavy breathing.

"What do you want?" Harris snapped.

"Same thing you want: a breath of fresh air," Josh said.

Harris laughed. "Don't think I don't know how much you're loving this."

"I don't know what you're on, man, but I don't like seeing my good friend this upset. Why is Natalie crying, Harris? What did you do this time?"

"We're getting a divorce. It's an upsetting process for both of us."

"Yeah, you seem like you're really unraveling," Josh said. "A yoga instructor, huh? You realize that you're *paying* her to make you feel better. Never thought you'd be taken so easily."

"You have no idea what you're talking about."

Eliana could hear Josh rolling his eyes, coupled with the

sound he made at the base of his throat when he was stifling a groan. She could see his face even as he stood far out of sight.

"I see you just as you are, *friend*: an overgrown, entitled frat boy with a Peter Pan complex. An insouciant *lobbyist* for real estate behemoths. Trust me, bro, I see you."

"You talk big now that you've hit pay-dirt with your comic book obsession, but let's not forget that you play *pretend* all day. I'm the one who has always had the grown-up job."

"A grown-up doesn't blow up his whole family over his own inferiority complex."

"It doesn't even occur to you that I could've fallen for her?"

"Hell no," Josh said. "You love yourself way too much for that."

When Eliana knotted her dark hair high on the crown of her head, she found her hands clammy and shaking. She had never heard them talk like this, had never known they could think like this. She thought back to a blur of countless meals shared – clanking cutlery and candlelight and laughter; she remembered the iconic picture of them all in their graduation gowns, arms locked and eyes glittering.

"Well, at least we can let go of this charade now," Harris said.

"What charade?"

"The one where you and I pretend to like each other."

"I'm your son's godfather. I was never pretending. I always liked you for *her*. That's what mattered to me."

Harris said nothing, but Eliana twitched as she listened to Harris crack his knuckles. She knew his expressions, too: the way his brown eyes darkened, the way his jaw flickered. She closed her eyes, but both men were still so visible to her.

"You don't believe me?" Josh asked, never giving Harris a chance to respond. "It's true. I remember the night I met you – when Eliana dragged me to some frat house to meet Natalie's new boyfriend. I initially made excuses to get out of it, but I was curious because Natalie – reliable, work-study Natalie –

didn't seem to pair well with a frat boy—"

"You can stop calling me that now. I remember that night, too. I might've worn a backwards lacrosse hat, but you were rocking purple hair and black eyeliner."

"That was my French New Wave phase. But we digress. I wanted to bolt as soon as I saw the garbage can full of red 'jungle juice.' You shook my hand too hard and talked too loudly and wanted Eliana to drink out of that cesspool, and I wasn't impressed. You remember the rest, right? Natalie was probably as uncomfortable as I was because she actually drank cheap alcohol. She had way too much, way too fast. She could barely stand. Some pledge was watching. I still think he did it on purpose – spilled his drink on her and tried to put his hands on her to clean her off. You got in his face so fast he went white. You insisted on walking her home. So, I insisted we follow you. We waited outside her dorm while you got her water and tucked her in. You walked yourself home. You were one of the good guys. Remember?"

"I remember," Harris said hoarsely.

"And who would've thought that *that* guy, the one who practically carried her home that night and proposed right after she found out she was pregnant and paid off her school loans and gave her the family of her dreams, that *that* guy would hurt her worse than anybody else?"

Feet scraped against synthetic wood. The ocean roared, its dark tide rising, inching closer.

"Turns out, you were the one we should've warned her away from."

The door slid open and closed. After a long moment, the door opened and closed again.

Suddenly very tired, Eliana entered the house through the basement door without a parting glance at the ocean. The basement hallway was narrow and cold. She shivered, teeth chattering, as she stood clutching towels that were sandy and matted with saltwater. Right then, Eliana had a fierce impulse to go home.

She fought the urge to flee from this drafty, weather-beaten house. She'd hoped that stocking it with board games, too much food, and good wine would be enough. Eliana could see now that this big house was nothing more than a sanctuary for broken people, a temporary shelter, but not a home. And no matter the money spent on this rental house or the time set aside to enjoy it, she couldn't pay for a peace that none of them believed in anymore.

And, as with any castle in the sand, it had never been theirs to own in the first place.

Chapter 14

Natalie pressed her cheek to Aaron's door. She knocked softly, careful not to rouse Everett, who was sound asleep right across the hall.

"Come in."

Natalie opened the door, turned toward Aaron, and came to a dead stop. He sat on the window seat, his knees pulled to his chin. Retreating taillights cast red shadows on his face. They were silent for a time, while Natalie watched him watch his father drive away.

"He's always leaving."

Natalie sighed. "Oh, sweetie. He has a lot of work to do."

"I don't mean this weekend," Aaron said. "I mean, like, always. He's never home anymore. Like, all of last year, he was gone."

Shifting her weight from one foot to the other, Natalie wriggled like a child. She couldn't believe that he'd felt his father's absence so acutely. After all, Natalie hadn't known that Harris had been gone until he'd said he was leaving her.

She chose her words carefully, nearly chewing on them.

"Your father and I have been talking about that," Natalie said, speaking slowly. "We're going to do better for you kids. You two are the most important people in our world. And if we haven't made you feel that way, then I'm so very sorry."

Aaron shook the hair from his face. "It's not a big deal, Mom. It's just my birthday, so ..."

"Not just a birthday. It's your thirteenth birthday."

Natalie crossed the room and sat down on his bed. She slid a present out from behind her back. "Every birthday is a chance to be more of who you were made to be. And I think, if you have a calling, you should follow it."

Aaron's brow furrowed, but he unwrapped the present hurriedly. As soon as he peeled away the wrapping paper, he smiled. His fingertips traced all of the component parts of the cardboard box: the watercolors, the pastels, the charcoals, the two sketchpads, three canvases, and the desktop easel. He hugged her hard.

"Thank you," he whispered, his words thickening in their embrace.

"You're very welcome. Goodnight, my sweet thirteen-year-old—"

"Wait," Aaron said, pulling away from her and staring intently at her with cavernous brown eyes. "Tell me the truth: are you and dad breaking up?"

She chewed her lower lip and looked away from him as her gaze settled briefly on the lake. The dark water shimmered, catching fragments of light from the homes encircling it. For only a moment, she watched the reflected light change shape as she straightened her spine.

When she answered him, Natalie looked him straight in the eye.

"We've separated," she said.

He caught a whimper behind his teeth. "Can't you work it out?"

"It's not so simple."

"It could be if you guys wanted it to be."

"I promise I wish it could be different."

"So. It's all done? Cracked in half?"

Natalie looked down at her cold, clasped hands. "I don't know. We're still figuring out what comes next."

And with that, she'd split the difference by spreading a lie too thin. She'd broken her promise to Harris by having the discussion without him, while also giving her son false hope for a different future. Her eyes misted over.

"Please don't say anything to Everett yet," she whispered. "He's too little—"

"Fine. Whatever," Aaron said, as he swept his gifts off his bed. He turned on his side, facing the window. He curved his body into a fetal position. When she touched his shoulder, he flinched.

"I'm so sorry. I know you're hurting, and I'm here—"

"Could you go? I want to be alone."

Natalie gave a curt nod and stretched her heavy limbs long before she stood. When she reached the door, Natalie turned back to him. "You can take all the time you need to sit with this news, but you'll never really be alone. Not in this family."

"We're not a family anymore," he said.

"Yes, we are," she whispered. "It's like what I told you about my mom: the love is what lasts."

Aaron shook his head. "Not the same. Your mom died, but we're all still here."

Though she opened her mouth in response, he popped his AirPods in and silenced her. She backed out of his room. Once in the blackened hallway, she braced her shoulders against the wall. Her shoulders shook while she cried without making a sound.

When he rolled away from her, peeling his hot, damp skin from hers, she shivered as a rush of cold air hugged her bare body. She scrambled for the covers, pulling a blanket to her chin. He stood at the window, naked and sculptural and hers, to pry the shades apart. Before he could reach for a curtain, Eliana pressed a button. When the shades parted, dawn's first light filled their room with a pale palette: violet layered with sparks of apricot.

Eliana smiled beneath a mound of tangled sheets and blankets, still warm with the heat they had made. She stretched long and took a mental picture of her husband. She promised herself she'd remember this quiet peace that felt like it belonged to them alone.

Their sunrise. Their ocean. Their world.

All too soon, the stillness cracked, and Josh came back to her. He wasn't smiling.

"I didn't have a chance to tell you earlier: the documentary was green-lit."

Eliana gasped. Her fingertips linked around his neck. "Joshua! That's amazing!"

"It is, but—"

"To think of all the work you've put into prepping this! This is nearly a decade in the making. It's incredible that it's finally happening!"

"Well, yes—"

She covered his mouth with hers. He pulled her close and then broke away, needing more air. He touched his forehead to her nose.

"Eliana."

"We need to celebrate!" she said, nearly squealing. "An actual party. And now that *that parasite* has left us, we might be able to have one. I'm so incredibly happy for you!"

"Eliana, please listen to me. There's something I need to tell you."

Something within her gut flipped, but she hardly noticed it fluttering through the random peals of laughter that wracked her in waves. She grinned. "I'm listening. Go ahead."

He exhaled. "I didn't tell you how hard it's been for me to find financing for this project. Everyone in this industry wants to keep me in a box. I've done one thing well – comic book superheroes – so they think it's all I can do. No one believed I could front a documentary based on the golden age of Mexican film. I've literally had people laugh in my face."

"Well, you're going to prove them all wrong. This is your second act."

"I had to put up collateral to demonstrate my commitment to the project."

"What?"

"It's the only project I've financially invested in, personally."

"Is that ... done?

"It's not uncommon," Josh said, before pausing. "Not often, no."

"With what money?"

"I sold the rest of the blue-chip stock that I inherited when my uncle passed away. I'm not sure if you remember—"

"Of course, I remember."

How could she forget? With school loans and minuscule incomes, they'd been living paycheck-to-paycheck in New York City. They'd had a studio apartment without a washer and dry-er. They'd rarely gone out for meals. They'd bought in bulk and saved their pennies and stayed in. They had survived together, always aware of the exact amount in their joint account.

Eliana could remember, vividly, standing in a grocery aisle and wondering if she could swing off-brand peanut butter. She wasn't one of those people who would toss it too soon. She would use her knife to excavate it, creating a kind of graffiti against the insides of a plastic jar. Even though she knew she wouldn't waste it, Eliana hadn't made the extra purchase. She had left with the contents of her grocery list, no more and no less.

When they received notice that Josh stood to inherit a small windfall, there was such a mixture of relief and guilt. Relief in being able to knock out two school loans in one fell swoop. Guilt because Josh could hardly remember the uncle who had never married, nor had children. He'd lived in Arizona. Josh had had to ask his mother for a photograph. They had framed it and put it up on their mantel, alongside framed MOMA gift shop postcard prints of artwork by Warhol and Rothko. Every single day, Eliana had said a prayer of gratitude for this man whom she would never know, could never repay, could never pull into their little family. And in time, she'd thrown peanut butter into her grocery cart without thinking. She'd thrown grocery receipts away without a second glance. She had ordered take-out. Overnight, their hours were saturated with such ease, such grace. It was the windfall that had changed their lives.

"What?" she asked again, blinking. "Why would you do that?"

"It made sense. Out of everything in our portfolio, it was the easiest to liquidate—"

"You didn't want to tell me," she breathed. "It's the only asset that isn't in my name, too. There was no way for me to know."

He didn't speak. She watched as he bounced his knee. His tell. She could see the first dewdrops of perspiration on his hairline. If she touched his palms, she knew she would find them damp. But Eliana did not reach for his hand.

"I knew you wouldn't be okay with it," he said finally.

"How could you do this?"

"You don't understand. Sometimes, it takes money to make money. I'm trying to be taken seriously, trying to build something from nothing."

"Don't patronize me. You lied to me, Josh. A lie by omission is still a lie."

He rolled his eyes. "Come on, now. You and I could both retire on what we have in the bank. Hell, the girls will be able to build a life on it as well."

"That's not the point."

"If that's not the point, what is the point?"

"The point is that you can't make sweeping financial decisions without me. Just because you're a bajillionaire doesn't entitle you to treat me like a child. You have to *talk* to me. We're supposed to be a team."

"I *am* talking to you. Right now," Josh said, his nostrils flaring. "And I'm not a bajillionaire. I'm a multi-millionaire. As are you. We're in this together. I made a decision predicated on protecting our future. Everything I've done – it's all for us!"

"You might've had good intentions, but you still did it behind my back. If you didn't think it was totally shady, you wouldn't be coming to me like this now."

"Listen to me: with the additional investment, I can buy the stock back in a week if that's what you want. Or we can invest the funds elsewhere."

"So, it's not theft if you put it back before someone realizes it's gone?"

"It's not theft because it's in my name! It was left to me!"

Eliana stiffened. "Then I guess there's nothing left to discuss."

She turned her bare back to him and elbowed her way inside her nightgown. There were tears in her eyes, but she could cry without making a sound. Her father couldn't abide a crying woman. He thought it was the height of manipulation. He thought it was a weakness. He thought it was every spiky word he could think, but the bottom line was that the tears were never true. Her father was so much with her here, in the spaces between the harsh words they tossed at each other. She shivered and wondered again why she had ever come back to this place.

"My mom wanted to go to breakfast this morning," Eliana said quietly. "I think you both should take the kids. All of the kids. Aaron would love the time with you."

"Eliana, come on. Don't be like this."

"And then I think you should go."

"I should *go*. Are you kidding me? You're kicking me out because I moved assets around? I haven't seen you in two weeks!"

"No. I'm *asking* you to leave because I need a minute to gather my thoughts."

"I never meant to hurt you with this."

"How exactly did you expect an ambush to feel?"

"This is not *us*. We don't leave fights in the middle. We

don't let things fester."

"Don't you get it?" Eliana said while she tied on a kimono robe. She pushed her hands through her hair, razing her nails against her scalp.

"Get *what*?"

"Never mind," Eliana said. "It's not a request, Josh. You need to go."

"Do you want to talk about it?"

Eliana sighed. "I've already said that nothing is bothering me."

"We're missing breakfast with your mom, your husband, and all of our kids. Brunch is your sweet spot, Ellie. I've never known you to miss brunch."

"I had something earlier," Eliana grumbled.

"Coffee," Natalie said. "So, you're functioning, but not at capacity."

Eliana shook her head. It wasn't yet nine o'clock and people ambled slowly across the sand. Beneath a blue sky scrubbed clean of clouds, gulls squawked and dove into the sea, pale spirals of ivory that stenciled ephemeral shapes in the sky.

"I also saw Josh's bags packed by the front door."

"Yes. Well. He'll be leaving after they get back."

"Are you really going to pretend everything is fine? With *me*?"

"Because you're always so extremely forthcoming? With *me*?"

Natalie's breath caught. Beside her, Eliana squirmed. She adjusted her sunglasses. She fiddled with her Panama hat, pulling it down low to shield her face.

"Sorry," she whispered. "My dad wasn't such a nice guy. Did I ever tell you that?"

Natalie snapped her neck to look at Eliana. "No. No, you didn't."

"I probably never said anything because your dad was ..."

"An alcoholic. A drug addict. An abuser. A philanderer."

"Right. Because your dad was all of those things, I never said that my dad could make life hard for me. He took care of me well enough, but he never *liked* me very much."

Natalie paused. "Is that why you don't visit him often?"

"No. Maybe. I don't know."

"I had no idea. Your family was so rock-solid. I envied you. I still do, if I'm honest."

Eliana laughed then, a mirthless, sharp-edged sound. "Andy and I were raised to keep up appearances, but my dad was always cold. Never nurturing. What bothered me most, though, was the way he treated my mom. She couldn't finish a thought without him interrupting her. He put her down. She was the punchline of his bad jokes. He made her so small that she disappeared, and our history disappeared with her. We only visited her family a few times. Never with him. I can't even remember Mexico. It was like life for her couldn't exist before him. Like she disappeared into her marriage. All my life, the one thing I promised myself was that I would never marry a man like him."

"Jesus," Natalie said, swallowing hard. "My dad was the same way. The belittling and isolation are all part of the control."

"I guess we were more alike than we thought the whole time," Eliana whispered, as she squeezed Natalie's hand. Natalie curled her fingers into Eliana's palm.

"You deserve better than whatever Josh did. I do know that."

"Me too."

They sat in silence for a long time, each tucking into their books and reading words that blurred together, drinking tepid coffee, and eating cold melon with their fingertips. Natalie kept sneaking glances at Eliana. She expected her to seem different, knowing this new truth, but her old friend looked exactly the same: her narrow nose, her long eyelashes, her high cheekbones. Natalie had always thought that Eliana was the type of woman who should've been carved into a coin, her profile forever incised into a precious thing that would endure.

Yet Eliana had an interior life that Natalie had never known. On impulse, Natalie scooted her chair as close to Eliana's as it could be. Their elbows touched. Natalie's eyes burned as she stared at their painted toes, still wiggling side-by-side in the sand.

"You've got to be kidding me," Eliana muttered.

Natalie followed Eliana's gaze. She sucked air through her teeth. There, on packed sand, a familiar woman jogged barefoot at a brisk pace. Natalie glared at her: this flame-haired stranger who had planted a flag in her childhood home.

"Of course, she's going for a jog with her hair down. Who could stand to do that?"

As if they had called her by name, the red-haired woman stopped running and turned toward them. She stood still. They watched her chest rise and fall. She took off her baseball hat briefly to smooth back her hair, before putting it back on her head and walking their way.

Natalie gasped. "Is she coming over here?"

"Looks like that's her plan. We still have time to run inside and lock the doors if we book it now. There's nothing quite as energizing as the urge to flee."

"The audacity of that woman."

"Right. We should go."

"I mean, she kicks us off of her property and now she wants to visit here?"

"Natalie, focus: do you want to talk to her?"

"Not at all."

"Then, you know, we should go inside now."

"No, that would be rude," Natalie said, sighing. "I won't stoop to her level."

Eliana sunk back into her chair with a low growl. She took a swig of coffee like a shot. Her lips pursed so hard that her face ached to accommodate them. The red-haired woman took impossibly long strides, and all too soon, she was upon them. Blocking out the sun. Standing so close that they could smell the salty-sweet musk of her perspiration. With every breath that Eliana took, she inhaled the scent of a woman she wished away.

"Hi there," she said. "I've been running, and I hate to run so much, but I've been looking for you both. I wanted to apologize for my behavior. My name is Allegra."

With that, she peeled off her sunglasses. Eliana and Natalie gasped. They *knew* her. Though they had certainly never met her, they'd grown up right alongside her. They knew her from magazine pictorials, television commercials, and internet ads. They knew her image so well that they could recognize whenever her copper-tinted freckles had been airbrushed away. They knew her changing faces: her shiny grins, her downcast eyes, her full pout. They knew her best two-dimensionally, as one might memorize the color and contrast of a painting.

And they knew her story, too. They knew that she had married a European count. That she'd been a party girl. That her kids had been taken away. That she was more private now. That she was fighting to get them back. They knew snippets of her story that they hadn't even sought out, as shells shimmer and beckon from ankle-deep water, best found when no one is looking for them. They blushed together now, to think of how well they knew her: a perfectly symmetrical face, a tall, exacting shape, and such a well of pain attached to it.

"Hello, Allegra. This is Eliana, and I'm—"

"Natalie. You're Natalie. I remember."

"We know who you are," Eliana said because it seemed the kind of thing to acknowledge. "We didn't recognize you then, but we do now."

Allegra's face softened. "That's good. Maybe my apology won't sound quite so crazy now. I've been followed everywhere. Men in fatigues have hidden in trees. Boats have followed me at sea. The pictures are worth more when my children are with me. When you came for a visit and wanted to see the inside of the house, I thought it was a ploy to take a picture that would net you a small fortune. But I found the heart the other night."

"The heart?" Natalie asked.

"Beneath my bed, there's a heart with 'Mommy plus Natalie' written inside. I found it and knew immediately that I'd made a huge error in judgment. I'm so sorry."

"The heart," Natalie whispered. "I'd forgotten about that. My mom knew that I hid under her bed sometimes. She drew the heart there to comfort me."

At this revelation, Eliana squeezed Natalie's hand. Allegra furrowed her brow, gnawing her lower lip and saying nothing.

"It was a game we used to play together," Natalie offered. "Hide and seek."

"Oh, that sounds very sweet. Is she staying with you on vacation?"

"She died when I was seventeen."

Allegra gaped slightly and then clapped her lips back together. She brought her hand to her chest.

"I'm sorry to hear that. It makes sense now – why you would want to return to the house. I feel terrible for sending you away."

"It's really okay," Natalie said. "You didn't know."

"In any case, I want to extend an invitation. My home is open to you whenever you want to come for a visit. I hope you'll feel welcome there."

"Thank you. That's very kind," Natalie whispered. Her eyes shimmered. She hated the tightness in her throat. The pain in her stomach. The way her chest heaved.

"We'd love to visit," Eliana said.

"My kids are actually away on a short trip with their nanny at the moment. You're welcome to stop by today if that works for you."

"I think that works for us, but what do you think, Nat?"

Eliana asked. "Are you ready?"

"I'm ready," Natalie whispered.

Without a word, they intertwined their fingertips.

"Really? Great! What time are you planning to come over?"

"Now," Natalie said. "If it's okay with you, now would be best."

Chapter 15

They walked out of the house right as Josh drove Natalie's car into the driveway. Natalie gave Eliana a sidelong glance, noting her folded arms and raised chin.

"I had a cape!" Everett yelled while he leaped out of the car.

Aaron rolled his eyes. "He means a crepe."

"Was it yummy, Bug?" Natalie asked, pressing a kiss to his cheek.

"It was *so* yummy."

"Last one to the beach is – well – it's Everett!" Aaron yelled before sprinting toward the house.

"Hey! No fair! How come you do that?" Everett yelled. He raced as fast as his legs could go, his face mottled with rage, until he saw Aaron waiting for him. Aaron held the front door wide open. Everett's face softened instantly, melting into a broad grin.

Gloria helped the girls out of the car. Silvia's face shone clean; her French braid coiled down her back like a rope. A satin ribbon, still perfectly knotted, bounced as she walked. Meanwhile, Lola looked like she'd slaughtered something and taken her teeth to it. Her mouth, rimmed in red jam, grinned widely. As Natalie appraised Lola, Gloria met Natalie's eyes with a rueful smile.

"Lola might require a bath before the beach. Would you mind taking them in for me?"

"Not at all. Come on, girls. Let's get you cleaned up."

When Natalie reached for them, they came to her. Silvia had been so shy in the beginning, so willing to cower behind Eliana's knees. Silvia held on to Natalie now with her fingertips, sneaking glances at Natalie while trying not to smile. Meanwhile, Lola bucked against the shackles of Natalie's grip. Each, in her own way, trusted Natalie completely.

It was worth remembering, in this summer of such steep losses, what had been gained. And what she herself had earned.

While they climbed the steps to the front porch, Natalie glanced back at the others. Josh and Eliana exchanged heated words close to the car. Gloria stood on the periphery; positioned out of earshot, she nonetheless wasn't missing a thing. A passing cloud fell upon them then, dulling their bright color. Natalie led the children away from it all.

Moments later, Josh stalked away from Eliana into the house. He didn't look back.

"What's that about?"

"Mom, stop," Eliana said. "Don't ask questions you'd rather I not answer."

"You asked him to leave. How could you? You're his family. He needs you."

"I know you've always cared about Josh, and I love that. But he and I are having some difficulties at the moment. We need some time apart to resolve them."

"Hear me now, child," Gloria said, grabbing her forearm and puncturing it with her short nails. "You are making a poor choice. Just like Natalie. It's become acceptable now to walk away and to find yourself and to wreck your family without even attempting to repair it."

"Natalie's husband left her for another woman! Harris is gone. What exactly is she supposed to do?"

"She could try harder. You both could."

Eliana pursed her lips. "I don't recall asking for your opinion, Mother."

"Well, maybe you should. Your father and I have been

married for forty-five years."

"Happily?"

"Of course, happily," Eliana's mother snapped. "What is that supposed to mean?"

Eliana shook off her mother's grip then. Absently, she rubbed tiny circles into the red marks on her arm. She looked past her mother to Silver Lake, where a grey heron ambled daintily by the water's edge. The morning had grown even warmer and brighter. Beneath her sunglasses, Eliana squinted against the blazing sunlight.

"Oh, come off it, Mom," Eliana snapped. "You're Mexican, and Spanish is the one language I had to learn in school. I don't know anything about you – not your family, not your home. You kept your stories from me like they only belonged to you, but it's my heritage, too. I can look you in the eye, but I still don't know where I come from. He did that to us."

"How dare you speak to me this way," Gloria hissed, shaking. "I could *scream—*"

"I know," Eliana murmured. "And now he's disappeared and there's no way to fix any of it anymore. It's okay. I would be angry, too."

Gloria's face paled. Her lips twitched with locked-away words. She rocked unsteadily. And then, as though remembering herself, she walked away without a spare glance.

Though enveloped with sticky heat, Eliana shivered. She crossed her arms across her chest. Eliana realized numbly that she had slammed a door. And now she stood on the other side of it, alone at last in an empty room. Waiting for somebody to come after her.

Just as they had done as little girls, Natalie and Eliana stood in front of the little house on Newcastle Street, hand-in-hand.

Lacy clouds hovered, draped across the endless blue sky. A handful of blocks away from the ocean, they were as comforted by its proximity as a child would be in earshot of her mother's idle chatter.

But there was the small matter of the house.

Natalie cleared her throat. "Do you want to talk about saying goodbye to Josh?"

"Nope."

"I suspected as much. I can't tell who's stalling more right now – me or you."

"Maybe we both are. Do you forgive me yet for wanting you to do this?"

"I said 'yes,' didn't I?"

"But are you ready?"

"If I waited until I was ready, I would never come," Natalie said. "Why am I so scared to walk up to this beach cottage? It's so lovely."

It was. The clapboard siding had peeled, the white trim was stained and chipped, and the front stoop was a leaning tower of loose stones. Yet, there were black-eyed Susans growing wildly, a tangle of peonies, azaleas blazing with hot-pink color, and great, hulking bushes of blue hydrangeas. Two small bikes leaned against the screened-in porch. Matchbox cars lay in the mulch bed. Natalie tried to summon her father's face, but his features were coated in shadow. Here, in this riot of bright color, he was fading.

"You're afraid of what you'll remember here," Eliana spoke low.

Natalie gritted her teeth. "I've spent forever running as far away from him as I could."

"I know. But what if, all this time, you've been taking him along with you?"

Natalie glanced sharply at her, though Eliana had already started navigating the driveway, cracked with chunks of loose gravel. They played "Follow the Leader" as well as they had done as children. Where Eliana wandered, Natalie followed. Then as now.

The door to the screened-in porch, wobbly and off-centered, screeched open. Allegra stood waiting for them. She had curled her long red hair and styled it into a soft side-ponytail. Delicate gold jewelry winked from around her neck, her ears, and her left ankle. She wore a long blush-toned dress. Her face was framed in light bronzer and heavy mascara. She smelled of orange blossoms. She appeared poised for a photograph that no one would take.

"Come in," Allegra said, waving them forward. "I was afraid you'd change your mind."

"Thank you for this," Eliana said, as she inhaled and stepped over the threshold.

Her eyes roved over a room that had changed its clothes. Teak furniture wore cushions in a navy medallion print. Alabaster lamps rested on white garden stools. A chandelier constructed from rope and candelabra bulbs hung from the ceiling. It all looked so different from the stained orange couches and threadbare hammock of her memory that Eliana nearly wept with relief. She turned to Natalie, who took in the changes with a thin-lipped smile and felt her own face fall.

"It's beautiful," Natalie said.

"It's so different from what we remember," Eliana said.

Allegra looked at them both uncertainly, her gaze volleying from Natalie to Eliana. "It's a start. I love the outdoors, so I work my way from the outside in. The inside is—"

"Exactly the same," Eliana breathed.

"My God," Natalie whispered. She clapped a hand across her mouth.

The two friends stood just beyond the doorway that opened into the family room. They might as well have peered through a portal back in time.

Natalie had anticipated a sort of mental unpacking. In her professional life designing homes for other people, she could easily gut a room in her head. She could mentally take down a wall, take a guess at where a support beam might be, and work around it. Natalie had known what she would've done to make the home current. Whitewashed walls. An open floor plan. A chunky island topped with sculptural light fixtures. Slip-covered couches and seagrass rugs.

What she hadn't counted on was a museum.

The walls were the same canary yellow. The fireplace's rust-toned brick had faded to peach. From their vantage point, Natalie could see the same sanguine fleur-de-lis wallpaper in the kitchen, the same linoleum floor. Impulsively, Natalie crossed the den swiftly and opened the closet door. On the inside were faded pencil marks, notations in her mother's hand: Natalie's height, her age, her name. She traced her own name with her fingertips, closing her eyes.

"Are you all right?" Allegra asked.

"She's fine," Eliana said. "She looks like she's going to vomit because she's remembering the time we paid off the neighborhood boys to watch us dance."

Unexpectedly, Natalie snorted with laughter. She chuckled with tears in her eyes.

Allegra grinned. "Sounds like quite the sight to behold.

"We were thirteen and absolutely terrible dancers."

Natalie nodded. "There was a lot of falling and getting back up and falling again – like watching a baby giraffe learn how to walk."

"And her mother was an artist who had a showing at a local gallery, so she was cramming in her artist way and had locked herself in the attic. While we were waiting, we choreographed a dance, asked some boys if they wanted to watch, and were straight-up rejected."

"I'm guessing that didn't stop you two."

"We took it in stride," Eliana continued. "We paid them, promised them snacks, and did our little performance. At the very end, this one did a headstand."

"You can do a headstand?" Allegra asked.

"No," Natalie said. "No, I can't."

"She crashed right into that fireplace and broke her wrist. Annabel was so angry, but she set her arm with paintbrushes and made us wait while she finished for the day."

"Did she kick the boys out?" Allegra asked.

"Nope," Eliana said, as they both laughed again. "We ate snacks with them and watched the *Romeo and Juliet* with Leo. *We* were the ones to send the boys home. Classic Annabel."

"I've met him," Allegra said. "He's a good guy."

"I'm shocked that you haven't dated him," Eliana said.

Allegra wiggled her eyebrows. "I'm probably the only one."

Their voices faded while Natalie crossed through the room to a back window. She closed her eyes until she could hear an acoustic guitar and the faint echoes of his velvet-toned voice. His melody. His chord progression. When Natalie opened her eyes, she could see her father singing under a dangling strand of white lights.

"And there was always music here, wasn't there?" she whispered.

Allegra and Eliana stopped talking to watch Natalie, her forehead pressed to the windowpane. When Allegra shot Eliana a questioning glance, Eliana merely shrugged.

There was so much to say. There was no way to know where to begin.

"He had the most beautiful voice, didn't he?"

Eliana clucked her tongue against her teeth. "He did."

"Who did?" Allegra asked.

"Her dad was the lead singer in a band called Adriftwood."

"Kip Stone? I remember him! I had their albums! I think they were bootlegs – sorry about that – but I did love them."

Eliana walked slowly to where Natalie stood. "There were always people visiting this place, a revolving door of artists staying for a day or a week, and always music in the backyard. I used to envy Natalie so much. She never had a bedtime. Never had to eat her vegetables."

"But I did anyway," Natalie said with a wry smile. "Because I cooked them. You eat your vegetables when you're the one who chopped them to pieces."

"Wait – so he died years ago, didn't he? He died and your mother, too?" Allegra asked.

"Yes. They both passed when I was a teenager."

"I'm so sorry," Allegra said softly. "I can't begin to imagine."

There was a long pause. A shifting of weight from foot to foot.

"Do you want to see the heart?" Allegra asked, her hands fidgeting.

Natalie nodded. "Very much so."

They climbed a narrow stairwell to the second floor and followed Allegra to the end of the hall. Inwardly, Natalie marveled that even the creaking of the floor could sound the same.

Allegra had updated the master bedroom. Its walls were a pale grey, while the ceiling had been wallpapered with dark sparrows. Mirrors caught the light from the open windows. A mound of throw pillows clustered atop the featherlight down comforter, all white and crisp and sumptuous.

"Was this the room where your mother would paint?" Allegra asked.

"No," Natalie said. "This was her – their – bedroom. Beyond those bookshelves, there used to be a short stairwell that would lead to the attic. She painted up there."

"And the previous owners put the bookcases over the door?" Allegra asked.

"No. My father did that. After my mother died, I don't think he ever wanted to see that room again. He put up the bookshelves and sold off the last of her paintings. It's all gone."

Without a word, Allegra embraced Natalie. Natalie patted her back, even as she pointedly raised her brow at Eliana. Eliana shrugged.

"Come," Allegra said, pulling away and dropping to her knees. Natalie followed suit.

Beneath the bed, Natalie found the heart locked into the drywall. Even as Natalie remembered tracing its edges compulsively to drown out the screaming downstairs, she found it jarring to see its shape again. Natalie touched her hand to it, tracing it once more.

"Oh, Mommy," she whispered, fresh tears coating her face. "Mommy, I'm home."

Just then, a crash resounded. Eliana cursed a litany of one-syllable words. Natalie jerked and bumped her head on the bottom of the bed. Allegra scrambled to her feet.

"What is it?" Allegra asked. "What happened?"

"I'm trying to figure that out," Eliana said while she rubbed her hands along the bookcase. "I leaned against this thing and fell because it was loose. It definitely wobbled."

Moments later, Natalie was surreptitiously wiping her face with her sweater when she heard Eliana yell, "Bingo!"

"This is unbelievable – there's actually a latch," Eliana said, while she pried the bookcase open. "Nat, this isn't a built-in after all. Your dad built a door."

"Oh, my goodness," Allegra whispered. She moved quickly to stand beside Eliana. Both of them peered into the dark attic stairwell, brushing aside cobwebs and dust flurries. Behind them, Natalie, overcome with vertigo, sank onto the bed.

"Well, we have to go up there," Eliana said.

Natalie rolled her eyes. "We can't be sure that the steps are sound."

"Are you honestly telling me you don't want to see your mom's studio?"

"We would be trespassing, Eliana," Natalie said.

Allegra waved her hand. "Oh, I'm totally fine with it."

"No disrespect to you, Allegra, but I was talking about my mom."

A woolly silence descended. Natalie looked at her hands. Eliana wriggled where she stood. Only Allegra kept peering into the darkness, allowing her eyes to adjust to the shadows.

"But what if your dad didn't lock away the room to bury it? Maybe he wanted to give you the chance to find it again," Allegra said. "If you have the will, Natalie, I have a flashlight."

Thirty seconds later, Natalie cast a wavering light that licked the forgotten corners of the attic stairs. Eliana held tightly to her hand, while Allegra came up in the rear. The flashlight's thin beam only filled the spaces where it landed. They could still see next to nothing.

Eliana bumped into Natalie for a second time, her chin aching, and cursed under her breath. "I distinctly remember a window. Am I making up the window?" Eliana asked.

"No. The view meant everything to her. It was her greatest inspiration."

Eliana scoffed. "*You* were her greatest inspiration, Nat."

Natalie didn't respond. Still blinded by shades of inky black, they heard the faint scratch of Natalie's fingernails coasting over wood. Metal clanging. Hinges whining. A crack. A bang. A sliver of light nicked the darkness, as sharp as a knife's edge. When Natalie finally pried the wooden shutters apart, scalding light flooded the room. And then, they could all see what lay before them. Large windows anchored a window seat. Though smudged with two decades worth of festering dust and grime, the view – the great sweep of their backyard, the treetops intertwined above fences, the roofs bleached by sunlight – opened like a shared secret.

All at once, the little house remembered to breathe.

The view was so compelling that, for a handful of minutes, they sat on the window seat and stared. It wasn't until Allegra turned back, absently fixing her ponytail, that she gasped. Natalie and Eliana glanced back over their shoulders and their mouths dropped open.

They sat surrounded by Annabel's life's work. Oil paintings. Watercolors. Sketches in charcoal and pastel. Unused, wrapped canvases leaned against easels dripping with color. A rag lay crumbled on a stool, dried into a fan's fold and neatly preserved. Natalie walked to the stool, grasped the rag, and brought it to her cheek. She glanced at the unfinished canvas that sat on her mother's easel. Natalie could decipher the ocean in the foreground, but behind it were faint, incomplete pencil markings.

"Her last piece. I've never seen this before," Natalie breathed, but too soon, she straightened her shoulders. "They're yours now, Allegra."

"What?" Allegra asked, blinking.

"It's your home. These pieces of art belong to you."

"Don't be absurd. These were yours all along, and they're still yours now."

Her heart racing, Natalie traced the pencil markings where clouds should have been. "Her last work was a watercolor. She loved working with watercolors. I love that I know now how she spent her last good days. Allegra, how can I ever thank you for letting me come back here?"

Allegra smiled. "I think we could have some of those paintings properly restored."

Tears pooled in Natalie's eyes, her watery vision softening colors and molding shapes into unknowable forms. She brushed her tears away. As her vision cleared, Natalie glanced at the wood frame of the attic's ceiling, at its spindly, rough-hewn bones. Wooden floors creaked with their weight. Dust swirled with their breath. And Natalie knew what she should do.

"I'm afraid that won't be enough. This is your house now and it should look like it belongs to you. To your family, not mine. I can help your home reflect your people."

Allegra furrowed her brow. "What are you saying, exactly?"

"What if I were to design you a house?"

Part Three

July

In the Japanese origin story of Tabanata, two lovers, Orihime and Hikoboshi, became besotted with each other and neglected their duties. Orihime's father, the Sky King, grew so incensed that she had stopped weaving clothing that he exiled the two lovers to the heavens. Orihime (represented by the star Vega) and Hikoboshi (represented by the star Altair) would be forever separated by the vast "river" of the Milky Way. However, the Sky King took pity on their suffering. On the seventh day of the seventh month, he ordered a flock of magpies (represented by the star Deneb) to form a bridge over the heavenly river, allowing the lovers to reunite.

On that day, when the cobalt-tinged Vega shines brightest, we are reminded that love exists out of time – no less magnificent when severed too soon.

Chapter 16

Natalie zested a lime over a bowl of fresh flounder. She wore frayed cut-offs. Her feet were bare. Her painted toenails were chipped. Saltwater had spun her hair into tight spirals. Beyond the deck, Natalie could make out Lola and Silvia flanking Everett, while they raced a battery of ragged waves. Beside them, Eliana clapped wildly.

"I'm done with the pickled onions," Aaron said, catching her attention while he screwed the lid of a Mason jar back into place. "Should I heat up the tortillas in the oven?"

"We have a few hours before we need them. You should go relax."

Aaron nodded and then paused. "You know, Mom, I like fish tacos better than hot dogs anyway. I think I'll like tonight's meal better than whatever we'll have with Dad this weekend."

Natalie plastered a smile on her face. Harris had intended to take the kids last weekend for a baseball game but had canceled on them at the last minute. She could recall the sketch of his flimsy excuses: too much work, too far of a drive. She had seen fire, her pupils dilating and her pulse ricocheting, when he'd offered an explanation. As soon as Harris had finished speaking, Natalie had hung up on him. They'd confirmed that he would take the children to Cape May via text message. Natalie was assured that Sophia would not be joining them.

"You're going to love a special weekend away with your dad."

"He didn't even show up last time," Aaron said. "I don't want to go."

"You'll have fun as soon as you're with him. He's your dad, and he misses you."

"Maybe I should stay."

The doorbell rang. Natalie nearly swooned with relief, even as such an ordinary summoning felt intrusive to her. They hadn't had a single visitor all summer. They had become so insular, relying on each other perhaps too much.

Aaron raced ahead to open the door. He stiffened at the sight of Allegra. Though Natalie had explained that she'd offered to redesign her childhood home for Allegra, Aaron remained skeptical. He couldn't understand offering to help someone who had turned them all away.

"Mom, your client's here," he called out.

"Allegra! It's so good to see you!" Natalie rushed into the room, smiling widely.

"I'm sorry to come to your house, but you said you found a gallery with experience in restoration. I didn't want you to leave this one behind. I found it in the attic closet."

At the word "gallery," Natalie flushed red. She ducked her head as she accepted the 11x14 canvas wrapped in brown paper. As she did so, two blond-haired children peeked out from behind Allegra's legs.

"Thank you all for bringing it by," Natalie said, bending low. "And who are you both?"

The children said nothing, though they blinked at Natalie with familiar, far-set, grey eyes.

"These are my kids, Jules and Delphine. Children, this is my friend, Miss Natalie."

"It's a pleasure to meet you," Jules said.

"Very nice to meet you," Delphine mimicked.

They each stood with one foot planted behind their mother. They reminded Natalie of captive birds, with every fine movement a flinch.

"Your mom has told me such wonderful things about both of you."

"She said you would make our house pretty?" Delphine asked.

Natalie chuckled. "No promises, but I'll certainly do my best."

Aaron raised his brow, his eyes twinkling with amusement. Natalie didn't know what amused him more, their thick accents or their vintage politesse, but she narrowed her eyes slightly and – without a word – shut him down. His smirk vanished.

"Would you both like to stay for a while?" Natalie asked.

"Oh no," Allegra began in a rush, "We wouldn't want to impose."

"No, it's okay," Aaron said. "I was going to shoot the ball around. Do you guys play?"

Jules's cheeks reddened. He shook his head. Delphine tucked her hand inside his.

"That's probably better – that way, when you beat me, you can be smug," Aaron said.

Jules grinned and tugged on Allegra's arm. "What do you think, *Maman*?"

"I think it sounds like you couldn't ask for a better teacher."

With a curt nod toward Allegra, Aaron stepped through the front door. Jules and Delphine quickly followed. Natalie and Allegra stood for a long moment on the porch. Aaron passed the ball to Jules and Delphine, alternating between them. After a moment spent watching them, Natalie guided Allegra inside the house. She made a beeline for the kitchen. "Coffee?"

"Please," Allegra said, as she eased onto a stool at the island. "This place is amazing."

"I know, right? I can't claim any credit. Eliana and her husband waved their magic wands to put all of this together for us."

"I know," Allegra said, attempting to hide her pink cheeks behind her mug. "I Googled you both. I now know that her husband is filming the latest installment of the Ecne Knight movies in France and that my Fairy Godmother is actually an all-star interior designer who has been profiled many times in *Brickhaven* magazine. I can't believe I didn't recognize your name."

Natalie grinned. "I can't believe I didn't recognize your face."

"You're too good for our little house, and we both know it."

"Don't be silly. I start to get a little edgy if I don't have a creative outlet. Besides, I left too much behind in that house. I'll finally have the chance to say goodbye to it now."

They went quiet then, soundlessly sipping coffee together. If either of them had the fleeting thought that this was rare – to find a friend where a conversational lull could occur without the urgent need to fill it – neither noticed the pocket of peace for long.

"You're clearly prepping for a party," Allegra said. "I should go."

Natalie blinked. Her gaze briefly followed Allegra's, as it alighted on the countertops around the kitchen. They were covered with bags of chips, crudités, a massive fruit plate, and a few boxes of crackers. A tangy, briny smell, emanating from the marinating fish, hung in the air.

"I'm really not," Natalie said. "It's a fancy version of family dinner."

"Pardon?"

"My husband – the boys' father – we're in the process of separating, and he's taking them away for the Fourth of July this weekend. I've never been without them for a holiday, so I was trying to plan something celebratory here. A festive sort of send-off, I guess."

Suddenly, Natalie felt a familiar heavy sadness return. Her shoulders slumped. Reflexively, she splayed her hand against her stomach.

"I'm sorry," Allegra said softly. "I had no idea."

"It's silly. I didn't want to cook hotdogs because I felt it was too traditional – I didn't want to overstep on their dad's time with them. I'm too freaked out to serve them nitrates today."

Allegra smiled. "It's not silly. I do the same thing. I always cook too much food for them, like I can keep them satiated long after they've left me."

"Yes!"

"Maybe the only good thing about my sociopathic, vitriolic ex-husband is that he's European, so the hot dogs and hamburgers are mine for life."

Natalie burst into laughter. Unexpectedly, a memory overcame her. Waiting for the arc of a wave. Shooting her flat hands out in front of her. Riding it to shore. Tumbling, spinning, flipping in its spittle and froth. Sinking into the sand like loosely stitched pockets. Fingers clenching. Toes curling. Climbing, crawling into the sand until the land flattened, until Natalie found her footing again. Never sure if she was freer on the sand or in the sea.

"You should come tonight," Natalie said.

"No—"

"Please? Come on. It would give you a break from that nanny."

A slow smile crawled across Allegra's face. "But you called it a 'family dinner.'"

"I know what I said," Natalie said. "And I'd like for you all to join us."

As Natalie strolled down Rehoboth's Main Street with a cup of coffee in hand and a canvas tucked under her arm, she bit back a wobbly smile. Her breath came short. Her heart raced in her chest. Her entire jittery being was a stark counterpoint to the sun-kissed families and couples ambling past her.

She scanned the faces of each person who crossed her

path. Invariably, they offered a lazy grin like a nudge. It was one of those rare, soft-focus mornings that looked like it wouldn't leave a mark. Natalie wanted to believe in it as much as everyone else did.

At the next shop window, Natalie surveyed her reflection. She wore a floral dress that grazed her ankles. Her hair had dried into ringlets. Her bare shoulders were marked by a woven latticework of uneven tanned lines. She hadn't thought to wear makeup beyond a swipe of mascara and a dusting of bronzer. With an unsteady hand, she applied some lip balm.

She took a deep breath, tried to smile, and turned onto Penny Lane.

Penny Lane was a pedestrian thoroughfare, lined with cobblestone. Shops sold trinkets like farmhouse signs and jewelry. A toy store beckoned close to a photographer's studio. Another storefront sold freshly squeezed lemonade. Natalie caught sight of a wooden sign swinging in the breeze: Backlit Gallery. She paused for only a moment before stepping inside.

Bells rang out when she pushed the door open. At once, Natalie lost her breath. She froze, now entirely still.

A man stood with his back to her, staring at a sprawling modernist mural. She knew his black hair, though his curls had all been clipped away now to a tightly cropped cut. She knew his crooked smile. She knew the white scar that she would find on his thumb – a fishing trip gone awry – and the smattering of tan freckles across his shoulders. He hadn't turned around yet, but she knew his blue eyes as well as her own.

Her fingers clutched the doorframe, her whole body itching to make a quick exit. He turned back toward the doorway and raised his brow. His blue eyes were exactly the same, still rimmed with green and flecked with gold. She fell into them exactly as she used to, forgetting everything she'd planned to say.

And then he gaped at her. Natalie shivered. He took a

step toward her, opening his mouth and closing it again, and stopped in the middle of the room. He gazed at her from underneath thick, black lashes. She remembered them, too.

"It's you."

"It's you," she whispered.

"I saw you the other night, but I never thought I'd find you here."

She exhaled. "The sidecar. I thought it was you. Thought I saw you leave."

"Once I saw you, I couldn't possibly have stayed."

They lapsed into silence. She scanned the walls, coated with large-scale, dripped-paint murals. While a scarlet flush raced from her chest to her face, Natalie looked away from him. Her gaze roved over the walls like the paintings could cue her as to what would come next. All the while, he stared at her unabashedly, like there was nothing else in the room to see.

"I hope I didn't overstep – buying you a drink when you were clearly there with a group of people. I saw you with them before you wandered over to the Oyster House. I couldn't help the impulse," he said, pausing. "You have a lovely family."

"Thank you. I can't remember the last time a man bought me a drink in a bar. At my age, it's flattering."

He grinned, still lopsided and rimmed with scant stubble. "I don't believe that at all."

Natalie reddened further. "So. This gallery is a dream. Is it yours?"

"Most of it. My dad is my silent partner, but I've almost paid back his investment."

Natalie smiled. "Good for you, Damon. I know how much you wanted to stay and make your life here. It's everything you wanted for yourself."

"This part went according to plan, but it's not everything I wanted."

She kept staring at his mouth, remembering it, too. She found she couldn't look away.

"But," Natalie began hoarsely, "you found a way to *stay*. You did do that."

"And you got the hell out as soon as you could, so I guess we were both true to our words," Damon said. Neither of them laughed.

"Maybe so, but I'm glad to be back for a season."

With a nod, Damon pushed his hand roughly through his hair. "Why are you here?"

"Eliana invited me to stay with her for the summer. She's a hard one to resist."

Damon grinned. "Eliana – wow. It's good to hear that you both are still close. Gives me hope for the rest of the world. But I meant to ask why you came to my gallery today."

"Oh, oh, of course," Natalie sputtered, flushing again and cursing the blotchiness that she could envision lingering on her cheeks. "I saw online that your gallery does restoration work."

"Yes, we partner with a local company. What kind of work do you need?"

"Well, I'm a designer now—"

"I know."

"You do?"

"I always wondered about you. Always wanted to make sure you were okay."

With a slight smile, she took a few steps closer to him. "I'm fine."

"You're more than fine. You have a stellar national reputation."

"Well, you know I wanted to be a curator for a museum, but life had other plans for me."

"None of my plans worked out like I thought they would either," he said, grinning now without his eyes. "I have faith that things work out exactly as they're supposed to."

"You always were an optimist."

"I just turned around to find my high school girlfriend in

my place of business. You make it easy to keep the faith today."

She smiled softly. She looked to her feet, thumbing her wrapped canvas all the while. She wasn't sure what to do with her hands.

"Is that the artwork you'd like restored?" Damon asked.

"Yes. It was one of my mother's pieces."

When he smiled, tiny crinkles fanned out from the corner of his eyes. "A favorite?"

"I'm not sure I've ever seen it before," she said. "I'm actually redesigning the cottage on Newcastle Street for the family that lives there now."

"Sounds like something you'd do. I still can't believe your dad sold it."

"You and me both. The other day, we stumbled on a whole treasure trove of my mother's paintings in the attic. All this time, I thought my father had sold them all away, but … I don't know now."

Damon whistled low. "Who knew Kip Stone could be a good man?"

Their shared silence filled the whitewashed space.

"Come on. Let's have a look at it in the back. I have an eye for an initial damage assessment, but obviously, we should get these pieces to the expert."

"It would be a big job, Damon. I've counted at least twenty pieces."

"It's not a problem. I'll make sure that we do whatever we can for you."

"Thank you."

She followed him into a spare room lined with tables. A sketch was unfurled on a drawing table. Framed pictures rested against the wall. Drip coffee burbled from a tight corner.

"This is our control room. I apologize for the mess, but this space isn't normally open to the public," Damon said, clearing his throat. "Should we have a look?"

Natalie nodded eagerly, and he carefully pried the brown

paper covering away from the canvas. She watched his hands work. His calloused fingers. His clipped, clean nails. They bent over the painting together, their shoulders touching, and she breathed deeply as she tried to remember if he smelled the same.

He tore the paper away, undressing the rough-edged canvas until it was exposed. Natalie gasped and, for a few bundled seconds, forgot completely that he stood beside her.

This landscape would prove to be a companion piece to Eliana's painting. Hers hinted at a storm brewing off the horizon, showing Natalie and Eliana playing in the sand as children. In contrast, this watercolor glowed with brighter colors and composite strokes. Here was a sunset Natalie couldn't remember having seen, yet couldn't believe she had ever forgotten. Shrieks of orange and pink colors splattered the sky, with dusk's violet color rising from the silver-toned ocean like smoke. She and Eliana sat together at the water's edge, gangly limbs entwined. It was masterful – Annabel had used their skin tones (olive and pale peach) to separate their forms, rather than a dark outline. But they nonetheless blended together as a cohesive whole, mirroring the sky's darkening color fading into the ocean.

It had been Annabel's last summer with them, and she had caught them linked.

Damon brushed a tear from her cheek with his thumb. Natalie hadn't realized she was crying. She leaned her head against his shoulder. He wrapped his arm around her.

"Tell me you're happy."

She blinked away tears. "What?"

"You wear a ring," he said quietly. "Tell me you're happy with him."

Natalie looked down at the diamond glinting, all sharp edges and faceted light, from her left hand. Her throat constricted. He tightened his grip on her shoulder, but she pulled away.

"I'm actually in the process of separating from him. I still wear the ring out of habit. And for my kids, my boys, because I haven't had the courage to tell them both the whole truth yet."

"Natalie, I know you well, and you've never been without courage."

Fresh tears sprang to her eyes. "I'm happy. I am. I'm blessed. We're all okay here, for this summer at least, in this small town. I'm just not sure what to do about the rest of my life."

"Then it's not time to think of the rest of your life yet. Think about tomorrow. And tell me that you'll come to dinner with me then. Please?"

Chapter 17

Eliana's hand opened and closed, as she expanded and contracted the image on Natalie's phone. She shook her head.

"Annabel, you ninja."

"Do you remember that day?"

Eliana nodded. "I think so. I think it was the last week before we left to start our senior year. Or, I should say, I left to go back to school. You went off to go on a festival tour with your parents. I remember being so jealous of you."

"Well, it didn't quite work out as planned. The tour was cut short when Mom was diagnosed with ovarian cancer that autumn. She was gone by the spring."

"I remember that, too," Eliana whispered. She draped her arm over Natalie's shoulders. Natalie encircled her arms around Eliana's waist. They set Natalie's phone aside, never realizing that they were mimicking the painting exactly. Instead, they watched as Allegra snapped photographs with her Nikon camera from the deck. The children were playing kickball in the sand, with Aaron serving as pitcher while everyone ran around him. Beyond their raucous game, wisps of clouds incised the sky with deepening smears of violet color.

"I think she was creating a memory to take with her," Eliana said. "I think she *knew*. I think she'd already begun to miss you."

Before Natalie could reply, Allegra swept into the house.

"I hope you don't mind me taking so many pictures. It's what I do."

Natalie smiled. "Of course, we don't mind. We just want copies."

"Not a problem. My kids are so happy here. Thank you for including us."

Eliana surveyed the room. Chips, cookies, and brownies littered the island. The vegetable platter had been left untouched; the cheese plate had been scavenged. Guacamole browned next to an empty bottle of Pinot Grigio. With a grin, Eliana reached for another bottle of wine.

"The way you take pictures seems so professional," Eliana said.

Natalie nudged her. "She does work with professional photographers occasionally."

"I hope I've picked up some tricks of the trade," Allegra said. "I've always hung out with them on my shoots more than the other models anyway."

Eliana nodded sympathetically. "So, you can eat from craft services without being shamed?"

Natalie nudged her again, but Allegra laughed.

"That, and it's always a nice distraction. Because I hate getting my picture taken."

Eliana and Natalie exchanged a glance. "But ..." Natalie began.

"But isn't that literally your entire job?" Eliana finished.

"Yes, and I've often wondered on the third hour of being too hot or too cold, half-naked and contorted in some weird position: how exactly did I get here?"

Eliana nodded. "Living in L.A., I think that all the time."

"It's funny the paths our lives can take," Natalie said. "I've made all these plans, and lately, I've wondered if any of the decisions were even mine."

Allegra accepted the glass of wine that Eliana held out to her. "For me, I was this awkward kid – 6'1", bony, these alien eyes – and some woman in a shopping mall told me I was beautiful. I didn't believe her, but I needed to believe that my life was bigger than a suburb of St. Louis. And even though I've never liked being the center of attention, I wanted a different sort of life. It was my exit strategy."

Eliana had walked over to the kitchen window, folding her arms across her chest. The children were playing dodgeball now, and their shrieks of laughter resonated like wind chimes through the open window. Eliana's brow furrowed.

"We're too far away," she said, swigging a sip of wine. "They're moving too close to the water. I'm going back outside to watch them."

Eliana stepped outside onto the deck. The sliding door closed behind her with a sigh.

"They're not even near the ocean," Allegra said. "Was it something I said?"

"No. Sometimes Eliana lives too much in her own head. You'll see."

By the time they both joined Eliana on the deck, her emotional state had flipped. When she turned back to Natalie, Eliana smiled so hard that both rows of white teeth shone, so hard that the muscles in her neck popped. Natalie squinted at her friend and tried to find her eyes beneath her sunglasses. But it was no use.

"So," Eliana began, "I want to know how a count from Luxembourg came to own a house in Delaware. And why our very own countess decided to keep it. Canapé?"

Allegra shook her head while shooting Natalie a glance. Natalie swallowed. She ached to be back inside the kitchen, to fall back in time and pinpoint whatever had triggered this high-pitched, false cheer. With a sigh, Natalie sunk deeper into her chair.

"There's no countess here. I lost the title when our divorce was finalized," Allegra spoke slowly. "Etienne went to Georgetown. One weekend, I'm told that he and some buddies rented the house. He bragged to someone that he could buy it. It wasn't for sale. He made the family an outrageous offer. It wasn't that deep. It was Etienne's usual recklessness."

"It's hard to believe that our little cottage was an impulse purchase," Natalie mused.

"Well, it backfired, as impulse purchases often do. His father called him a spendthrift and stuck the rest of his assets in a trust. I was actually the one who brought the most income to the marriage, but after lawyer's fees and maintaining multiple homes, I'm barely my own breadwinner these days. He likes to say he bled me dry."

In the silence that followed, they listened to the children's laughter.

"How did it come to be yours?" Natalie asked.

"I always loved it. I think he only gave it to me because he never knew that," Allegra said, as her voice fell away. "I would come here whenever I had a break in my schedule. And because our free time rarely overlapped, he wouldn't come with me. We never spent a minute here together, so it's one of my favorite places on earth. There isn't a patch of sand here tainted with his memory."

Somewhere close, an engine died. A car door opened and slammed shut. Allegra walked to the edge of the deck but couldn't manage a visual of the side of the house. She sighed.

Meanwhile, Lola – her ringlets flying, her dress rippling – tore off for the ocean.

"Lola!" Eliana screamed, shooting to her feet. "Lola! Get back here *now*!"

"I've got her!" Natalie yelled, though Aaron and Jules were already in hot pursuit.

Natalie and Eliana raced down the coarse wooden stairs. Natalie sprinted faster than them all. Allegra waited in the doorway, her hand resting on her heart, until Natalie had scooped Lola up in her arms. Even as Natalie scolded her, she peppered her small, heart-shaped face with kisses. Natalie brought her back to Eliana.

Allegra's forehead creased as she watched Eliana fall to her knees and embrace Lola intensely. Allegra watched Eliana's shoulders heave. She blinked rapidly and chewed on her lower lip, watching. She then turned away, disappearing into the house like a shadow into shade.

Minutes later, Eliana sat in an Adirondack chair on the deck with Lola wrapped up in a towel on her lap. The children played dodgeball. Aaron had strategically placed himself with his back to the ocean. The shrieks were subdued now, tempered with the remembered presence of grown-ups, but their game continued on. Still, Eliana could not seem to let Lola go. She locked her arms around her daughter, weaving their fingers into one clasped, knotted fist.

Natalie tried not to look at Eliana. Instead, she swept the ever-present layer of sand from the deck. When her ring caught the day's lingering golden light, she stopped to worry the diamond between her fingers. Natalie twisted it, revealing the pale tan line that marked her skin.

"I thought I would be peaceful here," Eliana said. "That it came with the house."

Natalie turned back to her, setting the broom aside and settling into the chair beside her friend. She watched Lola sleeping on Eliana's chest; they breathed together, each instinctively mimicking the other's rhythm.

"I know."

"And I thought it was all for you," Eliana said. "I was running so quickly toward you that I never stopped to think that I might be running *away* from something."

"I know."

Eliana sighed, a weighty rush of air. "This postpartum anxiety – well, it isn't so postpartum anymore, is it? My God, I hate it. Will I ever feel like myself again?"

"*Yes*," Natalie whispered fiercely. "Yes, I promise you will."

"I feel like I'm falling apart, like I've disappeared."

"That's impossible," Natalie said. "Because I still see you."

Eliana nodded, her eyes shining with tears. Silvia climbed up the stairs to the deck and smiled halfway at them both. When Eliana gave her a slight nod, Silvia rushed to her side and somehow managed to clamber up into the chair. Lola moved in her sleep as though endeavoring to make space for her twin, but did not wake up. Silvia's eyes drooped heavily as soon as she found space on Eliana's chest.

"This *is* peace, right now," Natalie whispered. "Hold on to it."

Eliana rested her head between her girls' cheeks. Natalie watched as Eliana grinned and a familiar dimple popped. A tightness within her own chest eased.

"Maybe we should have a girls' night this weekend, just you and me," Eliana said. "We could ask Allegra to watch the kids. She seems reasonably sane for a model."

"I doubt we can afford her hourly rate."

"Maybe she'll take pity on us? We did feed her. That has to be unusual in her line of work."

"Can't do it."

"You can't wallow this weekend. I won't let you. You have to let me take care of you," she said, her voice cracking. "The way you take care of me."

"That's not what I meant. I can't go on a date with you. Not when I already have one planned with somebody else."

Eliana blinked. "Say what now?"

From her vantage point standing behind a porch column, Allegra could watch him undetected. His driver had left, with a clap on the back and bills exchanged in a handshake. He pressed his phone to his ear. He bent to retrieve his bags often, but then stopped and straightened back to his full height with a sigh. He opened his mouth but closed it again without a word.

Allegra had watched him for five minutes now, though she had yet to hear his voice. He paced back and forth with his phone clamped to his ear, but his stride was slow, and his smile was loose. While she watched him shuffling his feet with his hands in his pocket, Allegra wondered if she'd ever seen a man listen so well. He nodded every so often, as though assuring whomever he was speaking to that he was still there, still hearing every single word.

She was used to being interrupted, her sentences dismembered to half-thoughts, with every directive followed by a clipped goodbye. She had learned to take orders well. Yet, Allegra couldn't remember the last time she'd been *heard*. Her exchanges with lawyers, agents, photographers, and of course, Etienne, were all hierarchical and mechanized.

He laughed then, a rich baritone of amusement that rippled out to where she stood beneath the eaves. Allegra tilted her head to the side, taking in the full measure of him. She decided that she liked life better this way – watching, as opposed to being watched.

Allegra always failed to realize the burden that she carried until she came back here. Her hair knotted inside an old baseball cap. Her eyes locked away behind dark sunglasses. Always, she endeavored to blend. Always, the camera found her. Even worse than that staccato sound of a non-consensual shot was the eerie inkling of being watched. A prickling on her neck. Her skin on fire. She would suspect she'd been spotted and recorded and – in a rush of paranoia – dart into the nearest building she could. Allegra never felt safe until she was wrapped in the snug enclosure of four walls, breathing better for a time – until the walls closed in.

He put his phone away. Lost in her own thoughts, Allegra had missed him ending the call. He started up the stairs. As she rose to her feet, Allegra wondered if this gentleman was Eliana's megastar producer husband. The one who had spun comic book stories into gold.

He bounded up the stairs, moving quickly. He didn't even try to knock, but instead grabbed hold of the knob. Allegra smiled. He had to be the husband.

Good for you, she thought, warming to him. *You're exactly where you belong.*

"Hi there."

He stiffened with surprise, his whole body jerking.

"I didn't mean to startle you," she said. She stepped out of the shadow, into the light.

Allegra watched as his lips broke open. His face paled.

"Huh? What? You, er, so, you're you."

Already extending her hand, Allegra grinned. It was the way of fame that there was an extra, loaded step in every greeting. Her face knocked people off-kilter, and it was her responsibility to attempt – with excessive friendliness – to reset their equilibrium.

"I'm Allegra. And you would be?"

"Wow. Holy. Just wow. What – what are you ... Why are you here?"

"I'm a friend of your wife."

He frowned. "I don't have a wife."

Allegra's hand dropped, untouched, to her side. Her confusion mirrored his own.

"I'm – I'm a friend of Eliana Rollins."

"My sister? *You're* friends with my baby sister?"

"Your sister," she breathed, her pulse quickening. "Eliana is your sister."

"Yes. Are you, um, an L.A. friend?"

"No," she said, shaking her head. "I'm a friend from here."

He blinked. "From Delaware? No kidding."

"Tell me everything," Eliana demanded. Her eyes glittered in the waning light.

"Well, there's not much to tell. You already know him—"

Before Natalie could continue, they heard voices, heavy footsteps, and an unmistakable, immediately-identifiable whistling.

"Ellie, Ellie, PB-and-Jelly, I know you're here somewhere! Where are you?"

Eliana gaped. Natalie grinned.

"Mom!" Eliana sputtered with a gasp. "She wouldn't dare send him!"

The screen door slid open. Andy stepped outside, a sheepish smile plastered on his face. He had his same essential Andy-ness about him: his dark hair tousled and his tie askew, his towering height and olive skin a near-carbon copy of his sister's likeness. But his hands were shaking. Allegra stepped outside behind him, her arms folded against her chest. Natalie's eyes darted between them both. She discovered a newfound respect for Allegra, as she appeared to be the one woman to have ever caught Andy off-guard.

Natalie leaped to her feet and embraced him. He lifted her to his chest, spinning her in a circle. He pressed a kiss to her forehead. "Always were a fighter, Nat," he said, with a voice that had the texture of crushed gravel. "If it's a war you're waging, you wear it well."

"I'm fine. Things are ... civil between us."

"That's good. I always like to hope for the best, even while preparing for the worst."

Eliana made a face. "That's a lawyer for you: always and forever a buzzkill."

"That's not fair, Ells Bells."

"You're right. You were too serious long before you passed the bar."

Andy furrowed his brow, releasing Natalie from his embrace. He knelt beside Eliana. Their pale eyes met. His glance took in the sleeping girls, the dodgeball game, and the full weight of dusk as the sky softened, saturated now with a violet color.

"It's going to be okay," he whispered. "Whatever it is, it's all going to be okay."

Fresh tears coated her eyes. Eliana looked away from him, though she reached out her hand. Andy took it. He then tightened his grip, holding on.

Behind them, Allegra scuttled down the stairs, head down and eyes downcast. She pulled her open sweater more tightly around her body. Allegra looked back only once, gazing at the tight-knit cluster of friends and family, and felt her cheeks grow hot even as her teeth chattered. She looked away then and lifted her eyes to the skies, already waiting for the stars.

Above her, Silvia's eyes fluttered apart. Face to face with her uncle, she smiled widely.

"I dreamed of you," Silvia whispered.

Eliana, her cheeks now tight with her tears, glanced at Silvia. Andy's breath caught. For a long moment, no one spoke – until Lola jerked awake, opening only one eye.

"Uncle Andy!" Lola shrieked, tumbling out of Eliana's arms. She climbed into his lap, smacking his cheek with a wet, loud kiss. "Can we be alien soldiers? Like last time?"

"That was my plan! How'd you know?"

"Because that's why you're here," Silvia said softly, her tongue tripping over consonant blends. "You came for us."

Andy touched his head to hers. "That's right, angel girl. I came for you. For all of you."

Chapter 18

Nightfall descended as clear as polished onyx, pricked with pulsing stars. Natalie stared out the kitchen window, aimlessly drying a dish.

"I think it's dry now," Eliana said, prying the dish from her hand.

"Where did they find that thing, anyway?"

Eliana shrugged. "Andy said it was in his room. He took it as a sign, I guess. It's a perfect night for stargazing. So cloudless and clear. My dad and Andy did that a lot together."

They watched as Andy taught Allegra and Aaron how to use the telescope. He gesticulated wildly, pointing out stars scattered across an inky swath of sky. They took turns, transfixed, as Andy patiently explained another world to them.

"Anyway, I'm still waiting," Eliana murmured.

"What?"

"Who's the guy? You said you have a date this weekend and you blushed as you said it, and don't say you didn't because we all know your embarrassed face could stop traffic—"

"Damon. It's Damon."

Eliana gasped. "High school boyfriend Damon? I remember him!"

Natalie rolled her eyes. "'Boyfriend' is a big word for two short summers. And the first summer was the only one that really mattered. I wasn't my best self for the last one."

"Your mother had died, Natalie."

"Yes. Well. I kept trying to end it, but Damon would always make me laugh when the conversation took a dark turn. And then, well, you know the rest."

"I know that it fizzled out during our first semester of college. You never told me why. I know that this is going to come as a shock, but you're a very private person."

"I had no idea," Natalie said, chuckling. "He was in Savannah at SCAD for a semester, but he left to come home. His father was sick. He wanted me to come visit, but my dad had sold the beach cottage and we weren't speaking. I was finally free. And I couldn't stomach the idea of visiting someone else's ill parent. Looking back, I treated him poorly."

"You were fragile, Nat. Porcelain-doll fragile. I'm sure he understood."

Natalie covered her face with her hands. "Maybe this is a bad idea. I *am* still married."

Eliana glanced over to Natalie's rings, winking from the white sliver of marble countertop. "Legally, yes, but marriage is meant to contain much more than one person's broken heart. You don't owe anyone an explanation. I'm so impressed that you reached out to him!"

"I didn't. I surprised him."

"Pardon?"

"I needed to have my mother's paintings restored, and his gallery does that type of work. I may have searched for him first on social media—"

"Well, look at you. Full of surprises," Eliana said, grinning wide. "It was fate."

"It wasn't fate," Natalie said. "I need a service that he provides. That's all."

"You know, I knew a girl once who would pretend that she didn't care about things. That way, if it all didn't work out in the end, she couldn't be hurt."

Natalie released a long exhale. "Well, she sounds like a perfectly well-adjusted person to me. Wise beyond her years."

"She's also stunningly modest."

More laughter. More dishes passed from hand to hand. More candles flickering fast from darkened corners. More wine being poured, the quiet chime of two glasses toasted without a word. Then the whisper of a door opening, the panting of breath, and the pounding of fast feet.

"Mom, guess what?" Aaron asked.

Natalie smiled. "What?"

"Andy showed us the Summer Triangle: 'Deneb, Altair, and Vespa.'"

"Vega," Eliana corrected.

"That's what I said: Vega. He called it an asterism because the stars don't actually go together – they're bright stars from other constellations. But Andy said they still do belong together because of how we see them. I gotta sketch it," Aaron said, sprinting from the room.

"Would you look at those two?"

Natalie followed Eliana's gaze to where Andy and Allegra stood side-by-side, their shoulders an inch apart. Her hair blew against his neck. His feet were planted beside hers.

Natalie shrugged. "Maybe they're entranced by the stars."

"Oh, he's entranced by something. My brother can make any space into a singles' bar."

"Not another word," Natalie said, hushing her. "Remember what he said to Silvia?"

"Okay, okay, Andy's here for me and my girls. Probably at my mother's instruction, but it's still a solid gesture. I'd be willing to bet though, that right now, he's also here for Allegra."

"He might not even recognize her."

Eliana fixed her with a look.

"You're right," Natalie said. "He totally recognizes her."

With no apparent sense that they were being watched, they spoke in profile. He put his hands into his pockets. She fussed with her hair. They parted ways with stilted gestures and a few muffled words. Allegra looked back at him, waving one last time, before walking away. For his part, Andy turned back to the stars. Natalie could've sworn she heard him whistling.

When Allegra started moving back towards the house, Eliana and Natalie rushed away from the window. They hurried into the family room, collapsing onto the massive sectional and pulling magazines onto their laps. Natalie flipped on the television.

They did notice the deep, rosy flush to Allegra's cheeks, but neither said a word to her about it. Natalie thumbed through her magazine, pursed her lips, and tried to keep from smiling.

Allegra cleared her throat. "I wanted to thank you both. This is the nicest evening I've had in – well, I can't remember the last time I had a night like this. We stayed too late."

"Not at all," Natalie said, beaming. "I checked on the kids a few minutes ago. They all fell asleep watching television in Eliana's room. I think they wore themselves out."

"Sometimes the best evenings come from tossing bedtime to the wind," Eliana said.

"Theirs and mine, too," Allegra said, flashing the grin they knew so well. "I'm going to go rouse my kiddos—"

"Want me to help you carry them out?"

They looked to the doorway where Andy stood, nearly filling its frame as he stretched to his full height. He stared at Allegra like he couldn't see past her. Eliana looked at them, her gaze drifting from one to the other, and then back again. She sighed.

As soon as Allegra left the room, Eliana narrowed her eyes. Natalie shrunk into her magazine. Andy turned away from them, locking the doors and flipping off the outside lights.

Natalie's throat tightened as she stole a glance at him. She had forgotten the way that Harris would shut down a house, as meticulously as he tucked in their children. Natalie leaned her cheek against the couch, pulled her knees to her chest, and closed her eyes.

"Don't even think about it," Eliana intoned.

Andy turned back to her, blinking innocently. "Beg your pardon?"

"You're not allowed to date my new friend."

"Why do you always assume an agenda? Maybe I was just showing her the stars."

"You've seen enough stars in your day."

"The Summer Triangle on a clear night is nothing to sneeze at—"

"You weren't looking at the stars, bro. Don't play with me. I see you."

"Then, you know I'm a decent, kind, hard-working individual."

"You are all of those things," Eliana said, nodding. "But you can't make a relationship work longer than two weeks."

"And the last thing Allegra needs right now is a broken heart," Natalie piped up.

"You both act like you know her so well, and it hasn't even been a month, right?"

"That's still longer than your longest relationship," Eliana grumbled.

"We know her well enough to know that she shouldn't be discarded," Natalie said.

"Well, ladies, your well-intentioned warnings came too late. I asked her out. She said yes. We're going on a date. Drinks. Dinner. A walk on the beach. But that isn't what this inquiry is about."

"It isn't?" Eliana asked.

He walked by her and dropped a kiss on her head. "You're changing the subject. We're sure as hell going to talk about what's bothering you. You can't avoid me forever."

Eliana turned away from him, pulling a blanket to her chin. "Just like Josh."

With wide eyes, Eliana snapped her neck to look at him.

"He's your husband. You can't avoid him forever, either," Andy said.

He pivoted, walking away from them. They listened as his footsteps echoed down wide, cold hallways. When he bounded up the stairs, taking them two at a time, Natalie could hear his lilting melody. Andy was definitely whistling.

Allegra's fingers shook while she tried to fasten a choker behind her neck. She cursed under her breath and glanced outside her bedroom window. Delphine and Jules played hide-and-seek, weaving in and out of blooming lilac bushes. They shouted in rapid-fire French that Allegra couldn't follow.

When Allegra heard Véronique coughing politely from the doorway, she immediately manufactured a smile. Even as she turned, however, her fingertips remained pressed to the windowpane. It was Allegra's way: to keep them as close as she could.

"Do you need help with that, *mademoiselle?*" Véronique nodded to the necklace.

"I do, or I need to choose a different necklace."

Véronique smiled. Wordlessly, she crossed the room, took the necklace in hand, and turned Allegra towards the mirror. They said nothing as her deft fingertips fastened the vintage clasp. Seconds moved like sieved water, running at a slow trickle.

"*Et voilà, mademoiselle.* You look like one of Degas's ballerinas."

Allegra tried to smile. "Thank you. And you shouldn't worry – it's only dinner with a friend. I'll come home early enough to tuck the children in."

"Perhaps, just this once, don't."

"I'm sorry?"

Véronique smiled, revealing the barest flash of neat white teeth. "When I was a little girl, my mother received a beautiful bird as a gift. Green wings. Red streaks. Black eyes. She set its cage by the window so that the bird could see the sky – as if a window could ever be enough for a bird, or for that matter, a girl. I asked to set it free, but my mother forbade it. She said it would die. For my part, I couldn't decide if my mother wanted to protect it or simply own another pretty thing. Because that's what cages do, you see: they protect, *mais aussi,* they entrap."

Allegra blinked. It was the most Véronique had ever said to her. "What happened?"

"I will never know what became of the bird, but I shall never forget its joyous song as I opened the door of the cage and then lifted the latch of the window. Nor the brilliant flash of color it made as it soared up into the sky. Free."

Eliana's forehead creased. "Does Silvia's breathing sound funny to you?"

"No. And you're a better person than me – I used to turn off Everett's baby monitor when I worked in the home office. If he wanted me, he had to put his lungs into it."

With a small smile, Eliana set the baby monitor down and raised the volume. When Eliana turned and glimpsed her friend, her breath caught. Natalie wore a midi-length sundress, pale pink and flowing and looped with a thin braided rope around her neck. Her hair, curled and captured in a messy, asymmetrical knot, revealed her round green eyes.

"You look beautiful," Eliana whispered.

"I'm too old for a first date."

"Not true. We're never too old to begin again."

Eliana's smile wavered, however. Natalie tilted her head to the side.

"Are you okay?"

"I'm fine," Eliana said before pausing. "I guess I thought

we would all grow old together. Retire somewhere hot. Drink cocktails by the pool. Complain that our kids never call. Golf."

"You don't golf."

"I could learn. My future octogenarian self wants to learn."

"You don't want me to go?"

"I *absolutely* want you to go," Eliana said. "A second chance with your first love? It's like a dream. I guess I'm still processing the person Harris turned out to be. Lousy friend, huh?"

Natalie's mouth fell open. "He broke your heart too, didn't he?"

"Maybe a little," Eliana said with a shrug. "I keep trying to hate him – because, frankly, he deserves it – but we all grew up together. I can't dislike him like I should."

Natalie sat beside her, resting her head on Eliana's shoulder. "Me neither."

Both of them sat quietly for some time, long enough to watch sunlight splatter throughout the room, to know the clouds passing over the sea for the long shadows that they cast.

"We've done everything together. I studied abroad in St. Petersburg for you."

Eliana arched an eyebrow. "I minored in art history for you."

"And I sat through too many subtitled art-house films for Josh."

"I still have a subscription to *Congressional Quarterly* for Harris!"

"Yes, we've done everything together, but let's not do this together."

Eliana snapped her neck to look Natalie in the eye. "What?"

"Don't blow up your whole world so we can be in the same season of life together."

Eliana jerked away. "Do you think I would actually do that – leave my husband to be more like *you*? To be single again?"

"Not exactly, but I do think that all relationships get old, and divorce can be contagious," Natalie said with a sigh. "I just hope that – in putting on this beautiful, borrowed dress and drenching myself in perfume and wearing lipstick like a co-ed – I hope I'm not making this out to be easy. Because it's not. It's terrifying."

"Here's the part where you tell me to call him back," Eliana said, narrowing her eyes.

"Andy had a point: Josh is the one man you can't ignore."

Eliana laughed acidly, nearly sputtering with sarcasm. "And now a thinly veiled reference to my father? You're on a roll today."

"That's not what I meant," Natalie said, eyes widening. "I was talking about the father of *your* children, Eliana. I don't want to see your family break apart the way mine has."

Eliana jumped to her feet. Natalie's eyes tracked Eliana as she paced the spacious closet.

"How come everyone gets to be mad but me?" Eliana demanded.

"What?"

"Andy stops speaking to women after two weeks of dating – the original ghosting no-show before Gen Z had a term for it. My mother has stopped returning my calls. You barely speak to Harris, and you're separating from him. My husband has wronged me, too, Natalie. I'm entitled to some time."

"That's true."

Eliana exhaled. "Thank you."

"But not completely."

"Natalie!"

Natalie raised up a palm. "I would've fought for my marriage had Harris not convinced me that there was nothing left of it. He left me, while Josh wants to come home."

"You say that like it's enough. Like it fixes everything."

"It's a start," Natalie said, raising her voice. "It's been weeks, and your husband is still chasing you. Why won't you let him catch you?"

Eliana muted a scream in the back of her throat. Pivoting

on her heel, she stormed out of the room, slamming the door behind her. Her bare footsteps smacked down the hallway.

Natalie took the baby monitor in hand and pursed her lips. She envied Eliana's certainty that she could slam a door, and someone would come after her. Natalie was trying to raise her children with the same inexhaustible devotion. How many times had she said that she would love them unconditionally? That her love for them was bigger than their bad mood?

But still.

Natalie tucked her hair behind her ears. Her hands shook from her internal simmering. And then Natalie, who had never once slammed a door, wearily rose to her feet. She took care not to step on her handkerchief hem, grabbed the baby monitor, and then walked briskly to her best friend, glowering in a distant room. Because Eliana was waiting for her.

Chapter 19

Allegra stepped onto The Cultured Pearl's rooftop deck like someone wading into water. With her height and her blazing red hair, she'd never been one who could blend into a crowd and had long dispensed with trying. She wore a simple, black sleeveless dress that hit her at mid-thigh. At home, in that last backward glance before exiting, Allegra had thought she looked elegant. A layer of black to frame her lithe shape. A black choker necklace around her neck. With a smear of lipstick and a near-empty envelope clutch, Allegra had felt like a girl again.

Now, pulling at her high hemline, Allegra wished she'd made a different choice.

Before she could retreat, Andy stood up from a gazebo. He flashed a grin. Allegra felt her face mirror his smile. Only a moment ago, she had been eyeing the patrons and wondering if anyone recognized her. Now, she forgot the rest of them.

When she reached the table, Andy gently helped her into her seat. He nursed a whiskey on ice.

"You are a vision."

"Like something out of a magazine?" Allegra asked dryly. "I'll have the Sake Sangria. Thank you."

The waitress who had appeared at her left them with a nod.

Andy smiled. "I guess compliments are part of the job description for you, huh?"

"I'm sorry. You were trying to be nice." Allegra said.

"I was trying too hard. I only meant to say that you look like a dream to me. It's surreal that you said yes—"

"That sort of compliment I actually *have* heard before—"

"Because I tried to ask you out years ago, but I chickened out."

"What?" Allegra asked, blinking fast.

"When I was in law school at NYU, a friend's older sister was studying at FIT and got us seats at New York Fashion Week. I have no idea why I said yes – that's the obliviousness of youth for you. Anyway, I saw you backstage at the Calvin Klein show. You were the closer—"

"You were *there*?"

"I was. Following my buddy like a lemming."

"And you were going to ask me out?"

"You were in the corner with cameras in your face. You looked so sad and cornered. I remember wanting to make you laugh. Want to hear what I was going to say?"

Her drink appeared before her. Allegra barely noticed. "Yes."

"I was going to say something like: 'I get it. I feel your pain. But I bet my shoes hurt worse than yours do.'"

Allegra grinned. "That was your opening?"

"See, I knew it never would've worked."

"I wish you'd talked to me."

"Do you? Well, I wasn't going to blow my second chance with you," Andy said. "Bottom line? I don't expect anything from you tonight. You said yes. It's enough for me."

"You're very sweet, Andy," Allegra said, smiling halfway. "But you make me nervous."

"I doubt that. But maybe you should put me in the hot seat. You can ask me anything."

"Okay then," Allegra said, exhaling deeply. "Eliana warned me about you. She said you would break my heart. Why would she say that?"

Andy winced, pausing only briefly to knock back a swig.

"Because she cares about you, and my relationship history

is … patchy, at best."

"And why is that?" Allegra asked, before closing her eyes. "Actually, don't answer that. I've been on the receiving end of one too many of these, and I got carried away."

"No, it's okay," Andy said, though he paused for a moment and looked down Rehoboth's bustling Main Street. He watched people while she watched him. Waiting. "I guess I don't want to recreate my parents' relationship. I'm too much like my dad as it is."

"What's he like?"

The light dimmed in Andy's eyes. He stared at his hands. "Cold. Aloof. Unreachable."

Allegra's forehead creased. "So, you don't get close to people in order to protect yourself from a perceived inability to get close to people?"

Andy barked laughter. "Well, when you put it that way."

"It sounds like you're scared of getting hurt," Allegra said. She waited until he raised his eyes to meet hers before speaking again. "It's okay. I'm scared of getting hurt again, too."

A rosy flush climbed Andy's neck. He quickly looked away, muttering: "I'm scared of being hunted down as well. If they ever create a sort of Yelp for ex-girlfriends, I'm screwed."

Allegra laughed. "Okay, your turn. Ask me anything."

Andy hesitated for a moment. "I only have one question."

"Sure."

"You're a fantastic mother. I've only watched you for a day, and I can recognize it because my own mom was incredible. You're present and involved and loving. So, why would you give full custody of your children to your ex-husband?"

"I didn't."

"What?" Andy asked, a clipped sound that rose above the din of conversation encircling them. His pupils dilated, watching her.

"It just sort of happened," Allegra said, her palms splayed. "The children went to Luxembourg for Christmas. I joined them late after a shoot in Indonesia. When I arrived, I discovered that the guest rooms in our second home had been redecorated as their bedrooms. Etienne had had their things shipped from New York. He ambushed me. He told me he would only live in Luxembourg. He said he wanted a divorce unless I quit my job. Because his job has always allowed him to stay put, he claimed that he'd been the better parent. And if I didn't acquiesce to his ultimatum, he would take the children from me."

"Did you challenge any of this?"

"I said that I was an excellent mother, that I love them desperately," Allegra said, her voice softening. Andy leaned forward to hear her. "But he had a file on me. He had hired private investigators. The pictures showed me leaving nightclubs late. I met agents and photographers there, but no one would've believed that I took meetings for work after midnight. It was all such damning conjecture. A random man standing next to me looked like a lover. A clumsy fall made me look drunk. Within forty-eight hours of handing me the file, he had leaked it to the press. It was a nightmare. I had never been in the tabloids before, and immediately I lost work. I barely had time to hunker down with agents and lawyers before my kids had started school again across the ocean. They were beginning a whole new life without me, while I left them with him to figure out a plan. And with each passing day that he had them, his argument for keeping them grew stronger – is this boring you?"

Andy looked up from his phone. He blinked.

"What? Of course not."

"You're playing with your phone while I'm telling you about my life imploding."

"Sorry about that. I'm listening. I wanted to check The Hague Convention."

"What? Why?"

"Because I don't think your ex-husband simply took custody of your children."

"You don't?"

"No," Andy said, his voice flinty. "I think he kidnapped them."

As Natalie stepped inside the Backlit Gallery, she gasped. Twinkle lights encircled the ceiling. Low, ambient music swelled. In the far corner of the room, a picnic blanket teemed with food. She saw a platter of fruit flanked by two copper Moscow mules. An artfully arranged cheese plate. Crudités garnished with fresh herbs. Plated crab cakes with lemons.

"Do you recognize it?"

She smiled as soon as she heard his voice. How many times had she pulled that voice closer, pressing her bedroom phone tightly to her ear and wrapping the cord around her wrist? How many times had she leaned against his shoulder in his ancient Jeep, listening to him speak with her whole body? His mouth on her ear. Her hand on his thigh.

Her breath hitched now, remembering.

"Do I recognize what?"

"The painting. Tell me where it takes you."

Following his gaze, Natalie stared at the painting hanging above their picnic. Her eyes darted over the broad brushstrokes. Streaks of silver augmented with bursts of white. Hard, spiky lines of green. Soft, pliable golden color. A spot of caramel. Another of speckled cream.

"Wait," she murmured, forgetting her nerves. "Is that a *horse*?"

"It is," Damon said, chuckling. "I knew you'd see it."

"It's Assateague," Natalie breathed, moving swiftly to stand before it. "You can see the dunes and the grass and the horse in the background. It's exquisite."

"It's a piece by a young artist. He's amassing quite the regional following," Damon said. "Initially, I thought I would take you out to a restaurant. When he delivered this piece yesterday, though, I thought I might take you back to the island instead. Minus the sand fleas at night."

They sat down on the blanket. "I haven't been back to Assateague since, well, you."

"I've gone back a lot, but our memories were my best moments there."

Natalie flushed, remembering their last night together. She recalled their tent, bleating fiercely in the wind. Their one sleeping bag. His hands roaming beneath her clothes. Her giddy laughter, a sound she had forgotten since she had lost her mother. She remembered marveling at the irony of it: that a flimsy tent could feel sturdier than the cottage she shared with her father.

It was the summer when they had fallen apart, disintegrating like paper in water.

Yet, that night had been watching the stars and listening to the wind and pitching a tent. Natalie had forgotten that night to feel guilty for laughing because her mother couldn't make a sound, to feel guilty for seeing a sunset because her mother wasn't there to paint it. There had only been the heft of his mouth and the safety of his arms. As the sun rose, Natalie had wanted to stay in that rose-gold hour forever, even as she itched to run and never look back.

"I do realize, you know, that you've lived a lot of life since our stolen summers together," he said, rousing her from her reverie and distracting her from the heat of her own red cheeks. "I want to know you beyond my memories. I'd love to hear more about your world as it is now."

"You mean – crumbling?"

He gave her a look and took her hand.

"You're still too hard on yourself. You're not failing simply because you're waiting for something new to bloom," Damon said quietly. "You said you have children?"

Natalie smiled. "Yes, two boys. Aaron is thirteen now and Everett is four."

"Two boys," Damon said, whistling low. "Well done. I know how much you wanted a family. They're lucky to have you for a mother."

"I'm the lucky one. Do you have children?"

"No," Damon said. "I was married for five years, but our paths diverged. She joined the Peace Corps, and she's very happy with her life now. We have a pact where she sends me postcards from every place she travels to. I'm proud that we've held on to our friendship."

Natalie blinked. "Wow. That's so, so ... Zen. At the moment, I'm proud of myself for returning his text messages without attaching devil emojis."

Damon laughed, a warm, liquid flow that drenched the room. When he stopped laughing, Natalie impulsively grazed his cheek with her knuckle.

"I have to warn you," she began, somewhat haltingly, "that I might not be ready for this."

He kissed the soft space behind her wrist, pulsing with jasmine perfume. "I'm not asking anything of you, Nat. I just want to be where you are."

"I don't know what to say, but I always forgot what I meant to say with you."

Damon nodded. "So maybe we won't talk tonight, then. Lie down."

"Pardon? I need you to take it *slow*, Damon. Maybe you're not following me here."

Damon laughed again and then he blew out the votives, one by one, before scrambling to his feet. "I have a surprise for you," he said, as he crossed the room in long strides. "We used to spend a lot of time waiting for night to come so we could do this."

He cut the lights. Her face burned in the darkness.

"Damon, is this some sort of trust exercise?"

She found his laugh first, deep and velvety and low, right beside her. She felt around the picnic blanket until she found his hand, and then she clutched it tightly.

"Lie back," he whispered.

With a sigh, she lay down. Their shoulders touched. He clicked the button of a small remote control. Immediately, Natalie gasped. She clapped a hand across her mouth.

Natalie didn't know how she had failed to notice it: the painting mounted to the ceiling. The unframed, textured canvas was framed by crisscrosses of spotlights, shining upon it from the gallery's corners, and doused with bold splotches of color. Heartier than ink. Looser than oil. The splattered circles bloomed like navy stains on a dove-grey background.

Damon then pressed two more buttons on his remote control. Her breath hitched.

Debussy's "Clair de Lune" wafted from hidden speakers. A star projector blinked to life. Constellations roved over the walls, gathering momentum with the piano notes, until the light and the music moved as one. And once more, they were under the stars together.

"Is it too much?" Damon asked, his voice hovering above a whisper.

Right then, Natalie peeled her gaze away from the stars, and her eyes traced his darkened profile. She was overcome that he had done this, all of this, for her. She'd been discarded. She'd been devalued. She'd grown used to the discomfiting sense that she herself was not enough. And while she knew she might never know exactly why Harris had betrayed her, Natalie rarely gave a thought to his failings. She hadn't ever blamed Harris like she had herself. Instead, she regularly engaged in an unfair, open-wound inquiry, parsing apart everything that might be wrong with her. Because it must have been her fault that she lost him.

And now, here was this man who had poured her a drink. Cut fruit. Made drinks. Arranged appetizers. Broiled crab cakes. Mounted paintings to walls. Transformed a gallery to the inky, wide expanse of sky that nightly shrouded the ocean. He had done it all for her.

Without a word, Natalie climbed further into his arms. She took his stubbled, sandpaper cheeks in her palms, folded her mouth over his, and opened to him. He startled for only a moment, before wrapping his arms around her hips and pulling her against him. It was brand-new for them both, but also like slowly remembering the lyrics to a song they used to know. Humming the sound. Mouthing the words. Turning phrases over the tongue. Riffing on it.

His hand pillowed her head. Her mouth pressed against his throat. Their urgent, muffled sounds hid beneath the piano's rising timbre. Their warming bodies rolled now with the rhythm of the ocean, overlaid with passing stars.

With a sigh curled in her throat, Eliana sat staring into the baby monitor, listening to her daughters breathe. She hadn't yet touched her penne pomodoro, nor had she sipped the wine she swirled in her glass. She was burrowing deeper into a blanket when her phone buzzed.

> *Whenever you want to talk, I'm ready. I'll wait for you forever. I love you, Eliana.*

Reading Josh's message, she pursed her lips. They'd spoken, of course, though they talked exclusively about their children. She'd sent him pictures of the girls playing in the sand, splashing in the water. He'd read them bedtime stories. The girls cried that they missed him, whimpering after they hung up the phone. They seemed to forget him after a few readings of *Goodnight Moon*, which made Eliana want to cry for the emptiness, the sheer lack of him.

Eliana pulled her knees to her chest. As she tossed her phone aside, her eyes narrowed on the fireplace. Flames danced, controlled and predictable, from faux wood. Eliana tilted her head to the side and tried to think of how to say "fire" in every language she knew. In Spanish: *fuego*. In German: *feuer*. In Russian: *pozhar*. In Mandarin Chinese: *huo*.

"*Le feu à l'intérieur*," she whispered in French. *The fire inside.*

Because that was what it felt like deep within her. English, a Germanic language replete with spiky syllables, didn't adequately capture the seductive, silken quality of the anger she nurtured toward her husband right now. Eliana could understand now how people held grudges for a lifetime, how they could stay angry forever – feeding off poison in indulgent, parasitic pleasure. She knew that this stalemate of theirs was trench warfare. But still.

Eliana was angry, had never been quite so angry. She could feel the fire within ravaging her insides, eating away at her even as it metastasized. It was not unlike cancer, this burden that she refused to set down. It was a sickness of her own making.

Just then, Eliana stepped outside of herself. She could see a woman sitting all alone in a too-big house, immobilized as she watched a fake fire burn. The woman pressed a baby monitor tightly to her ear – waiting for someone to need her. And Eliana realized then that her life had never veered so far from the way she thought it would go.

Chapter 20

His mouth was moving. He had put his phone away. Allegra, however, couldn't hear Andy above the ringing in her ears. She closed her eyes.

"You okay?" Andy asked.

Allegra nodded numbly. "That's a big word to throw around," she finally said.

Andy didn't speak for a long moment. He chewed the inside of his cheek, assessing her. She felt his gaze pour over her, not unlike the photographers who marked up her likeness, indicating where her image should be retouched. Allegra squirmed. She wanted to leave.

"He threatened you, didn't he?" Andy asked.

"He threatens me all the time. I've been advised to let it go."

"You need to find new representation," Andy said firmly. "Someone proactive. Beyond that, you need to start a journal and document it if he acts abusively toward you. You need to ask for help from law enforcement immediately if you feel at risk."

"Would you possibly," she began, tucking a stray hair behind her ear, "consider representing me?"

"I can help you find someone, but I can't be your lawyer."

"Why not?"

"Because I don't want to represent you. I want to date you."

He held out her sweater for her like he could embrace her with it. As he smoothed the fabric along her shoulders, Natalie looked back to their picnic. Thin tendrils of smoke wafted from extinguished candles. They had shared a piece of tiramisu, and Natalie couldn't drag her gaze away from that one small plate flanked by two forks.

"To think, you even mixed me a greyhound. You remembered my very specific tastes from well before I had a legal I.D."

Damon smiled. "How could I forget a girl who makes a cocktail like an aging bartender?"

"They were all from old movies," she said, nudging him with her hip. "I loved anything as long as you wouldn't have found it on the festival circuit. Anything that wasn't theirs."

"Or, you were an old soul. Even then."

Her breath hitched. "Thank you for this evening. I'm so appreciative of it all."

"You deserve so much more than you know."

"Damon," she said, resting her hand on his chest. "I do need to say one thing."

"Don't end it yet, Natalie – not when we haven't even started."

Natalie paused. She blinked rapidly, searching his eyes. "That's not what I meant. I was going to say I saw the drink on your Instagram feed. I've been keeping up with you for years. Maybe I was looking for an excuse to come back, but it isn't luck: me being here with you—"

"The hell it isn't. I've never felt so lucky," Damon finished, exhaling. "The stars are on my side."

She stared at his mouth. Before a thought could flash, Damon lowered his head to hers. Their lips met, merging and softening and opening. When he pulled away, her chest heaved.

"I came tonight because I thought you would distract me from my messy life."

Damon smiled. "Really? How'd I do?"

"You – you're so much more than a diversion. You're the whole point."

His smile vanished. Damon pulled her tightly against him. He tangled his fingers in her hair, its careful knot having been dismantled on the floor. Standing in the doorway of his gallery, Damon appeared to hesitate before opening the door. Natalie noticed his stillness and grinned.

"Five more minutes," she said.

"Five more minutes," he agreed.

As shared laughter wafted between them, he took her face in his hands. It was a phrase they'd repeated countless times in their youth. And this was all Natalie had ever known: holding him tightly before reluctantly letting him go. She hoped he felt the longing to stay, too.

"I know you're not in a position to make promises," he whispered.

She arched an eyebrow. "But?"

"Promise me we'll last beyond summer this time."

Natalie kissed him, then, knowing that he wouldn't believe a promise she'd broken years ago. But she felt his grip tighten on her waist and she leaned into it, letting him hold on.

Andy reached for her hand as they wove through the crowds congregating on the boardwalk. He found a spot on the boardwalk by a group of collegiate revelers. With his arm draped over her shoulder, Andy held her close.

On a patch of sand beyond Rehoboth Avenue, shadowy figures prepared the fireworks.

Allegra could feel the crowd's anticipation rising like heat. Yet with her head against Andy's chest, with her ear privy to the thrumming of his heart, she ignored the other people. Instead, her gaze drifted to the ocean. The night's black veil shrouded the water. Finding the delineation between sky and sea required other senses, assessing the water's movement and its noise. Its dimpled waves. Its hushed roar. Its raw, hidden power.

"Do you really believe I can get my children back?"

She had asked the question without thinking. She didn't realize that she'd been pondering it, that she was near-dizzy with this kernel of hope – not until the words had left her mouth.

"I'll always believe that what is right and true has the best shot."

"I haven't told the truth in some time," she said, pausing. "Not even with my own name."

"Your name?"

"When I started modeling, my agency gave me a name that they said could stand alone. I've spent most of my adult life trying to be worthy of it."

He smoothed a hair from her forehead. "What's your real name, then?"

"Jane. Plain Jane Riley from Missouri," she said, smiling ruefully.

"Jane. I like it. It suits you," Andy said. "I was actually named Andres. My mother's Mexican, and it was her father's name, but I've always gone by Andy."

"Why?"

He sighed. "It was easier. But I've always wondered if it's possible to be really known without your real name."

At once, she looped her arms around his neck like she'd done it a thousand times before. He kissed the sides of her lips first, before progressing to her neck and her cheeks. By the time his mouth found hers, she had glued herself to him. Later, she would remember that moment as a homecoming, heady with a sense of déjà vu.

Fireworks erupted in a cacophony of sound and color. Reflected, fiery steaks of gold and red splashed the boardwalk with bold color. Golden light set the Star of the Sea building ablaze. All around them, people gazed upward, scouring the sky for eruptions like falling stars.

Allegra didn't see it.

Her eyes hung closed. Her arms coiled within his. He took his time as he kissed her, setting their pace. She followed his languid motion, as though they were dancing. For the sparest moment, she lost track of the time, the crowd, and even her own unrelenting pain.

But Allegra had always lost her peripheral vision in love, in lust. She, who had spent the bulk of her adult life in the public eye, was normally finely attuned to the gnawing sense of being watched. Paparazzi shots of her sold well because they rarely captured a good image of her. She was *that good* at protecting herself. A baseball hat would obscure her face. A prominently placed arm – raised as though blocking a shot – would sever a photograph. Always, Allegra wore sunglasses, glaring through them with her lip curled.

Tonight, however, Allegra never noticed the handful of phones shining her way. She was moving toward him, rather than away from everyone else. Her guard was down. By the time Allegra and Andy had pulled away from each other, catching their breath with soft laughter, text messages had been sent. A bidding war had ensued. Already, underpaid interns were sleuthing the internet, frantically trying to identify a man by only his shadowed profile.

For their part, Andy and Allegra held hands, their wrists swinging. Andy whistled, while Allegra tried to smooth the crooked grin from her face. While he walked her home, they barely had a passing thought for anyone else in the world.

But the world, ever hungry, was coming for them.

Eliana sat on the deck wrapped in a cashmere shawl, her bare feet curled beneath her, and sipped a glass of Malbec. The promise of tears burned her eyes, but she would not cry.

She jerked as the screen door slid open behind her.

"Hey you," Natalie said.

"It's the Fourth of July! Why aren't you off celebrating?"

Natalie shrugged. "I told Damon I needed to be home early enough to see the fireworks with you. It's tradition. He understood. After all, he was there."

Tears clouded Eliana's eyes as she thought back to the many times she had clustered on the boardwalk with Natalie. She remembered the later years, too, when she and Natalie and Josh and Damon had claimed their patch of sand. Lying on their backs. They hadn't only been waiting for a fireworks display. They'd been on the cusp of the rest of their lives, waiting to begin.

"I'm sorry," Eliana said.

"I'm more sorry," Natalie said. "You absolutely get to be angry with him. I know I am."

"You don't even know what he did yet."

"Doesn't matter. I know you," Natalie said, before pausing. "Look, I know you've hated it when I've isolated myself over the years. I'm used to dealing with things on my own, but that's no excuse for not reaching out. You're the one who's kept this friendship alive and kicking. Not me. When you asked me for advice after that bad playdate, I almost laughed. Because you're not just my best friend, Eliana – you're my *only* friend. I don't know how to do this."

Eliana touched her hand to her heart. "Natalie," she whispered.

"But I do know *you*. And that's why I found this thing with Josh alarming – it's so out of character for you to bottle things up and stonewall and ice a man out. That's something *I* would do. I was worried I was rubbing off on you."

"Thank you for telling me how you've felt. You're a wonderful friend and none of this is your fault," Eliana said, as she chewed on her lower lip. "We're in this rut, you see. If I tell

Josh why I'm angry with him, he'll tell me exactly what I want to hear to fix it."

"But you won't trust his apology unless he comes to it on his own."

"Yes," Eliana breathed, as she finally exhaled. "*Yes.*"

Eliana smiled then, her spine loosening. She watched as Natalie poured herself a glass of wine. Natalie swirled the Malbec in her glass, giving it legs. Eliana noted the high color of her friend's cheeks. Her loose hair. Her inflamed, naked mouth.

"It was a good date, wasn't it?"

"It was an epic date," Natalie whispered. "But it's not only him – it's this place. All the time I was here, I was plotting to get out. Thank you for bringing me back."

"Oh, Nat," Eliana said. "Don't thank me when you're the one doing me a favor. I don't know how I would get through this season without you."

"We'll figure it out. We always do."

Above them, fireworks bloomed like flowers, explosive fragments falling away like wind-blown petals over dark, ruffled waves.

"Where did he take you?" Eliana asked.

"He made a picnic and turned his gallery into a planetarium. Want to hear the rest?"

Eliana pointedly turned her chair away from the fireworks display and toward her friend. Behind her, pyrotechnics thundered. She reached for more wine. "Tell me everything."

"I kissed him first," Natalie said, as she brought her hand to her cheek.

Eliana grinned. "I was hoping you would say that."

Moonlight cast shadows throughout Allegra's room. She could hear the celebratory shouting outside her window. The popcorn intensity of DIY fireworks set off in the streets. A shriek of joy here. A car's deep bass notes pounding there. For once, Allegra had been a face in the crowd, too. She had been *out there*, as excited and anonymous as everybody else.

Her phone vibrated. Allegra smiled like he was right there with her, reaching across the coverlet for her hand. Andy had already called twice. The first time, he'd called ten minutes after kissing her goodnight. The second time, he'd waited an hour and had caught her curled up with a book in bed. They'd talked for another hour. And now, here he was, calling again.

Without opening her eyes, Allegra brought the phone to her ear.

"I guess you can't sleep either, huh?" she asked.

"I just finished my breakfast. You won't imagine the trash I've read with my coffee."

Her eyes shot open. "Etienne."

"Allegra," he said. "I had hoped to start the day with *The Economist*, yet here I sit, reading about a tryst with the mother of my children and another man."

She sat straight up in bed, pinching the bridge of her nose.

"If you don't want to read about me, take me off your Google Alerts."

"I am only checking in. My children are in your care, are they not?"

Allegra raised her chin. "*Our* children are sound asleep in the next room. They spent the evening in the capable hands of Véronique. You remember Véronique, don't you? The nanny you chose to raise our children instead of me?"

"Clearly, they are not your priority. Careful now. Don't force me to reclaim them."

She thought then to Andy's hazel eyes, rimmed with a deep sable color. His furrowed brow. Her cold hand, slowly warming in his. His low, serrated-edged words.

I think he kidnapped them.

"Yes, our children live with you most of the time," Allegra said quietly, pausing for a long moment. "But, for tonight at least, I'm with them and far away from you. I'll take it."

Through the phone, Allegra could hear something fragile smash. His breathing grew labored. He hissed, a grating, serpentine sound.

"You will not see him again. Do you understand?"

Her heart pounded so quickly that she felt its reverberation in her core. Allegra placed a hand over her stomach. She swallowed, saying nothing.

"End it," Etienne growled. "End it, or I will *bury* you. Worse than that – I will make certain that you are forgotten. When I'm done with you, no one will ever remember your name."

"That doesn't matter to me. No one really knows my name anyway."

For the first time, Allegra hung up on the father of her children. Her hands quaked as tremors wracked her joints in waves. She closed her eyes tightly, willing Andy's face into her mind's eye. She envisioned him as he had been only a few hours ago: sitting across the table from her, holding her gaze and speaking with firm, quiet authority.

Write down everything.

With a deep breath, Allegra turned on the light on her bedside table. She retrieved a blank notebook from the drawer. She dated it in careful handwriting and painstakingly documented his toxic, threatening language.

As Allegra tucked her notebook away and turned out the light, she was viscerally aware of feeling *seen* even in her solitude. Her notebook would bear witness to her pain. She wasn't alone anymore.

And, in time, Allegra could sleep.

Chapter 21

As often happened when Natalie designed a home in her head, big dreams met cold, hard reality. Budgetary constraints. Tight timetables. Ultimately, Natalie had been forced to scale down her plans for Allegra's cottage. Allegra, grateful for every idea, had insisted on paying Natalie for her time. Instead, they compromised with joint manual labor.

And so, on this, the first Tuesday morning after the holiday weekend, they found themselves painting glossy indigo color onto the walls of Allegra's library. In the kitchen, contractors jackhammered the linoleum floor and peeled away the faded wallpaper. Outside, through a wide set of double-hung windows, their children – still speckled with blue paint – played tag in the backyard. On the patio, Véronique poured them all lemonade.

Allegra could hardly keep the smile from her face. She had met Andy for an early breakfast at Egg this morning. She and Véronique had given each other pedicures. She and the children took turns in an ongoing Scrabble tournament. Mercifully, Etienne had never bothered to call her back. Natalie had begun to make her home beautiful. A giddiness, a buoyant fluttering, rose from deep within her; Allegra didn't trust that the feeling would last, but she would sit with this goodness, as rare as a powder-winged butterfly alighting in her garden, for as long as she could.

"Jane," Natalie murmured, while she trimmed the edges of

a new built-in bookcase. "I like Jane."

"I don't know if my agent would agree with you. Jane requires a last name, and it doesn't exactly fit with the image of a globetrotting supermodel."

"I think you can have both worlds," Natalie said. "No one can ever take your career, your talent, and the life you've built away from you. But you don't have to hide who you are and where you've come from, either. People can't know you unless you let them see every side."

As soon as she finished speaking, her breath caught. Her heart throttled. She trained her red face on the blue wall, away from Allegra.

"I hadn't thought of it that way," Allegra said, squeezing Natalie's arm. "Have I thanked you enough yet for doing this to me?"

"Allegra, you're the easiest client of my professional life, and you're covered in blue paint! I never meant when I offered this for you to have to *do* anything. And I'm sorry for taking you away from your children while you have them."

"That's okay," Allegra said while glancing at Aaron, Jules, and Everett playing catch. "I think it's time for us to let other people in. We've been a tight little tribe for far too long. They need friends, and so do I."

"Us too. I think we'll all be happiest if we expand our idea of what a family can be."

"You could do that. Or, you could paint a room," Allegra said with a wink.

Natalie laughed. "It's true – this is my happy place. I'd forgotten how much I like playing with color. Normally, I don't have time for much of this anymore. I delegate now."

"Isn't delegating supposed to make life easier?"

"It is, but I've assigned away a lot of the work that I love to do."

"Well, you're the boss, right? Take it back."

With a start, Natalie stopped painting. She stared at the

thin brush, saturated with dusky blue paint. She turned it over in her hand, as though seeing the sinewy liquid for the first time.

"Mom? Are these the photographs you wanted to frame?"

Aaron stood in the doorway delicately pinching two 11x14 black-and-white prints of Delphine and Jules. Delphine, kneeling in late afternoon light, blew a dandelion. A confetti of delicate ivory fluff matted her face. Jules, balancing on a slim surfboard, rode a wave into shore with his arms outstretched. His mouth opened in laughter as he locked eyes with the photographer.

"Aaron, put those back," Natalie said sharply. "We're guests in their home."

"I wasn't snooping! I saw these against the wall in the hallway. Besides, weren't you telling me you were going to ask Miss Allegra about framing her pictures?"

"Yes, but I hadn't actually asked her yet."

"Oh. Well. This is awkward."

Natalie's face had caught fire again, her cheeks stained with red splotches. Watching her, Allegra suppressed a smile and spoke quickly. "Aaron, that was very thoughtful of you. I had forgotten where I put those prints when I was moving things out of the way for the contractor."

"No problem. Want me to put them somewhere less ..." he began, as his eyes circled the room, "blue?"

"The coffee table in the family room?"

"Good idea," Aaron said with a nod. He took a step to leave, before turning back. "You know, these might look better with some color."

Natalie sighed. "Aaron, these are her *private* images."

"I *know*, but I thought it might look cool to *apply* color. You might dig it, Miss Allegra."

"This is Miss Allegra's house, not mine anymore—" Natalie began.

"I love the idea," Allegra said.

"You do?" Natalie asked.

"Really? No lie?" Aaron demanded.

"No lie, but I'll only proceed on one condition."

"What's that?" Aaron asked while Natalie looked on with wide eyes.

"I want *you* to be the one who makes them better."

As the girls played with dolls (one a princess, another a super-hero) under the umbrella, Eliana and Andy played catch with their lacrosse sticks. Eliana had been irritated when Andy had foisted the lacrosse sticks upon her – interrupting her effort to reheat a mug of coffee in the microwave. He wanted to play though, and when Andy wanted to play, the man couldn't wait.

Eliana was surprised now to find herself enjoying their volley. She leaped to pluck the ball out of the air, swiftly cradling it in its pocket. With a forward-flick of her forearm, Eliana launched the ball back to him. He caught it, rocked it back and forth, and tossed it back.

"Want to tell me why you're so angry with my brother-in-law?"

"Not particularly."

"You know, I'm on borrowed time every moment I'm on vacation. I only have until the weekend to be here."

"Let's talk about it tomorrow, then," Eliana said, firing the ball back at him.

Andy let the ball fall into the sand. "What'd he do, Eliana?"

"You're not going to think he did anything wrong. What he did makes good financial sense."

"Go on. If you're wrong, you know I'll let you know. It's basically in my job description as your brother."

Eliana smiled through thin lips. "Do you remember the blue-chip stock his uncle left to us?"

"Sure. Josh paid off his student loans with that, right? And you guys bought the Volvo."

"Right, at the time, it was a game changer," Eliana said. "My name wasn't on the stock, obviously. It wasn't a bequest to me. Anyway, he decided to put up his own money to try to net more investors for his documentary project. Bottom line: he sold the stock."

Andy was silent for a long moment. "Without telling you?"

"Without telling me," Eliana said. "Josh thinks I'm angry with him for not telling me."

"But that's not why you're really mad."

"No."

"You're mad because that's exactly the kind of shit Dad would've pulled."

Eliana's eyes filled with tears. "Yes."

Andy dropped his stick to the ground and pulled her to him. Her shoulders heaved as she wept against his chest. Waves of tears pulsed through her. She could not stop them.

He held her tightly while the waves crashed close. It was the way of nature to go on, indifferent to the ebb and flow of any one person's interior life. Seagulls scavenged in the dunes. Sand crabs burrowed beneath shifting sands, their spindly antennae guiding them back toward the ocean. Sunlight flashed. Sea oats waved. And then her reserve of tears dried up.

"Did you ever tell him about Dad?" Andy asked finally.

"Not really. I always assumed that he understood. I mean, we grew up together. Mom and Dad moved us back to the States for my last two years of high school, and I dated him for most of it. And then Josh and I never left each other's side, so he saw everything up close."

"You can't make that assumption. Dad knew how to turn it on for an audience, and he always loved Josh," Andy said, furrowing his brow. "You have to talk to him about it."

Eliana's face darkened.

"I'm going to go check on the girls," she said, ducking beneath the umbrella's shade.

He left them, then. After climbing the stairs to the deck, Andy retrieved his phone from the picnic table. Andy took a deep breath and thumbed through his contacts list until he reached a familiar number. The number rang only once before his call was answered.

"Josh? It's me. And goddamn if you don't owe my little sister an apology."

Chapter 22

Before joining Everett, Lola, and Silvia on the porch for breakfast, Aaron passed Natalie a sketch he had completed of Natalie's left hand. Then he walked away. Natalie gasped, stunned by its detail. He had drawn her hand bent over a sketchpad, a paintbrush hooked beneath her thumb. She noted a familiar smattering of freckles by her wrist. Her ragged cuticles. Her stained fingertips. Curiously, in the picture, Natalie still wore her wedding rings.

But then, Natalie was not left-handed.

"So, I think the key to actually enjoying pancakes as an adult is waiting until your children are finished – really, totally finished – with their pancakes, before partaking of your own plate," Eliana said, between gulps of coffee. "Otherwise, you have a perfectly good pancake that you never get a chance to taste. You've gotta protect your pancake, right?"

"Right," Natalie said absently.

Through the open kitchen window, they heard mild chatter from the porch. From her vantage point, Natalie could see Everett race his car in circles around his plate. Beside him, Aaron stared down at his phone. He frowned at whatever he found there.

Eliana sighed. "Remember at the beginning of the summer when we said they couldn't have phones or toys at the table? It's like *Lord of the Flies* out there."

"Do you want me to take their toys away?"

"Did you hear what I said about protecting my pancakes?"

"I spoke too soon. Maybe we're all stuck in a vacation-mode rut."

"Well, *we* certainly are," Eliana asked, between stolen bites of a misshapen mistake-pancake. "But you? You took on a job for free. You're being extremely responsible in reconnecting with your first love. You wear hardly any of the free clothes I'm offering you. And you're pouting over your pancakes and coffee. Face it, Nat: you might be beyond help."

The doorbell rang.

Eliana rose. "I'll get it."

It rang once more, and then again. As the doorbell rang for a fourth time, Eliana scrambled to her feet. She rushed to the foyer. Eliana flung open the front door, intending to give a delivery professional a lecture on patience. Instead, she gaped.

Josh knelt on bended knee, as he had done years ago during a snowstorm in Moscow. They'd stood in Red Square, the domed Cathedral of St. Basil the Blessed towering over them, snowflakes tumbling and swirling and gathering amidst slick cobblestones. He'd had a ring, a modest sapphire that Eliana refused to 'upgrade,' which he had held out to her in his open palm.

Marry me, Eliana. Marry me, and I'll give you the whole, wide world.

Now, Josh clutched a bouquet of peonies. When he spoke, his voice shook.

"I'm so sorry, Eliana. I had no idea how much I hurt you."

Her breath caught. Her nostrils flared. *Andres David Smyth,* she thought, *I will kill you.*

"I'm not your father. I'll make mistakes and apologize for them a thousand times over. But know this: you're the love of my life, and I would never, ever try to hurt you."

"You already said you were sorry. You don't need to do it again."

"Like hell I don't," Josh said. "Look, I don't know how to do this, Eliana. My dad had a normal job with a normal schedule, a week of vacation each year, and a solid 401k. I have no idea how to manage this financial windfall or this weird profession. All I know for certain is that I can't do it without you. There's no point to any of this without you and the girls."

"I'm sorry, too."

"You are? For what?" Josh asked, his eyes widening.

"I'm sorry we didn't come with you. I think I was tired of following you."

"Eliana, you were never 'following' me – we're partners."

With a jolt, Eliana's lips fell apart. She went still. And then she wrapped her arms around Josh's waist, resting her head against his chest.

"I didn't know I needed to hear that," Eliana murmured against his pounding heart. "My dad never had partners. He had disciples."

Josh kissed her head. "We walk *together*. Where you go, I go."

Eliana smiled as tears pooled to blur her vision. "And where you go, I go."

On the edge of dunes peppered with sea oats, Andy and Allegra ate crepes between sips of coffee. When Andy had surprised her early with a warm bag from Sunshine Crepes, Véronique had whisked her out of the house. As Allegra had waved goodbye, Delphine and Jules had settled into the couch for a lazy breakfast of cinnamon rolls and cartoons. Véronique had shot her a sly grin. Her children had not yet known a world where crumbs could disappear into couch cushions. She would never have expected Véronique to be her best ally in giving her kids a normal life and in nudging Allegra toward a new normalcy, too. But here they were.

"What do you think of this morning's dining establishment?"

Allegra grinned, while her eyes roved over Dewey Beach's fine, golden sand. "I do like a table by the window, and I can't think of a better view than this one."

"And no need to worry about any ill-mannered patrons snapping our picture."

Allegra winced. "I'm still sorry for ... everything."

And she was. In the last seventy-two hours, Andy had been identified as an attorney who specialized in securities law. Little information beyond that and his gym membership had been provided. Two women who had briefly dated him had said that he worked too much. The vultures had soon pivoted to connect the dots from him to Eliana and Josh. No one had contacted his mother or researched his father yet, but Allegra knew it was coming.

The breakfast dates had been her idea. Allegra had found that photographers often slept in, and she'd spent much of her adult life exploring cities with the rising sun.

"You keep saying that," Andy said. "You have nothing to apologize for."

"You don't feel like you're being picked apart?"

Andy shrugged. "I'm not all that interesting, and my colleagues – except for some spot-on jokes that I'm out of my league – could care less. Besides, you're worth the extra, er, *logistical* effort. I promise to be especially boring to throw them off our scent."

"I appreciate that," Allegra said, chuckling. "I'm always trying to offer them my most vanilla self, too. No luck yet."

Andy sobered. "Has Etienne contacted you again?"

Allegra stared at the coffee cup in her hands. She had known that he would ask and had already decided what she would say. "No," she said. "No, he hasn't."

Her phone seemed to burn through the back pocket of her cut-offs, then. After a brief reprieve, Etienne had come back. His bold-faced name coated her missed calls list like graffiti tags. She had saved each voicemail, but she would not have her past relationship seep into this one like a contagion. She'd already lost too many people due to Etienne's antics. She would not lose this one. She tried to smile.

"So, I read what they had on you."

"Did you? Well, if it's true that I'm a workaholic, you should know that it's only because nothing else – or, I should say, no one else – has ever piqued my interest."

"That's not what I meant. How is it that you grew up all over the world?"

"Ah, that," Andy said. The muscle in his jaw worked.

"You said your mother's Mexican?"

"She is, and my dad's American. He was a real estate developer. He bounced from hotel chain to hotel chain, so we followed him. Eliana was always my own personal translator, our linguist sponge. I preferred math – no translation required. It's the reason we're so close, I guess. We've always had to lean on each other."

"Why did you spend your summers in Delaware?"

"Because that's what my father did as a boy. Everything we did was for him."

Allegra paused for a moment, biting her lower lip. "And that's how you met Natalie?"

Andy nodded. "As soon as Eliana started looking for her, my parents made sure to rent places near her parents' home."

"Small world," Allegra murmured. "I still can't believe that her dad was Kip Stone, lead singer of Adriftwood. I had a few of their albums. On vinyl, no less. Did you ever meet him?"

"I did."

"Did you like him?"

"No."

Allegra stopped chewing and followed his gaze out to sea. They watched as a barge made its way south, framed against the horizon line. He squeezed her hand, smiling briefly.

"Are you close to your family?" he asked.

Allegra nodded. "More so now than ever before. For a long

time, they didn't understand my job. They're very conservative. My swimsuit pictorials always led to some difficult conversations. Eventually, our relationship improved."

"What changed?"

"More clothing," she said, and they both laughed. "Actually, I think my first spread in *Vogue* forced them to take it seriously. I remember my mom said that the clothing reminded her of fine art. When I insisted that it *was* art, she said that meant I was a painting that had 'come alive.' That was maybe the best conversation of my life."

"She must know that these creatives couldn't realize their vision without you."

Allegra flushed. "Just wet clay. Waiting for hands to mold me," she quipped.

"No," he said. "You're so much more than that."

With a soft smile, Allegra tipped her head back to kiss him. His day-old stubble grazed her cheeks. She inhaled the coffee on his breath, the scent of his sunscreen, and kissed him deeply. When she reluctantly pulled away, she found the breeze colder than she remembered only a second ago. She heard his breath catch before he spoke.

"Do they like Etienne?"

Allegra paused for a millisecond. "Not at all. They never did."

"Do they know how bad it got?"

She shook her head. As her lips trembled, it became clear that Allegra couldn't speak anymore. Andy pulled her into his lap. He pressed a kiss to her head and brushed sand from her legs. In silence, Allegra leaned back against him, releasing a tightly held breath.

"It sounds like they're proud of you, as they should be."

Against his chest, Allegra sighed. "Maybe. But my mom also told me to make a change."

"Is that why you moved here?"

Allegra nodded. "I needed a home. We all did."

With his head resting on her head, Andy smiled. He held

her hand and kissed her cheek.

"Well, I like your vision so far, Allegra. What else have you got?"

"Sword," Lola said.

"Wand," Silvia countered.

"Dinosaur."

"Unicorn."

"LEGO house."

"LEGO *castle*."

Lola nodded. "Okay. LEGO castle."

Eliana chuckled as her girls watched the clouds glide across the sky, a procession of anonymous stratus shapes ready for their identification. Two pairs of bow-lips shouted into the wind. Four arms, sticky with peanut butter and sand and sunscreen, reached out like the clouds themselves could be pocketed.

At the water's edge, Josh jumped in shallow waves, motioning for Everett to join him. From Everett's perch atop a mound of dry sand, he shook his head again. With sinking shoulders, Josh took Everett's hand. Together, they walked back to their umbrella.

When they reached her, Eliana tossed Josh a towel. Everett immediately wedged himself between Silvia and Lola. Lola nudged Everett in the ribs.

"What you think, Eh-vit?" she asked, pointing to a particularly lean cloud.

"Pirate ship," Everett said.

"Yes! Pirate ship," Lola agreed.

Josh sat down beside Eliana, shaking the sea from his hair, and reached for her hand. All morning, Josh had reached for her. For her part, Eliana searched him out everywhere – the house, the beach, the sea – in a kind of game to prove to herself that he was actually there.

"A storm's rolling in," Josh said, nodding to grey clouds buffeting the horizon line. "Soon, but it's not here yet,"

She leaned her head against his shoulder. He rested his mouth on the nape of her neck, pulling a stretch of wet fabric away to reveal her tan line, and swiped his mouth across her skin. Eliana shivered, suppressing the urge to kiss him back.

"Do you know what I realized in France?"

Eliana blinked, taken aback. Her neck still winked with his heat. "What?"

"You understand the life our children will lead better than me."

"That's not true."

"It is," Josh said, punctuating the statement with a nod. "You know what it's like to live nomadically. I couldn't understand why anyone wouldn't want to vacation in the south of France, but then I realized: you've already lived there."

"I only spent a year in Provence," she said, as her hand disappeared into his. "Besides, I haven't been to any of these places with you. You help me see everything with new eyes."

"And I love that you want to see it with me," he said, kissing their intertwined fingers. "Still, maybe I should defer to your judgment more when it comes to the girls. Take the Academy, for instance. I know that you pushed hard for that school for its flexibility."

"Or maybe I've looked for a way to belong through them."

"Is there something wrong with that? I never feel like I belong unless I'm with you."

He took her hand. On the navy-toned rim of the horizon, a swollen rain cloud opened. They watched rain ripple, pocking darkening water, and instinctively moved closer to each other. Their fingers remained coiled together. Near their feet, all three children had fallen asleep.

"What do you think? Should we try to beat the rain, or should we stay awhile?"

Eliana raised her chin to the sky. "It's only a little rain. Let it come."

"It's raining!" Aaron shouted. "We need to move. Go!"

Delphine and Jules collapsed into laughter, tripping over their feet after him as they raced into the house. Raindrops gathered momentum, while dark clouds coalesced overhead. Véronique, wrinkling her nose at the gathering storm, hurried after them.

"We should go inside, too," Natalie said.

"You're probably right," Allegra said, though she didn't move from the back garden where they had been arranging azalea bushes for planting. She gazed back to her house. Natalie had commissioned a pergola for the backyard. Workers had quickly extended the stone patio as well, softening its stark edges with small boxwoods and urns spilling over with geraniums.

Having recognized the soft, contented expression on Allegra's face, Natalie smiled. She had forgotten how rewarding it could feel to make an old space new.

"If you want to stay productive, we could go wallpaper that powder room," she offered.

Allegra chuckled. She had fallen in love with hand-painted, lavender chinoiserie wallpaper, but hadn't wanted to use it at first. Allegra wasn't certain that it flowed with the coastal décor she'd requested. Natalie had reminded her that they weren't designing a spec house to flip; they were designing for her family, for what their story had been and all it had yet to become.

It should reflect your heart, she had said. *The things you don't say out loud.*

In the end, they chose the wallpaper.

Thunder clapped. Lightning blinked. Natalie took Allegra by the elbow and together they raced back into the house. The head contractor, Joe, ducked his head out of the kitchen. "Hey Natalie, are you okay if we check out for the day? We have the cabinets in. We're all set to lay the soapstone countertops tomorrow."

Natalie nodded. "I can't believe how much progress you've made. By all means, get home before this storm gets going."

"Thanks," Joe said. "The kitchen should be back in full working order by the weekend."

Before Allegra could respond, Véronique lifted her eyes from her embroidery. "We are *fine*. We will do as you Americans like to do and – what is the expression? – order out for pizza."

Joe laughed. "You and me both, Veronica."

Véronique's eyes narrowed. "I have no need of your extra syllable, young man. There is no 'a' at the end. I am not Italian. I am not English. I am *French*."

His eyes twinkled, while he and two other workers quickly gathered their tools. "I know, ma'am – *madame*," Joe said. "I promise – this is the last time you'll have to remind me."

Before he could go, Allegra lightly tapped Joe's arm. He turned on his heel and reddened, as he always did when his eyes directly met hers. "Yes, *Allegra*?"

"I understand that you're replacing the doors next week?"

"That's right. We'll get this place better insulated, and we'll replace most of the internal doors of the home as well. No more squeaky hinges for you."

Allegra opened the closet door. "That's all well and good, but not this one, okay? It's very important to me that this door stays."

"Understood, Allegra. We'll leave that door alone."

Behind her, partially hidden in the shadowed doorway of the blue library, Natalie clapped her hand across her mouth. Her eyes misted over. Just then, she could smell magnolia in a room that had neither open windows nor fresh flowers in a vase. She watched as Allegra brushed her fingers across Natalie's childhood growth chart, her fingertips touching Annabel's handwriting. Natalie rested her head on the open doorway.

To soothe her thundering heart, Natalie brushed her palm across the library's blue wall until it came to rest on the space where she knew the support beam to be. And there she stayed.

Much to the joy of the three toddlers, Andy shook off the rain like a dog. Lola, Silvia, and Everett squealed with delight as recycled raindrops sprinkled their skin. As Andy kicked aside his flip-flops in the front hall, he pressed his finger to his lips. He knelt. They circled him, squirming in anticipation. He opened the bakery box he had been carrying, revealing oversized chocolate chip cookies.

"Time to spoil your dinner," Andy whispered. When the children paused with giant eyes, he wiggled his eyebrows. "Go on now. Get after it."

Shrieking with laughter, the children each grabbed a cookie and took off sprinting. Andy chuckled to himself. He had just broken off the corner of a cookie, popping it into his gum line and letting it macerate there, when he caught sight of Eliana.

She was leaning against the hallway wall, her wet hair knotted into a low bun and her arms folded across her chest. Furrowing his brow, Andy chewed his cookie like it was cud.

"You're too thin," he said. "I can see your hip bones through your dress. You need to eat. Cookie?"

For a long moment, she said nothing. Her lips quivered.

"Josh is here," she said.

Andy swallowed. "What?"

"Josh flew in from France. He's here now."

"Well, that's an unexpected surprise—"

In a few long strides, Eliana crossed the hall. She wrapped her arms around his waist. She knocked the wind out of him.

He held his breath as he held her. When Eliana pulled away from him, Andy was stunned to find her smiling. Her grin radiated its own heat, her teeth shining like a beacon. Playfully, she punched his bicep, even as she clutched him tightly with her free hand.

"Thank you, Andy," she said, emphasizing every word. "Thank you so very much."

Chapter 23

Natalie stepped out of the bathroom dressed in a white jump-suit. She wore her hair pulled back at the sides, curled and rippling. As she slipped her feet into gladiator sandals, Eliana whistled appreciatively. Natalie flushed scarlet. Eliana doubled over with laughter. Impulsively, Natalie hugged Eliana in a tight squeeze.

It had only been a handful of days, yet Natalie couldn't recall the last time she had seen Eliana so happy. She laughed easily. She ate hungrily. Whether wrapped in a blanket on the couch or walking on the beach, Eliana scanned her surroundings with glittery eyes, having lost her faraway gaze for the cleared-eyed awareness of whatever rich moment enveloped her.

"You look beautiful," Natalie whispered.

"Me? I'm not dressed for company," Eliana said, rosy color blooming on her cheeks. "*You* look beautiful. But how do you feel?"

"I think invigorated," Natalie said. "Are you annoyed with me for asking you to babysit? Josh has only been here for a few days. If anyone needs a date night, it's you two."

Eliana wrinkled her nose. "Don't be ridiculous. My hus-band walks red carpets for a living. I've had my fill of date nights. All I want is to be normal together. I want that sweet hour after the kids go to sleep. Just the two of us."

Natalie felt her smile waver and locked her grin into place, her facial muscles straining. She remembered that hour. She hadn't realized how much she'd missed it.

"What's wrong?" Eliana asked.

Natalie bit her lip and looked away. "I feel guilty leaving the boys. Next weekend, they're with Harris in Potomac. I'm not sure that I should be—"

"Missing a meal with them? Missing one bedtime? And after Harris has barely seen his children this summer," Eliana said, rolling her eyes. "You deserve a break, too. You should be forgetting Harris's name and painting on a bold red lip and spraying perfume all over your—"

Natalie held up a hand. "Settle down, Ellie. I fully intend to make curfew."

"Besides, I'm going to owe you some free babysitting anyway," Eliana said, clearing her throat. "Would you be angry if the girls and I were to join Josh in France for a week?"

"Of course not! I think that's wonderful!" Natalie exclaimed.

"But if we leave next week, it would overlap with Harris's weekend. I don't want you rattling around this big house all by yourself. I feel like I'm abandoning you."

"Don't be silly," Natalie said, smiling brightly even as her pulse quickened. "We'll be putting the finishing touches on the house, then – it's always a mad dash. I'll be fine."

"But I can't leave you now – not with your marriage ..."

Natalie took Eliana's hand in hers. Splashes of golden light drenched the wall. Through an open window, seagulls cawed their staccato song. A breeze kicked up, ruffling leaves. Traffic hummed. Water lapped. Natalie collected these raw, unfiltered sounds, just as she pocketed cast-off shells and pilfered them from the sand. Soon, she would take it all with her.

"Did I ever tell you that I called your mom a few times when my mom was sick?"

Eliana's eyes grew large. "No."

"The first time was right after her biopsy. That horrible autumn. I was so scared of the results. My dad and I were waiting in silence. I didn't know who to call, but I knew I needed a grown-up. An actual adult. She made me feel better, better than anyone else could have."

"What did she say?"

"She said 'whatever it is, already is.' That there shouldn't be anything scary about giving something a name. Because you can't solve a problem unless you know what to call it."

Eliana paused. "So, what do you call it right now?"

"An ending. We've separated. In time, we'll divorce."

"I'm so, so sorry, Natalie."

Natalie smiled as she touched the naked sliver of skin where her wedding ring had been. A pale ring of color had browned in the sunlight, now nearly matching the rest of her.

"Don't be. We see what we want to see. And all I see, all around, are new beginnings."

Natalie ambled around Silver Lake, taking her time to notice the dappled light checkered across the water's edge. The gnats circling the sea grass. The ducks disappearing beneath the stone bridge in neat, angular lines. The pebbles she kicked aside, and the fragrant air she took within. She had told him to meet her on Lake Drive, not wanting her sons to see a strange man take her out on a date. But maybe, too, Natalie had needed the walk.

As she crossed the road, a breeze cut in from the ocean. She closed her eyes to it, welcoming the blast of sea air. When she opened them, Damon had stopped the car beside her. With a broad grin, Natalie climbed inside his Jeep.

"You still have a Jeep, huh?"

Damon grinned. "You know how I like country roads. Or, even better, no road at all."

She folded into him, smiling when their mouths met. They kissed long and deeply and pulled away too soon. She was hyper-aware of his rapid breathing, his quick pulse, and his dilating eyes. Sheepishly, Natalie thumbed her lipstick from his mouth.

"I forget myself around you," she muttered.

"So far, I'm game for all of your impulses."

Natalie laughed. "I bet you are."

"You kiss just as well as I remember, Nat. You can kiss me anytime you want."

"So noted. Are you going to tell me where you're taking me yet?"

"Where's the fun in that?" he asked, as he eased the car back into traffic.

"You know that women like to prep for dates, right? The prelude is part of the evening. I like to know that I'm dressed for the right occasion."

"You look beautiful. You always look beautiful."

Natalie's face blazed its blush. "Thank you, Damon, but you didn't answer the question."

Damon cast a quick glance down to her feet. As his eyes tracked the ties of her sandals, he rested his hand on her thigh. Instinctively, she moved closer to him, her shoulder resting against his. He dipped his mouth toward her neck. "Let's just say that you wore the right shoes."

Just as they had done as teenagers, Natalie and Damon rushed too quickly down the dock of the Rehoboth Bay Marina. Damon led the way. His hand engulfed hers, clutching her tightly. When Damon stopped at the end of the dock, Natalie lost her breath.

His was one of the last slips. Within the berth, a 35-foot fishing boat, sparkling white and trimmed in blue, bobbed on a gentle, low tide. A cheese plate and fresh fruit waited in the lounge area. Sparkling cider had been put on ice. A box of Sperry's, topped with a bow, rested on a cushioned bench. Spotting them, Natalie grinned and nudged him.

"I love a boat shoe, but are you so sure you remember my size?"

"I remember everything about you. You're the one person I've never been able to forget."

It was astonishing. To hear these words in real-time. To survey the scorched earth and bear witness to the crater-sized hole that she'd left in his life. To realize that her stomach could still flip. To feel the sunlight on her face, the wind tousling her hair, and water lulling her into the blurred space that rounds out a dream. To know that she could kiss him. To know how hungry she could be for that and for more, so much more.

"You know what, Damon? I think I missed you, too."

When he pulled her against him, she collapsed. His mouth moved on hers. His hands skimmed her back. His calloused fingers tangled her hair. He was the first to pull away – remembering before she did that the marina was only as private as a parking lot – and he tipped his forehead against hers. It was an act of resolve, this damming up of such potent force. She had forgotten that Saturday could be spent this way.

"So, a question for you," Damon began, as soon as he found his breath, "and there is no wrong answer: you can sit down here and enjoy the breeze and snack until your heart's content, or you can climb up with me and I'll let you drive."

She followed his gaze. The cockpit hovered above them like a castle's turret, its fishing rods as spiky as spires. A ladder glinted in the waning sunlight, beckoning.

"Don't you dare leave me behind again."

"Atta girl," Damon whispered.

He climbed the ladder first. Upon hearing the engine roar to life, Natalie cast off the bow and stern lines. As Damon eased the boat away from the dock, she joined him in the cockpit. He wrapped his free hand around her waist.

Natalie kissed the underside of his chin. "Now will you tell me where we're going?"

"Right where we left off," he said, as together they eased the vessel into open waters.

"You cannot keep a man waiting," Véronique intoned, clucking her tongue against the roof of her mouth. "I can see him now sitting in his car in the street. *En seul.*"

Allegra laughed. "V, he is early. I'm exactly on time."

Véronique tilted her head to the side while openly appraising her. Véronique frowned.

"And he leaves tomorrow, *oui*?"

Abruptly, Allegra's smile faded. "Yes, he's back to work in the city on Monday."

Véronique scoffed. "American vacations are truly *ridicule*. One week? In France, there would have been protests. You cannot conduct a love affair in only a week! *C'est impossible!*"

"We're not in love. We're, you know, hanging out."

"This man has seen you every single day. He is making plans."

"Or he's simply making the most of his vacation."

Véronique smoothed a stray hair from Allegra's face. "Here is what you do: you take one of your earrings and you leave it in his car. If he is a gentleman, he will bring it back to you."

"I'm too old to play those sorts of games, Véronique."

"You must always play, Allegra. To play is to live."

Allegra fingered the gold filigree earring dangling from her left ear. She sighed.

"*Joie de vivre* never translates well to English," Véronique said ruefully. "Listen, Etienne has taken so much: your children, your work, your reputation – yet, through everything, you can keep your joy. Promise me you'll try."

Allegra's breath caught. "I'll try."

The sun hadn't yet begun its descent. Golden light glinted off the boat in icy clarity. As they linked hands, Damon steered his boat into the open-mouthed Rehoboth Bay. They accelerated, as wind throttled past and ribbons of whitecaps snarled in their wake. The inland air hung heavy, saturated with the indole scent of the surrounding marshland. They circled past Angola Landing. They decelerated somewhat into Herring Creek. As they passed the Island in Narrows, Natalie grinned. She knew where they were going and what game they would play.

"So, you tell me, Nat: what's the port of call?"

"St. John?"

"In New Brunswick? We'd freeze in that water," he said, wiggling his eyebrows.

"I meant the *island*, silly," she said, nudging him. "Bermuda, then."

"Still alarmed by the Triangle. Do better."

"How about Charleston?"

"Nah. The low country marsh is different from ours. Bugs are bigger, too."

"Palm Beach?"

"You trying to make me sweat?"

"I don't care where we go, Damon," she said, taking his hand. At this, his eyebrows knitted together. "I've never cared. And neither have you."

Because the point had never been to arrive. The point had only ever been to drop anchor somewhere, shedding minutes and waiting for the rest of their lives to begin – and to know the relief that comes from not waiting alone.

"... at which point, I've been standing in the hot sun for hours on this godforsaken boat, and nothing is biting. So, I turn to her, slurring from heat stroke, and pass out cold on the deck."

Allegra covered her face with her hands, shaking with laughter. "You didn't!"

"I did. When I came to, still holding a fistful of squid, the teenage first mate told me that I was 'out like a trout.' Probably not the first time he'd told that joke, but everyone laughed. When I came home – still mortified and sunburned beyond all good sense – my dad put his arm over my shoulder and said, 'Son, some men can catch fish. And some men, like you and me, have figured out how to pay them for it.' "

"And the girl?"

"Never returned my call."

They were dining al fresco at the Back Porch Café, their feet intertwined beneath the table. With her shoulders rocking, Allegra tried to affect a sad face for him, but she chuckled through pursed lips. "And that was the closest you ever came to a summer romance?"

"It is. One bad date at seventeen. I learned my lesson."

Allegra raised an eyebrow. "Opting out doesn't sound like you."

"What does sound like me?"

"I don't know. Casanova? Lord Byron? The former prime minister of Italy?"

Andy barked laughter. "I'm not that bad – I promise. When I was young, I never saw the point of beginning something with an ending in mind. I still don't."

Allegra squirmed, her cheeks flushed with deep color. "But the other women?"

"A holding pattern. I never really *began* anything with any of them," he said, as his eyes darkened in the setting sun's shifting light. "Not until you."

"It's only been one week."

With a soft smile, Andy brought their linked fingertips to

his lips. He rested the back of her wrist against his mouth. She shivered, goosebumps alighting down her arm. "I want you to know how much you mean to me. I went into this with eyes wide open. I know that you're a mother, that you're crazy famous, that your former relationship presents complications—"

"That's a remarkably diplomatic way of saying that my life is in shambles."

"It's a period of transition," he said firmly, holding her hand even as he sipped his gin and tonic. He cleared his throat. "You still haven't heard from him?"

"Nope," she said, releasing his hand to reach for her glass of white wine.

At least it was true. Aside from Etienne's initial outburst after seeing the image of them together, Allegra had heard nothing from him. They communicated entirely through Véronique. He had made no new demands. She had offered him no new information. All was still.

And yet, this quietude had the same charged air as the loaded hours before a storm. The animals seeking out higher ground. The birdsong suddenly gone. As the natural world hushed, the only thing left to do was to wait. She could not act until he acted. And so, in a cuticle-shredding state of hypervigilance, Allegra waited to react to him. It was her normalcy. Allegra had realized that much of her adult life had been spent holding her breath, waiting for whatever fleeting illusion of safety would give her the chance to exhale.

"Promise me you'll tell me if he threatens you."

"You leave town tomorrow, Andy."

"In every way that matters, I'm not going anywhere. I *can* protect you from him."

Her thoughts latched onto Jules and Delphine. Their light hair and their far-set, grey eyes, and their soft hands in hers. She swallowed, suppressing the sudden burn of tears. She was memorizing them because that was part of waiting for Etienne's next move: remembering them, their tiniest, loveliest details, before he took them away again.

"No," she whispered, her mouth drooping. "You can't."

"For the love of God, I need a whiskey, stat. Two fingers. Neat," Josh said, shaking his head as he walked into the kitchen. His polo shirt was soaked. "I had forgotten how hard it is to bathe the girls together. Silvia was fine, but I'm pretty sure that Lola tried to snorkel."

Eliana laughed. "It's the catch twenty-two of twin bath time: separate baths take forever, but it's harder to keep them alive together."

"I think I'm the only one who actually got clean."

Eliana looked up at him through her eyelashes. "I don't mind you in a wet shirt."

"You'll say anything to get me to handle bath time," Josh said, though he swept her up in his arms and held her there. He spoke into the crown of her head: "I've missed this so much."

"Me too."

"Our binding agreement is officially in full force now, right? We won't ever go more than two weeks without seeing each other again."

"Never again."

In one fluid motion, Josh lifted her into his arms. Laughter bubbled, rising and expanding, within her. "What are you doing? You're going to pull something!"

"Just realized that I never carried you over the threshold. Any threshold."

"Perhaps because our first apartment was a fourth-floor walk-up?"

Josh carried her to the couch, collapsing into it with her. After he had handed Eliana a glass of wine, he draped his arm over her shoulder. He reached for the remote control. She burrowed deeper against his chest. He turned on *Philadelphia Story* but paused the movie before it could continue. A muscle in his jaw ticked.

"I should've carried you. Knowing what I do now, I should've been better to you then, and I'm going to be better now. I'm going to be everything that you deserve."

Eliana looked at him. "This is all that I need, Josh. *This* is everything."

"You deserve more than warm wine and a movie you've seen a thousand times. In Moscow, I promised you the world. I'm not sure that I've delivered yet."

"This. Is. Everything. You. Are. Everything," Eliana said, punctuating every word as she straddled him and kissed his throat. "But maybe we should wait on the movie."

Chapter 24

The tide was low, and the moon was high. Hours ago, they had dropped anchor on a sandbar. Natalie closed her eyes now against the cool wind, its ragged chill like paintbrush strokes against her cheeks. Her eyes opened as his boat dipped into a maritime stillness – which was not stillness at all, but a caress of rocking and heaving and riding the bay's endless swells. Peace came with the inevitable union of her breath to the water's flow, her body calming as it had done when she had rocked her infant sons. Her pulse slowing. Her thoughts evaporating. Her thousands of sharp-edged anxieties quieting into a rare, fine rest.

"You haven't said much since we ate."

She jerked at his voice. Briefly, Natalie had forgotten that this boat, with this blackened bay and this firefly-studded marshland, was not her own. She'd forgotten the shrimp pa- ella he'd cooked for her, as infused with Old Bay seasoning as it had been with traditional saffron. She'd forgotten the Berg- er's cookies, the conversation, the sunset's last screech before darkness fell like a sigh. She had forgotten he was even there.

Natalie had been thinking of the life she could have had here: riding out every season on this spindly, marsh-edged peninsula. She could only speculate as to how happy she would've been or what their relationship would've become. They might have had a loving home, fulfilling work, and even children. But then, their children would not be *her* children, (God-breathed and fated and deeply wanted.) Her chest swelled with the sharp edges of a passing dream; she shook her head as though climbing out of a trance.

"I'm tired," Natalie said. Because it's the thing women say when there is too much else to say. Because the vault had snapped shut.

With a quick nod, Damon cleared his throat. "So, I did a thing."

"What?"

"Years ago, I missed you and went looking for one of your dad's songs."

Her eyes narrowed. "What has my dad ever had to do with me?"

"It was the closest I could come to you," Damon said, sighing heavily. "Do you remember that one night at your beach house with Adriftwood playing, dancing to their song 'Yellow Dress'? There were twinkle lights. We pilfered their boxed wine. Well, I did, while you drank a gimlet. You were actually wearing a yellow dress."

"Was I?"

She tried to remember but could only vaguely recall dusk like a violet blanket. His woodsy cologne. His hand on the small of her back. While she remembered Damon twirling her, her yellow skirt flaring, she also remembered how closely her father had watched her. And how she'd pointedly ignored him, choosing to bask instead in the attention of someone else.

Anyone else.

"Yes. I think that's why he played it. Anyway, in looking around this old record store in Savannah for 'Yellow Dress,' I found a recording of a very rare song."

"What song?"

"It's called 'Natalie.'"

At once, her hands shot to her cheeks. She looked away from him.

"Have you listened to it?" Damon asked, speaking quickly.

"Nat, you *need* to hear this song. It's one of the few where the lyrics and melody were all his own, so it stands to reason that it was his gift to you. Hold on. Give me a minute to get set up."

"Damon ..."

But her words fell away. He glanced back at her, their eyes meeting for a long moment before he ducked below deck. Minutes later, the raw notes of an acoustic guitar bled into the marsh's cacophony with its cricket song and its distant boat traffic and its splash of bay water.

Her father hummed a few bars before he sang. He hadn't hummed to her since she was a girl; it was a sound Natalie had never known that she remembered, preserved with a gossamer-thin hold in her grey matter. With those first vibrating notes, her eyes filled with tears.

Soon, Damon was beside her, his arm snaking around her. He was holding her close and stroking her hair and tucking her head beneath his chin. And then, they weren't alone anymore. *He* was with them. His inimitable, velvet-toned voice. His astonishing range. His music unleashed from his mouth, from his fingertips. His stolen breath pulled from the rich, dappled spaces between his words. His words had not been lost with his brief, ill-fated life after all. Because he was here, right now, singing her a lullaby:

> *For my girl,*
> *I wanna build a better world (for you),*
> *For my girl,*
> *Only a kinder, gentler world (will do),*
> *But we're broken and we're tired,*
> *Beaten, burned, and wired (black and blue),*
> *So I'm gonna have to be a better man,*
> *'Cause I'm the only one who can (for you.)*

They sat in silence. As the bootlegged recording faded, Natalie could hear little beyond the ringing in her ears. The thundering of her heart. The chattering of her teeth. She said nothing, though she rested her head on Damon's shoulder. She set her hand, wracked with tremors, on top of his. Damon kissed her forehead, smoothing her brow.

"Does it matter?" Damon asked finally. "That once he wanted to be better for you?"

"I don't know," she whispered, as her eyes filled. "Because I remember too much."

Beneath a sky lacquered in cobalt, the beachfront home cast its shadow toward the lake. Natalie shivered in the early morning breeze. While her sons played basketball, Josh buckled his girls into their car seats. Meanwhile, Eliana worried the stack of bracelets encircling her wrist.

"You're sure you don't want me to stay?"

"Absolutely. I'll be fine."

"Because I can cancel everything. This is basically one long office Christmas party where I'll be making small-talk and checking the time. All that but with two toddlers."

"Maybe the sparkling Mediterranean Sea and the freshly baked croissants alongside those little cups of strong coffee will help?" Natalie murmured. "And give a girl a little credit: I *can* be alone. I just haven't had to do it in a while."

"I know you can," Eliana said, before pausing. "You know, maybe you should start listening to his songs again. Not just 'Yellow Dress' or even this new 'Natalie' but all of them."

"And why would I do that? We've been over this: the music has nothing to do with the man. I remember what happened before 'Natalie.' The reason he felt he had to write the song."

"Which you won't talk about—"

With a glare, Natalie yanked her shirt out of her skirt and lifted it to reveal scattered white scars on the small of her back. Eliana gasped.

"Jesus," she whispered. "He did that to you? What *is* that?"

"He cracked an acoustic guitar against the wall, then on my back. A vintage Gibson Les Paul Tobacco Burst," Natalie said. "A day after the fight where he gave me the cigarette burns, I tried to defend my mom when he was pummeling her. Again. And he turned on me. Again. Afterward, he cried for days. He was really sorry. He was always sorry, eventually. But he was probably more sorry about the guitar. He said he might write me a song."

Eliana swallowed. "I thought I knew all your scars."

"No one knows me that well," Natalie said. "And if you're asking me to listen to his music again, you don't know me at all."

"I do! I understand why you don't respond to journalists and why you don't keep in touch with his bandmates and why you don't care about the reunion tour and why you hate his fans—"

"Do you?" Natalie asked, her question a rising growl. "They've made a god of him, Eliana. It's not fandom. It's idolatry. They've made a god of an abuser – whose crazy antics with drugs and destruction on the road, by the way, should've clued everyone in. They've romanticized his self-sabotage. When he had public breakdowns, they threw more money at him. They gave him a pass for *life*, and they still do. All because the man could sing a pretty song."

"Natalie, you know very well that *I* am not *them*," Eliana said, half-shouting. Josh lingered by the car door's open mouth. Everett and Aaron's bouncing ball went still. "I know how he hurt you. All I'm saying is that you've closed yourself off to the best of him. Maybe he couldn't be a father to you. Maybe the only thing he could do was write you a song. And if that's all he could do for you, then I think you should hear it. I think you should hear *all* of it."

Eliana left her then. They never said goodbye, and Eliana thought she had said too much.

Josh made his rounds. He embraced Everett first and then Aaron, taking care to whisper something in their ears. When he reached Natalie, Josh simply touched her cheek.

"Try 'Windblown,' " he said. "It's always been my favorite."

Always. Favorite. Her cheeks burned hot and blazed beacon-red at the treachery.

"I've heard it," she said flatly. "It's about autumn and dead leaves."

"It's about *you*. Everything he wrote was about your mother or you. You or her. Take it from a fellow creative: there is no genius without inspiration. Those songs are yours, too."

Chapter 25

"No, you don't have to get married. You can do whatever you want."

Delphine nodded. "*Exactement.* That's what I hope. I want to travel and study and be free. I don't want a fairytale, *Maman.*"

"If you want to see the world, then the world is yours," Allegra said, as she deftly fishtail-braided Delphine's hair. "But you should know that real love doesn't feel like a trap—"

Her breath caught. Delphine's pale pink bedroom overlooked New Castle Street. Together, she and Delphine sat in the window seat, idly sipping juice and coffee. They were lingering inside the elliptical mother-daughter chat that she coveted, that she would secrete away. She could be nourished on these crumbs all winter. This languid, bilingual exchange. The silken softness of Delphine's hair in Allegra's fingertips. Allegra missed nothing and prized everything.

Yet now, as two familiar men exited a black sedan, Allegra felt her insides go ice-cold. Her heart erupted into a manic pounding.

"*Reste ici,*" she whispered. "Do you hear me? Stay here, Delphine."

"*Oui,*" Delphine whimpered because she had seen them, too.

It was a marvel that her voice could be so calm while her every internal support was caving in. As she raced out of the room, Jules met her in the hallway. His eyes were large. She took him in, with his bedraggled hair and wrinkled pajamas, and clutched him tightly.

"What will we do?" he asked.

"Go be with your sister. Keep her calm, Jules, and keep away from the window."

"*Oui*, okay. *Maman*, please don't let them take us."

She kissed the crown of his head. Her tear ducts burned, but she knew better than to indulge them. A loud pounding pulsed from the front door. Jules bolted toward Delphine's room. Allegra heard him lock it. At the sound, she raced down the stairs.

She stepped into the family room to find Véronique in the doorway. Véronique spoke to the two men, Etienne's muscled fixers, from a cracked door. They shouted at her. Véronique shouted back. Allegra furrowed her brow, trying but failing to parse apart the fast French. She repeatedly heard one phrase, as though a mantra: *les enfants*. The children.

"*Un moment*," Véronique said, before snapping the door shut.

The room was dark, musty, and frightening. Véronique had already shuttered every blind and pulled every curtain. Without asking, Allegra knew somehow that the older woman had already locked every door. She also knew that the men were casing the house, circling like rabid, predatory animals. If there was a way in, they would find it.

"I never thought he would do this," Allegra whispered. "He caught me by surprise."

"It is his way. His only strategy."

"I thought I would have more time. This is happening too fast. I don't know if there's a way to keep them in the country."

"There may be, but I think we must not let your children see these men threaten their mother. I think it would be best if we go."

"I can't lose them three weeks early. It's not fair," Allegra said, blinking back tears.

"Shhh," Véronique whispered, as she embraced Allegra. "It will be different this time. *Je te promets*. Because this time, *chère* Allegra, you will have me."

"What?"

Véronique pulled a piece of scratch paper from her pocket and passed it into Allegra's hand. "*Prends* ça: my private phone numbers. I shall call you. Twice a day, every single day, I shall call you. This is what Etienne does not realize: that now you have an ally."

"Are you serious?" Allegra breathed.

More banging rattled the back door.

"Yes, but you must let us go now. It is crucial, I think, to appear obedient."

"You won't forget? Your promise?" Allegra's words were whimpers.

"The children are safest in your care, and I want them with you," Véronique said firmly. "It is the responsibility of one woman to extend a hand to another, non? And now, because this will be our true goodbye, you must make a promise to me. You must promise to live, to play, to laugh. You can be sad, *bien sur*, but if you live within sadness for too long, you miss too much. It is a half-life. Your children do not want such sadness for you. They love you. For you and for them, you must live your life."

"*Mon ange*," Allegra whispered, and then again in English: "My angel."

The little house shook with the fists battering its door, but Véronique gathered Allegra close and whispered soft platitudes in her ear – *ce sera bien; nous sommes bien* – and let Etienne's men carry on shouting from the garden.

With her chin raised high, Véronique let them wait.

Somehow, ten minutes later, Allegra found herself hugging her children goodbye. There had barely been time to brush their teeth, make them a snack, or complete the braid by tying a grosgrain bow into place. Her children wiped away their tears.

"*Je t'aime, mon petit prince*," she said, loudly enough for the two men to hear. She hugged Jules tightly and whispered right into his ear: "It will be different this time, my love."

All too soon, Jules ducked into the car, still glowering at the two men flanking them. Delphine would not uncoil herself from Allegra's waist. She cried big churning sobs, which echoed so loudly that a few neighbors opened their windows. Across the street, an elderly couple stepped out onto their front porch. A jogger stopped across the street to watch.

"Everything all right over there?" he shouted.

"Leave us!" One of Etienne's men spat out.

But the jogger did not leave. Instead, he brought his phone to his ear.

"*Il est le temps d'aller,*" Etienne's man muttered before translating: "Time to go."

Allegra knelt down, resting her forehead against Delphine's. Through mercifully dry, red-lined eyes, she smiled. "We don't need to be sad," she whispered. "I'll always be there for you, *ma fille.* We'll make our own fairytale, remember? Someday, we'll all be free."

Allegra's voice cracked, then. She couldn't continue for fear of spilling over with tears.

"*Je te comprends, Maman,*" Delphine whispered. "I love you."

"I love you, too."

As Delphine reluctantly broke her grip on her mother and ducked into the car, a police cruiser turned onto their block. The jogger trotted to meet it. Immediately, the man standing next to Allegra leaped into the driver's seat and started the engine.

"*Allons-y, les gendarmes!*" the other man shouted, as he grabbed Véronique by the wrist. "The police! Go, go!"

The car moved closer. One of the men dragged Véronique around the car. He shoved her toward the back before jumping into the passenger seat. Before stepping inside, Véronique paused inside the open door and arched an eyebrow toward Allegra.

"You can be certain that I will give *Monsieur* Etienne a

full accounting of our holiday with you, *mademoiselle*. We will remember *everything*," Véronique spoke loudly.

She snapped the door shut. Instantly, the car careened out of the driveway, though the menacing man took great care to drive away slowly. He stopped fully at the stop sign. He eased gingerly into traffic. Allegra waved, though the windows never opened to receive her goodbye. The tinted windows completely concealed her children, but Allegra imagined them with their noses pressed to the glass. And so she blew kisses that could not reach them. She smiled, though she wanted to cry. She straightened her spine, controlled her face, and played her part.

As soon as they disappeared from view, the police cruiser pulled into her driveway. The jogger trotted along next to it. Allegra tried to affix a smile to her face, but she shook.

"Is there a problem, Officer?"

"You tell me. Everything okay here, ma'am?" the officer asked.

"Did you know those guys?" the jogger asked breathlessly. "They seemed pretty scary."

Allegra shrugged. "They work for my ex-husband. It was a custody exchange. As I'm sure you can imagine, it's always an emotional goodbye for me and my children."

"Where does your children's father live?" the officer asked.

"Luxembourg."

The officer whistled. "We only have jurisdiction to act while they're in the country, or better yet, this state. If you felt threatened at all, there are people who can help—"

"I'm fine."

"Wait a minute, you look familiar," the jogger chimed in. "Are you a model?"

The officer peeled off his sunglasses. His eyes met hers. There was no escaping his hard gaze. Allegra, her face streaked with dried tears, squirmed where she stood. He waited.

"My children's father has full custody," Allegra said. "There's nothing to be done."

The officer raised his brow. "You don't even want to try to stop him?"

"Do you think I could get an autograph for my girlfriend?" the jogger asked, having fished a tattered, sweaty napkin from his pocket.

Allegra smiled, trying not to scream. "Look, I understand your concern, but I have a private custody agreement with my ex-husband, and you're standing on my private property. At what point exactly does policing veer into harassment?"

The men went quiet, stiffened, and exchanged a pointed glance.

"I'm fine. We're fine. It's all fine. Please go now," Allegra said, as her voice cracked. She turned away. Once inside the house, she slammed the front door and slid down the length of it. She heard the police cruiser's engine roar, and then its sound receded. Finally alone, Allegra sobbed. Sticky with tears and sweat, she trembled. She was coughing mucus, dizzy with nausea, as though the loss of her son and daughter had made her ill. And all the while, she thought back to what she had told the officer, a brittle smile pinned to her recognizable face.

I'm fine. We're fine. It's all fine.

Even under the hard shell of a leaden sky, twilight arrived with its golden hour. Packed, wet sand glowed, effervescent with shine and bejeweled by half-hidden shells. Seagulls circled overhead. Sand crabs burrowed into the shoreline. Sunlight winked from gathering rain clouds.

"Come on, Everett," Aaron said. "Wade up to your knees. We'll hold your hand!"

Everett shook his head. "No! Don't want to go in the water."

"C'mon, you can't go to the beach and not get wet!"

As she lifted Everett onto her hip, Natalie raised her brow. "You were scared, too, once. He'll swim when he's ready."

With a shrug, Aaron skidded away from them on his skimboard. Waves left markings like splatters of paint, and the tide continued its rise. Everett shivered in her arms.

"Let's get you warm, Bug," she whispered.

Moments later, Natalie had wrapped Everett in a towel. He curled up in a chair while she gathered their things. With a yawn, Natalie checked her phone. Her hand stilled. The lone text message was a succinct kick to the gut:

Etienne's men came for the kids today. They're gone.

Without another thought, Natalie acted on impulse. Her fingers fumbled, nearly dropping her phone, until they flew. She paced in the sand. Andy answered on the second ring.

"Natalie?"

Natalie exhaled. "I didn't know who else to call."

Upon arriving in Nice, Eliana itched to leave the airport. She could already smell the tumbling, purple bougainvillea through the recycled air. Her girls lurched in her hands, squealing caricatures of her own excitement. While waiting in the baggage claim, Eliana received a single text message from Allegra and gasped aloud.

"What is it?" Josh asked, his glance sharpening.

"It's Allegra. Etienne took the kids early. They're gone."

Josh could only shake his head. He pulled her into his arms. Neither knew what to say when there was nothing that could be said and nothing at all that could be done.

Allegra hadn't answered Andy's calls. She had no idea what to say to him. Instead, she had had far too much wine and far too little food. As though behind a veil, she slept fitfully.

Through sheets of rain pounding against her windows, Allegra might have heard a distant knocking. She might have heard his voice calling out to her. She might have seen her children too, but they slipped out of her reach as soon as she extended a hand to them. It was difficult, in this murky marshland of her own making, to parse reality from dream. Allegra was too bone-tired to care. She imagined she would want to get back to sleep as soon as she woke up, anyway.

She might've heard a crash. She might've heard him call her name.

When her eyelids fluttered apart, she saw Andy stripping out of his wet suit jacket.

"How did you get in?" She whispered the question.

He smiled halfway, as he loosened his tie. "Rushed the backdoor."

"You were able to break the door?"

"We'll never know. You left it unlocked."

At 2 AM, her bedroom lights were still blazing. One by one, Andy killed them all. He kicked off his loafers. Now clad in his undershirt and boxers, Andy climbed into bed with her. He yanked the covers up to their chins.

Allegra tunneled closer, hungry for his warmth. "You came," she whispered.

He winced. "I hate that it comes as a surprise to you."

"My children … they're gone."

"I know," he whispered, as she collapsed in his arms. "But I'm still here."

Eliana brought a strawberry to her mouth and sighed. Josh played with the girls in an infinity pool. Behind them, limestone cliffs disappeared into the azure Mediterranean Sea. Palm trees flanked their view. Bougainvillea climbed the stone wall surrounding their villa, its veranda punctuated by potted olive trees. When Eliana breathed deeply, she could smell the tiered lemon grove on the grounds. Her eyes were attached to the liminal space, creamy with sparse clouds, where sea met sky. Everywhere she was surrounded by verdant, coastal beauty.

And yet. Tears filled her eyes as she stared at her children and thought of Allegra.

The villa's manager, Antoine, shadowed their family; when she felt his eyes on her, she brushed her tears away. She faked a smile and forced a sip from the cocktail he had crafted.

"*Monsieur*," Antoine said, waving toward Josh. "*Monsieur, ils sont ici.* They're here."

Chest-deep in water, Josh froze. "They're early," he said.

Eliana stifled a sigh. She fixed another smile on her face. She wasn't expecting him to go back to work within hours of their arrival, but these things couldn't be helped.

"Thank you, Antoine," Josh said, as he handed Silvia off to him. Antoine wrapped her in a towel as though he was swaddling an infant. "Would you give us a minute, please?"

"Of course," Antoine said. He then attempted to wrap a towel around Lola, only to find that she had ducked under his arm like a running back and bolted into the house. Taking Silvia by the hand, Antoine charged after Lola. "I follow the girls!" Antoine called out.

Eliana collapsed into peals of laughter, suddenly giddy with sleep deprivation. When Josh opened his mouth, Eliana held up her hand. "I know, I know, you have to work."

"I don't have to work. Do you remember when Andy called me and told me what was bothering you, and you were so grateful to him for overstepping?"

"Ye-es," she drew out the word.

He grimaced. "Well, I might have overstepped."

Lola then raced outside, trailing her sopping towel. "Ganny's here!"

Eliana rose to her feet. "Mom?"

As though beckoned, her mother then stepped out onto the veranda, her father hunched against Gloria's left arm. Silvia assisted in the effort to guide her grandfather. "I help," Silvia said. "Mommy says it's sih-ippery."

Eliana folded her arms against her chest. Hovering in the background, she recognized her father's caregiver, George. Antoine fluttered around them, wringing his hands in the periphery.

"Perhaps, *monsieur* would like a chair, *oui*?" Antoine asked. "Something to eat?"

Gloria shook her head. "Thank you, but we've been sitting for so many hours. We would rather stand. Oh, David, can you believe that view? It's like a painting."

But Eliana's father wasn't looking at the view. He gazed instead down to Silvia, smiling such that his eyes crinkled into pleats. "Thank you for helping me," he said.

"You're welcome," she said. They all leaned closer to hear her.

David knelt toward her. "And tell me, what might your name be?"

Eliana flinched. A heavy silence followed his words. It was George who ultimately stepped forward, a gracious, practiced smile playing across his lips.

"Silvia," George said. "Her name is Silvia."

As she pursed her lips, Eliana could feel Josh's eyes upon her. She did not look at him.

Chapter 26

"What's in it?" Allegra asked, eyeing the green drink warily.

"Well, that's a trade secret. It's my own hair-of-the-dog. Totally medicinal."

Allegra took a polite sniff before setting it down. It smelled vaguely ... weedy. Allegra's stomach flipped slightly at the pungent drink, so she turned instead to the plate of scrambled eggs and toast. She took a bite. Forced herself to chew. She tried to smile, but winced instead.

"Thank you for making me breakfast, though it was unnecessary."

"Stop. You deserve somebody to take care of you through this ... crisis."

And there it was: the dark, knotted truth that sat between them. Her children were gone. Allegra wasn't sure when she would see them again. She set her fork down.

Andy pulled out a chair opposite her, took her hand, and raised her knuckle to his lips. In spite of the grey veil encircling her, Allegra smiled. Her head hurt. Her stomach churned. Dark circles shadowed her eyes. Even so, he had stayed. Andy, freshly showered and crisp in a blue polo shirt, had dressed to meet a day she would've rather avoided entirely.

He looked like hope to her.

"You should've called me."

"It was too soon."

"No, it was *late*," Andy said, holding her gaze. "Tell me something: I know Etienne surprised you yesterday, but has that been your only contact?"

"The day after the pictures of us were released, Etienne was very angry."

Andy closed his eyes. "I'm sorry."

"Don't be. I'm not. Whenever I think of you, I just feel lucky."

As soon as she spoke the words, Allegra knew them to be true. She went still. She then sat up a little straighter, caught off guard by her own fire. In a slow-burning epiphany, Allegra realized that Etienne had failed in some crucial way because Andy was still there with her.

And so was she. *I'm still here*, Allegra thought. It felt like no small victory – to be on the other side of a bottle of wine, eating the meal this man had cooked for her, sitting in a patch of warm sunlight.

Andy pulled her into his lap. "When I was a boy, my parents took me to Churchill's War Rooms in London. He needed a bunker, safe and sheltered from the Blitz, to carry out an invasion of France. Because you can't win a war while you're ducking for cover. Do you know what I see in your home renovation? In the new paint colors and the kitchen appliances and that half-finished portico thingy? I see your safe place to land. Your haven. You have your bunker."

Allegra felt something within rise, as a balloon will leave the earth when its gas meets flame.

"My bunker," she murmured, with the faintest wisp of a smile trawling across her face.

"You're safe now," he said, his voice breaking. "Here, you can win the war."

Allegra tilted her head to the side. "So, what would Churchill have told me to do now?"

Bracing his weight on his forearms, Andy leaned forward.

The light in his eyes flickered and danced. "He would've said: 'If you are going through hell, keep going.' "

Honeyed rain dribbled across windowpanes. All was quiet in the villa. Eliana sat in an empty library with a mug of hot coffee, a soft throw around her legs, and a book splayed open on her lap. Her family had succumbed to jet lag, leaving her in solitude as they napped.

It should've been perfect, but Eliana had reread the same paragraph three times.

Eliana couldn't sleep. She seethed at Josh. She couldn't fathom that he would invite her parents to accompany them on their one true family vacation this summer without a word to her. Again, he'd made a significant decision without her input.

In this cliffside villa overlooking the Mediterranean, with its porous entryways and vibrant hothouse plants, Eliana couldn't seem to get warm.

Just then, Beethoven's Fifth Piano Concerto wafted toward her. Eliana stiffened. She craned her neck to gaze around the baby grand piano obstructing her view. And there he was. He had changed in small ways, with his back slightly stooped and his hair now white, but his presence was the same. He still took up an outsize amount of space in the room.

His caregiver, George, soft-shoed around the periphery of the library toward her.

"Your father couldn't sleep, so I brought him here. Playing the piano comforts him."

"Is he feeling all right?"

"He's fine. He seems happier than I've seen him in a long time, particularly while he was watching your daughters play in the pool earlier. Today has been a good day."

"And does he – does he ever remember me?" Her voice faltered. "Or any of us?"

George hesitated. "Alzheimer's is a progressive disease, so bear in mind that your father spends a significant portion of the day unable to engage as he once did. He misplaces things. He forgets names and faces. However, he also lives inside of memories that bring him great joy. So, while he forgets, he remembers, too. It's called 'the long goodbye.' "

"I understand," Eliana whispered. Her eyes glittered. Around them, his music rose and fell, powerful even in its interludes of quiet melody. "But how does he remember how to play?"

George shrugged, his smile soft and open. "The mind is a marvelous mystery. It helps to be grateful for what remains, rather than to focus on what's lost."

Eliana nodded. "If you'd like a break, I can watch him for a while."

"That would be great. Thanks," George said, his muscles loosening.

"Thank *you* for everything that you do for him all the time."

"It's a pleasure to watch him," George said. "Most days, he's easy."

Eliana's eyebrows shot upwards. *Easy?* Her dad was many things, but *easy*? As she let George's comment echo within her, George turned back to her in the doorway.

"Keep in mind: he may not remember everything, but he still carries you with him."

Eliana couldn't speak. She gave him a clipped nod and George scuttled away, his face flushed. Eliana closed her book. She moved slowly across the library, as though making careful, cupped-hand strokes through water. He didn't stop playing. Even when she took a seat beside him, her father kept playing. She knew the piece well enough to hear its denouement. She closed her eyes to enjoy the ending. In time, Eliana lost track of time.

When it was gone, she missed it.

"That was beautiful," she whispered.

"Thank you," David responded, smiling. "It's my favorite thing to do."

"You're very good at it."

David cleared his throat as he stared at his fingertips, still lingering on cold piano keys. "Those little girls who were in the pool – are they your daughters?"

Alongside the sharp physical pain in her chest, Eliana swayed with vertigo. She fought the urge to walk away from him and nearly gritted her teeth as she forced herself to stay. This time, Eliana would not leave him.

"Yes. Their names are Silvia and Lola. They're fraternal twins. Very different."

His gaze latched onto the middle distance. "I have a daughter. Eliana."

"Eliana," she repeated, as her breath hitched. He had always called her Ellie. Her cheeks burned before asking a question like dipping a toe into ice-cold water. "What's she like?"

"Oh, my Eliana is easy. I never worry about her," David said before pausing. "Her brother, Andy, he's the unpredictable one. He's already changed his major twice. He can't keep a girlfriend or a career path, but I have faith that he'll get there. His heart is golden. That's what you do as a parent: you hold the faith that they'll find their way."

"He's lucky to have you believe in him so much," Eliana sputtered. She remembered their raised voices behind closed doors. Their knife-edged looks. Their coldness.

"My daughter, on the other hand, she's as tough as nails. We can drop her anywhere. She learns languages on the spot. She can talk to anyone. The world is hers for the taking."

Eliana wrapped her arms around her middle. "And ... have you told her this?"

"No. I want to raise a strong girl, not an entitled one."

Eliana nodded. Tears coated her eyes.

"I tell my daughters every single day that I love them," Eliana said hoarsely.

She didn't think he'd heard her. He had started a sonata. The tinny thundering swept them both away from this astoundingly beautiful place to somewhere even more fleeting and exquisite. Moments later, he spoke, his voice dancing above a whisper's blurred edge:

"That's good. Maybe, that way, they'll say it back."

"You're positive that you have this under control?"

"Oh, ye of little faith, not to worry. I've got this."

"Maybe we should wait for Joe."

"Not unless we're waiting for him to admire my handiwork."

Andy stood on a stool in the breakfast nook of her kitchen. With his tongue poised between his lips, he screwed the beaded chandelier into place.

When her phone buzzed, she flinched.

Andy, his fingertips interlocked with strands of beads high above his head, paused at once. His expression darkened as he watched her.

"Who is it?"

"It's Natalie."

Instantly, Andy let out the breath he'd been holding. His muscles relaxed.

"She was wondering if we could come over to watch the kids for a moment. Something unexpected came up. The subsequent three text messages are her apologizing profusely for asking for help because something unexpected came up."

"Maybe I should be the one to go," Andy said quietly. "It's a bit soon for you, isn't it?"

Before she could respond, he stepped down and flicked the switch. Light shone, warming the small kitchen. Allegra's breath caught.

Andy grinned. "Told you I could do it."

"You're right. I never should've doubted you."

"Speaking of chandeliers," he said, before pulling a gold lattice-work earring from his pocket. "If you wanted me to come back, you could have asked."

Rosy colors filled her cheeks. "What? Oh, my earring! I hadn't even realized it was missing. Thanks for bringing it back to me."

He cupped his hands around her face and brought her mouth to his. The warmth they created, golden and restorative, spilled through her body. She arched against him. He pulled her hips against his. His mouth soon trailed down her neck, grazing the mound of her breasts through her t-shirt, while his hands gripped the small of her back. Until something stopped him. He pulled away from her, panting. When she opened her eyes, her dilating pupils voiced questions she couldn't put to words.

"Not today," he whispered, shaking his head. Offering a tremulous smile, he furrowed his brow. "You know, I've had toothbrushes planted in my bathroom, but I've never met a woman willing to part with her jewelry for me. Guess this means you like me, huh?"

Allegra smiled and rested her head against his chest. He pulled her close to him.

With her head over his heart, Allegra thought of Véronique. She couldn't wait to tell Véronique that he'd brought the earring back. Véronique had already texted to let her know that they had landed in Paris and that they would be transferring flights to Luxembourg shortly. The children had cried, but they'd rallied on the long, transatlantic flight. They'd missed her, but they were okay. Allegra loved the unremarkable details: the snacks they'd eaten in the airport lounge, the movie that had played on the plane. It was more than Allegra could've ever hoped for: to have an intimate connection to her children's everyday life.

Allegra straightened her spine and grinned, suddenly bursting with energy. "If we're going to watch these kiddos, I need to grab a shower first. I smell like stale wine."

"Are you sure? Don't you need some time?"

"Nope. What I need most today is to beat Aaron at 'Horse.'"

"You're not going to beat Aaron at 'Horse.' No one beats Aaron at 'Horse.' "

"Chalk drawings on the driveway with Everett then, while you play with Aaron."

"I don't know. 'Horse' with a basketball phenom can't do much for my pride. I managed to install the chandelier without electrocuting myself. Maybe I should stop while I'm ahead."

Allegra turned back to him in the doorway. "Maybe you should come get clean with me and raise your spirits before you're trounced by a thirteen-year-old. I'm no broken bird, you know."

She winked at him. His lips parted.

At the top of the stairs, Allegra laughed aloud when she heard his heavy footsteps, taking the stairs two at a time and rushing after her.

Natalie was rounding the corner into Penny Lane when her phone rang. She paused near Fun For All Toys, easing closer to a brick wall to allow passersby enough space to amble, and reached for her vibrating phone.

"Diana Weatherly," she said. "It's good to hear from you!"

When she heard Diana laugh, Natalie imagined Diana in her element. She would be sitting in her sun-streaked office in Arlington. Sipping a small cup of espresso loaded with sugar. Feverishly eyeing the magazine's layout taped across her office walls like a flimsy mural. They had history. They'd both been young mothers together, trying to forge their paths in competitive industries. But they hadn't spoken in some time – not since before the pandemic. Natalie flushed, a climbing, beacon-red glow, to think of all that Diana didn't know.

Because her old friend wouldn't recognize the life that Natalie now led.

"I've missed you, Nat."

"Me too. I know I've promised to call and grab a drink, but there's never been any time. I'm sorry it's been so long."

"Don't give it another thought – we were both too busy trying to keep our careers afloat during the pandemic. It's been forever since I've reached out. And I hate to be transactional about our friendship, but I'm calling because I'm desperate."

"Is everything okay?"

"The couple we profiled for our August digital edition forbade us to include their home in *Brickhaven*. They've threatened legal action if we move forward as planned."

"What happened?"

"Another messy divorce," Diana said, sighing. "And, while the editors are all in agreement that we should proceed with what we have on record, I'm concerned about burning bridges long-term. I'd rather let it go, and this is where you come in."

"Me?" Natalie asked, blinking.

"We've already showcased your work twice in *Brickhaven,* so this is me unabashedly exploiting our professional and personal relationship. I know that Birdie commissioned you to renovate her property in Potomac, and I was wondering if you think she might be interested in us profiling her home? I know it's a huge ask."

"She might be, but you'll have to ask her," Natalie said. "Birdie fired me."

"Are you serious?"

"She opted to go in a different direction."

"And which direction was that?"

"That last I heard, Scandinavian."

"Bullshit," Diana snapped. "There's no minimalism or functional simplicity to Birdie Wellington."

"In any case, I'm sure she's hired another designer if you—"

"No. There's no way I'm giving that woman more publicity after she fired you."

"I'm sorry I can't help you. After my past profiles in *Brickhaven*, I've had such an uptick in demand for my business. Believe me, I hate that I have nothing to offer."

"It doesn't matter. I'll think of something. In any case, do you want to meet for coffee?"

Natalie smiled. "I'm actually on vacation right now. How about I call you when I'm home again?"

"I'm already looking forward to it," Diana said, before pausing for a beat. "And, Nat? I've met Birdie. Someone like you should never let herself be limited by someone like her. Take care. We'll talk more when you get home."

Home. Natalie kept circling to that heavy, singular word. She didn't know what would become of her home. She didn't know if she carried it with her, not unlike a crab slogging through sand with its shell until that could be shed for a more suitable carapace. And if a home could so easily be cast aside, did Natalie's work – her well-honed eye for color and symmetry and line – even matter?

Natalie reached Damon's door. As soon as she stepped inside the gallery, though, her ricocheting thoughts ceased.

Her mother's paintings, watercolors and seascapes and portraits and pastels, and even precise, pointillist beach scenes, encircled her. With her hand covering her mouth, Natalie ambled into the middle of the Backlit Gallery as though half-awake. She spun slowly.

"You're here," she whispered. "You're right here."

The scent of magnolia blossoms thickened in the air. She closed her eyes.

And that was how Damon found her. Having heard the door's hanging bells chime, he'd strode into the showroom.

There, he found Natalie. She was a vision to him, with her cut-offs and her Dogfish t-shirt and the strings of her bikini tangled up with loose tendrils at the nape of her neck.

He cleared his throat. "I'm sorry to make you rush over here like this."

She opened her eyes and shook her head. Where possible, the paintings had been framed. The largest canvases, particularly her mother's vast, abstract sunsets, had been left untouched and raw. They dotted the white gallery with clamorous color, making the quiet room loud.

"Damon – it's just – it's magic," Natalie said hoarsely. Her throat felt raw. "You've made her work brand-new again. How much do I owe you for this?"

"I won't accept anything. Not from you."

"Please? I know that we're dating now, but this is too much."

Damon shook his head. "Face it, Nat: your money's no good here. The only problem is that I have a showing for an artist this weekend, and workers are coming this evening to begin mounting her work."

"So, you need me and my mother out of your hair?"

Damon winced. "I would keep them here, but I'm afraid something will be damaged. We only hold work temporarily for artists' showings. There won't be room."

"Of course," she whispered, as she burrowed into his chest. Her mind spun in circles, trying to envision a new place for her mother's work. But she had no home anymore to offer Annabel.

"So, we're dating, huh?" Damon teased, effectively shaking her out of her own head.

Natalie smiled at him. "Maybe that's the wrong word. Can we even use the same word we used as teenagers? It's been so many years that we might need a new language."

"As long as you're talking about me, you can call us whatever you want," Damon whispered into her ear. His breath tickled the pale hair on her neck. Natalie shivered in his arms.

When he whispered, she strained to hear him.

"What was that?"

"I said 'sell it.' Annabel Huxley has a substantial regional following, and not just because she was married to the elusive Kip Stone of Adriftwood. On this peninsula, your mother is an icon in her own right. The work in this room is worth a small fortune, and that fortune should belong to you now. Her masterpieces are your birthright."

"It's an idea, but I need a minute to process it."

"Take your time," Damon said, sighing. "But I hate how often this happens."

"What do you mean?"

"Many artists aren't recognized for their contributions during their lifetimes. It's a maddening near-miss. Particularly when I think of your mother. Had Annabel realized the commercial success that she deserved, she would've had better options. She came so close. If she'd sold even five paintings for what they're worth today, she would've been free. And you would've been free, too."

When his arms wound around her again, Natalie rested her cheek on his shoulder. She then locked eyes on an 11x14 pencil sketch. She could see her mother's skill in the rendering, the control of her line and the texture of her shading. It was a depiction of Annabel's studio window. Other paintings rested in various stages of completion beneath the open window, evoking the neat effect of smaller, weighty paintings within a light sketch. However, her other paintings were a distraction. A tease. The focal point of the sketch was the robin standing in the open window, staring directly at the viewer with a steady gaze. Presumably, the bird could have flown away at any time, yet it stood with its talons planted and its wings drawn.

The bird, hovering on the precipice between captivity and freedom, stayed.

All of a sudden, tremors overcame Natalie. She shook. Damon pulled her closer, believing she was cold. Sparks pulsed along her spine. She felt the urge to scream, to cry, to laugh. With shiny eyes, she raised her head from the soft curve of Damon's neck.

"I have an idea," she whispered.

Chapter 27

The sun rose, hidden by a blanket of dense fog. Through her open window, Eliana watched the fog ascend like smoke, obscuring towering cliffs and the unending azure color of the Mediterranean Sea. The fog acted as a sleight of hand, erasing the surrounding bright hues and numbing the senses, too. Eliana sipped strong coffee swaddled in a bathrobe. From her balcony, mist spritzed her face, and gathering clouds threatened their release, but Eliana made no effort to move. She'd never known Nice in this grey veil, and she liked the town more for it. Even Nice, it would seem, could get itself into a funk.

"You're sure you don't want to come back inside?" Josh asked as he took a seat across from her little bistro table, watched her look away, and sighed. "I'm sorry. Again."

Eliana swallowed. She had slept so hard and for so long that she felt hungover this morning. Her head pounded, as her body itched to shed this accumulation of time zones, the hours that she'd compressed together. Not for the first time, Eliana thought that traveling was its own kind of modern gluttony: stealing hours that were never meant to belong to you.

"Why did you invite them?"

Josh tensed. "I acted impulsively."

"You were the one who most supported me when I stopped speaking to him."

"And I would agree with you all over again," Josh said.

"Your father's behavior was inexcusable. However, I've had this one thought that keeps nagging at me."

"What's that?"

"He hurt you, but you're the only one who remembers it."

Leaning forward, Eliana pursed her lips. Josh hunched forward, his elbows on his knees, as he tried to meet her where she was.

"He was so horrible to me."

"I know."

"I mean, I had just given birth. I was weak. They were so little."

"I know," he said, sighing shakily. "I almost lost you – all three of you."

Eliana swallowed. "I've been so busy hating him when maybe I should have been mourning him. For as long as I've known him, it's like he's worn armor and it's all been stripped away now. Here's this kind man who loves to talk about his family and play the piano. He just doesn't recognize me."

"Oh, Eliana—"

"But he does *remember* me. Sort of. He remembers some of the good things. It's so strange – like a window into him I've never had before."

"Well, going forward, you can dictate the kind of relationship that we have with your father. We're partners, remember? Wherever we go, we go together."

Eliana stole a sharp intake of breath. "I'm glad to hear you say that because now I have a massive request."

"What's that?"

"I'd like to move back east to be closer to my family. All of them," she said, bracing her shoulders. "Is it possible?"

He paused for a long moment, tilting his head to the side. His lips curved into a smile.

"I think so," Josh said, as he took her clasped hands in his. "I said I'd give you the world. You were the one who had to decide where you wanted to be."

Friday came too fast. All too soon, Natalie received a clipped call from Harris, informing her that he was ten minutes out. Everett raced out the front door, abandoning his fork to his plate of eggs and toast. Together, Natalie and Aaron juggled the boys' suitcases in his wake. As Natalie descended the front steps with Aaron, her chest tightened.

Natalie had the same tingling sensation that she remembered from childhood. Her father's car would pull into the driveway of their tidy colonial in St. Michaels, having returned from months of touring, and the bottom would fall out of her stomach.

And now, Natalie fought a wave of vertigo as she trudged onward, wishing instead that she could lock a door.

When Harris pulled into the driveway, Natalie gripped the luggage tightly. He parked. Their children raced to greet him. Harris sank to his knees, gripping them in a long embrace. Watching them together, her stomach lurched. Harris's brown eyes shimmered in the sunlight. Their eyes met for a brief moment. Her throat hurt then, and she looked away.

She gazed at Silver Lake. A female duck, lashed with muddy brown color, materialized from the reeds. Soon, seven fuzzy ducklings followed suit. Far ahead, the mallard duck raised his burnished-emerald head and determinedly paddled to the front of their procession, as though clearing their path. Natalie watched as the ducklings trailed them, keeping close in a tidy V until they disappeared under the curved bridge.

When she turned back to Harris, he was already buckling Everett into his car seat. She flinched. Aaron, who had come to stand beside her, leaned his head against Natalie's shoulder. Though her eyes burned, she tried to smile while she rested her head on his soft, unruly hair.

Harris finally joined them. His brown curls and dark eyes and his freckled forearms all seemed slightly foreign to her now. Was this really the same man who had asked her to marry him amidst the red cliffs of Sedona? The same man who had held her hand under the table, as she unsteadily signed the agreement for her first business loan? The same man who had grudgingly put up every holiday decoration, who had overseen the math homework she so despised, who had made her coffee every morning?

He still resembled the person she'd once known, but this man wouldn't look at her.

Harris smiled at Aaron. "I'm all set, Bud. You ready to head out?"

"I'm not going," Aaron said.

Harris blinked faster. "What do you mean? You have basketball camp on Monday, remember? You're going to go off with your buddies for a week and do what you love to do."

"It isn't what I love to do," Aaron said. "It's what you love to *watch* me do."

"Aaron," Natalie breathed.

"Daddy!" Everett screeched from the car. "Daddy ... where are you?"

"Natalie, what's going on here?" Harris demanded.

"No one asked me what I want to do – no one ever does, and I don't want to go."

"Son, we paid good money for that camp, and you're going to go. That's the plan."

"What about our plan?" Aaron shouted. "You were supposed to see us two weeks ago, and you didn't! You don't do what you say you're going to do, so why should I?"

Natalie inhaled. "Aaron, we've talked about this already: Dad was very busy with work and very sorry that he couldn't get away, but he's here now and he loves you and it's time to go."

"Mommy, where are *you*?" Everett called from the car, his voice trembling.

"Right here, Bug!" Natalie called out. "Everything's okay!"

"He's just jealous, anyway."

"I beg your pardon?" Harris's eyes widened.

Without a word, Aaron unzipped a bag and retrieved his basketball. He set his jaw, dribbled in place for a second, and shot an easy, lazy three-pointer from the edge of the lake. When he turned back to them, he glared at Harris.

"You're jealous because you've never been able to do that."

"Aaron!" Natalie sputtered.

"Aaron Blackburn, get in the car right this minute!" Harris yelled. "You're going to camp and we're leaving *now*. Not another word!"

But Aaron trotted up the steps of the front porch. Tears glistened in his eyes.

"I'm not leaving!"

"Aaron—" Harris growled.

"Okay!" Natalie yelled. "Okay."

"Okay?" Aaron blinked, sniffling.

Harris snapped his neck in her direction. "Okay?"

"If he doesn't want to go to camp, he doesn't have to go to camp," Natalie said.

"Natalie – what the – this is my week!"

"It's not your week with them when you're sending them away to camp."

"For Everett, it's only day camp! He's four. He's spending the evenings with me."

Natalie rolled her eyes. "Semantics."

The front door slammed shut. Everett had started to scream, to weep, to cough. Natalie rushed to his side, wiping away his tears with her thumb.

"Hey, Bug," she whispered, touching her forehead to his.

"I want get out now!"

Natalie shook her head. "No, Bug. You're going to go take a special trip with Daddy."

"Can you come?"

"No, this trip is extra special – just you and Daddy. You're going to go home and eat Daddy's pancakes and sleep in your big-boy car bed and go to art camp. It'll be *so* fun."

Everett stared at her, his dark brown eyes (his father's dark brown eyes) considering. He gnawed on his lower lip. "What 'bout Aaron?"

"He doesn't feel well, so he's going to stay here with me. Okay?"

"Okay," Everett whispered, exhaling. "I love you."

"I love you, too. Be brave, Bug," Natalie whispered. She kissed him, already shaking with the weight of her unshed tears, and shut the door.

"That's enough," Harris said in a low voice. "That's quite enough."

"What?"

"'Be brave'? I'm his *father*, Natalie. You've had the entire summer with them, and this week is mine. I can spend it with them however I want – taking them to a ball game, sending them to camp, hot-wiring cars – however I want. I'm their *father*."

He slammed the car door shut. In a swirl of dust, flying pebbles, and screeching tires, Harris careened out of the driveway. Natalie could see Everett, his small face pressed to the window. She raised her hand to wave goodbye. He pressed his palm against the windowpane. Natalie stood still, shoulders shaking with silent sobs, until they were out of sight.

"Hey, Mom!"

Natalie's neck snapped as she looked back to the house. Aaron stood on the front porch.

His chin quivered while he exhaled a ragged sigh. "Thank you."

They were breathless, slick with sweat, each braided into the other's arms. Andy nipped at her shoulder. Allegra brushed her lips against the underside of his chin, chafing her mouth on his stubble. With a loose smile crawling across her face, Allegra rolled over, burrowing her back against his chest, and pulled his forearm more around her.

As they watched the sunrise through the screened-in porch, Andy kissed the crown of her head, the back of her neck, the ridge of her collarbone. Allegra nearly purred with contentment.

"You're my new favorite way to wake up," Andy said, his voice groggy and soft.

Allegra laughed. "It's not quite waking up when we never went to sleep. Have I thanked you yet for coming back to me?"

"A thousand times. You don't need to thank me. I'm exactly where I'm supposed to be."

He took her face in his and kissed her deeply. Allegra had never known that a kiss could extend so far beyond her mouth. She eased closer to him, eager to return all that he was giving.

Her phone buzzed from the coffee table. It was Andy who pulled away.

"You should check that," he said. "Might be your kids."

"Probably not. They're always pretty respectful of the time difference."

Still, she grabbed hold of her phone. In the dim, pink-tinged light, she squinted at the blue screen. Allegra found images documenting an event with Etienne's family. A sea of familiar faces, dripping with jewels and dressed in bespoke clothing. Catered food in silver service. Another small chateau, its manicured lawn rippling against an elegant, perfectly proportioned garden. Ignoring the aristocratic backdrop, Allegra only had eyes for Jules and Delphine. She took note of their tight smiles, their hooded eyes, and their intertwined fingers. Her heart pounded.

And, of course, there was Etienne's caption: *A beautiful*

day spent celebrating my mother's birthday. The children missed you. This could all be yours again. Pity the children who must live their lives without a mother.

"It's from him, isn't it?"

Allegra swallowed. "It's like he can sense whenever I'm starting to be happy again."

"Don't let him ruin it."

"You make it sound so simple."

"Can I see the text?"

Wordlessly, she handed it to him. His eyes narrowed as his fingers flicked across the images, across Etienne's words. With his free hand, he pulled her closer.

"Tell me this: how do you normally react when he baits you?"

"I suppose I take the bait. I'm emotional, but deferential, too. Begging and pleading. He holds all the power, and I do my best to kowtow to him."

While he settled his chin on her head, Andy stared out the big bay windows that faced the screened-in porch. "One of the most harrowing nights of my life happened when I was seventeen. Natalie and Eliana were twelve. Natalie's parents had invited us to stay for dinner, and I was so amped for the whole thing. The entire band was there, including their opening act. The alcohol was free-flowing. One continuous pour. There was an impromptu concert in the backyard – way louder than normal. Like they were all taunting the neighbors to call the police. I loved every minute. Couldn't believe that adults lived that way.

"But then Natalie, still the oldest twelve-year-old I've ever met, told me to find Eliana. She was missing. After a few minutes, I found her: stupid-drunk and talking to a man in his forties. Right before I got her out of there, I saw Kip spit at Annabel, Natalie's mom. Annabel slapped his face. The music went silent. Everyone was watching them, but no one seemed surprised. They'd all probably seen worse from those two.

Anyway, Annabel and Kip disappeared while I scooped up Eliana. It still kills me that I left Natalie with them. That *that* was her home.

"On my way out, I saw Kip and Annabel right there, inside the screened-in porch. Dancing to 'Muse.' They'd left this wreckage behind, but they didn't seem to care. They were dancing to a song he wrote for her. What kind of jackass dances to his own song?"

"My God. Poor twelve-year-old Natalie. I can't even imagine."

"Can't you?"

Allegra turned away. When she spoke, her voice was hoarse.

"I do know that song," Allegra said, and then she began to whisper-sing: "*When night falls, the moon all black and new, it's you, it's you; In this maze of empty halls, when the floor falls through, it's you, it's you; I'm beyond the pale and you're my holy grail, all that's good and true. I have my short fuse but now I have my muse, and I know exactly what to do. It's you, it's you—*"

Andy pressed a finger to her lips, effectively shushing her.

"I don't know your ex, but I've seen toxic relationships. I've seen love knotted into hatred. Some people feed off that energy. All we can do is offer them as little fuel as possible."

"You make it sound so easy," she whispered. "How would you respond to Etienne?"

"I would thank him for the pictures and turn off your phone."

Allegra blinked. "That's it?"

"That's it. Anything more feels like tossing a cup of gasoline into a dumpster fire. And remember: Véronique will tell you if something is wrong with the kids, so you're free to not be at his beck and call anymore. You can ignore him."

Allegra's fingers moved across her phone in a flurry. She started smiling when she turned off her phone. Allegra then grinned at him, her white teeth shining.

"I like that you called him a dumpster fire."

Andy laughed. "You like that, huh? Well, I have metaphors

for that P.O.S. for days—"

She pressed her finger to his lips, effectively shushing him. She arched an eyebrow.

"Etienne who?"

After she whispered the question, Andy cupped her chin, brought his lips to hers, and tugged on her lower lip with his teeth. He tented the blanket around him. When their skin touched, Allegra's breath hitched as she closed her eyes.

Against her will, the hook of "Muse" reverberated within Allegra, its lyrics pulsing louder than her own heartbeat:

It's you, it's you; I love you; it's you, it's you.

Chapter 28

Beneath a pale, blue sky marbled with clouds, they sketched in silence. Aaron depicted a still life of seashells stacked in a glass bowl. Natalie worked on an abstract version of a fleur-de-lis. On the table were two empty glasses of orange juice and a half-eaten Dutch baby, cold now in a cast-iron skillet.

Just then, a crescent of silver flashed from the ocean.

"Aaron," she squealed. "Look, dolphins!"

He tore off for the beach. She raced after him: down the stairs, through the dunes, across the beach, until they had charged ankle-deep into calm surf. They stood shoulder to shoulder and watched a pod of dolphins leap from the water.

"Your dad would've loved this."

Aaron shot her a look. "Dad? He never even takes us out on the boat."

"Because he has to work, but he loves the water, marine life, the natural world."

"He never told me he likes dolphins."

"Well, he keeps a lot to himself – like another guy that I know," Natalie said, as she nudged him. "When we went on vacation together in college, Dad woke me up super early one morning, drove me to this gorgeous beach in Puerto Rico, and we watched baby sea turtles crawl out to sea. They had just hatched, and they knew exactly what to do. It's one of the most beautiful things I've ever seen."

"That was Dad's idea?" Aaron asked, his eyes widening.

"We don't even have a dog!"

Natalie's gaze fell then. She looked at her toes, at the countless bubbles swirling around her shins. A sand crab scrambled against her skin. With a sigh, Natalie realized that Harris would've loved to watch it move. To be there, too. What had he whispered to her that morning?

Even the smallest beings matter, Nat. Their contribution to their habitat isn't diminished by their size. We're all connected back to each other.

Natalie sighed. "Your dad always wanted to get a dog. I always said no."

"Why?"

"Before I had an office, I met clients at home. I wanted everything to be perfect there."

"But when I'm making art, you tell me that the most important thing isn't how it looks. It's how it feels."

"That's true," she whispered. Her misty eyes skimmed the horizon line. "Trust me when I say this: your father would still love a dog. He has a big heart for even the smallest living things. And you should know this. You should know exactly who he is."

Eliana tiptoed into the kitchen and sighed with relief to find it empty. As she poured herself a cup of coffee, she heard the front door open. She listened to Josh greet Antoine, their muffled exchange of pleasantries. Eliana sipped the coffee quickly, snatching a rare moment of solitude before she was surrounded once again. Josh turned a corner and held up his hand.

"I gave Antoine the afternoon off."

Eliana exhaled. "Thank goodness for that. Greta's already made us the most amazing-smelling ratatouille for dinner, but I told her to leave early, too. I suppose I was hoping for ..."

"An evening alone with our family?"

"Something like that," she murmured.

"Well, I don't think that's too much to ask," Josh said. "I'm sorry I had to work longer than expected today. We're having issues securing the permits required to film in the city. It probably comes as no surprise to you that France requires a small mountain of paperwork."

"My parents used to complain about the red tape when we lived in Provence for that year," Eliana said. "I remember the lavender fields. They remember waiting in lines."

"So, you're not angry with me?"

"Not at all," Eliana said. As she answered him, she was stunned to realize it was true. She'd spent the day reading to her father and watching her kids splash in the pool with her mother. It had been an idyllic morning and also, Eliana realized, the only one of Josh's work trips where she hadn't been left entirely alone.

Josh grinned. With his arms wrapped around her, Eliana could feel his muscles loosening.

"I smell coffee," he whispered.

"Not only coffee, but Greta's almond croissants."

His eyes rolled back into his head. "Forget that I ever complained about the French bureaucracy. I can wait in any line, so long as I can eat like this," he said as he crossed the kitchen and helped himself to a warm croissant. Together, they walked outside onto the veranda.

For a time, they watched luxurious yachts sail. Farther out to sea, fishing boats returned with their catch from beyond the horizon line. Sunshine lacquered the water, burning their eyes.

"I think we should talk."

"As a linguist, I don't know of another English phrase that instills as much fear—"

"Not about us," Josh said, chuckling. "About Natalie and Harris."

"What about them?"

He paused. "I'm not sure that we've done enough for them."

"What do you mean? We invited Natalie to stay with us all summer to sort things out."

"That's what I mean: we've taken a side."

Eliana's mouth hung. "We took the only side we could. He screwed up. I'm not going to suggest that my best friend stay in a bad marriage."

At once, Eliana stood up, only to sink back down in her own chair. She sipped her cold coffee. Josh leaned forward on his knees, opening his palms to her.

"You know I'm not one to defend Harris, but I'm concerned that he's unraveling."

"Josh, stop. You were the only one who saw him as he is. You were right about him. Harris is the most pompous, selfish, sanctimonious—"

"Yes! Agreed! He's all those things, and he's always been all those things, but not with Natalie. Never with Natalie. With Natalie, he's always been ... better."

Abruptly, Eliana could see Harris and Natalie dancing at their wedding, his hand on the small of her back. She could see them in their shoebox apartment outside of Arlington; she could see him bringing her crackers and ginger ale, as Natalie writhed in bed suffering from hyperemesis gravidarum while pregnant with Aaron. The flushed pride on his face at Aaron's basketball game. Everett on his shoulders, their two faces laughing, posing in front of Baltimore's Inner Harbor. The text Natalie had sent of them in quarantine: all three guys playing a board game on the floor of their basement, grinning and tousled and content.

"I was talking to George about your dad," Josh said haltingly. "Apparently, when your dad said those things to you after the girls were born, he was likely in the early stages of dementia. George said that many people become angry when they start to forget things and lose control. Often, they lash out at those they love. They rage out of fear."

Eliana turned away from him, burying her face in an empty mug and glaring into the crystal-clear sky, her eyes trying to rend a hole into its aquamarine expanse.

"The day we cut him out of our lives, we didn't have all the facts," Josh said. "There was a story within a story. And maybe, beneath the betrayal, Harris is hiding another story, too."

He kissed her brow, her eyelids, the sides of her mouth.

"Ask me to stay," he whispered, as he tipped his forehead to hers.

With her eyes closed, Allegra smiled. "Can't do it. You have to go back to work, and I have to figure out life on my own. Besides, stay too long, and you might get sick of me."

"Impossible."

She pulled away from Andy, finally opening her eyes to him. He stood solidly planted in her driveway. Workers bustled around the property. They hammered the pergola. They cleared weeds from her flowerbeds. They painted the trim ecru white. Allegra hardly noticed the noise. She couldn't take her eyes from Andy, believing that as soon as she did so, he would be gone.

"I was thinking though," Allegra began casually, "that maybe I could come visit you in the city? That is, if you want the company."

"I definitely want the company, though I'm not sure I can wait that long."

He kissed her then like they were entirely alone, behind a locked door impenetrable to the outside world. She kissed him back with all she had to give.

Moments later, Andy started the ignition and pulled out of the driveway. Allegra waved him off. Her cheeks ached with the raw memory of saying goodbye to her children. That same ambling speed. That same right turn. That same sense that the ones she loved had not merged into traffic but had been swept away by a rising tide.

Once back inside her home, Allegra went upstairs with heavy footsteps. Every muscle ached. She pushed open the door to Delphine's room. It was late morning, and together, Natalie and Aaron had finished the first application of violet paint.

"It looks great," Allegra said, and she meant it. She loved the dusky, soft color, like something stolen from an early evening sky.

"I thought you'd like it," Natalie said. "It felt apt. The shade is called 'Delphinium.' "

Allegra's breath caught. "I love it."

Aaron's glance darted between both women. "Okay, then," he muttered. "I'm out."

"Thanks for your help!" Allegra called to his retreating form. She turned back to Natalie. "I was surprised to see Aaron here this morning."

"Me too," Natalie said, before sinking onto the tarp-covered window seat. "Oh, Allegra, I don't think I'll ever get used to this. Our first hand-off went horribly, and it was all my fault."

"What happened?"

"Aaron announced that he didn't want to go to camp. I was so stunned that, before Harris could even respond, I told Aaron that he could stay with me despite what we'd agreed. Can you believe it? I don't know what I was thinking."

"Hey, be kind to yourself. You've never done this before."

Tears pooled in Natalie's eyes. "And the whole time, Everett was screaming to be let out of his car seat, and I couldn't pick him up. It was like I'd decided to make Everett the peace offering. I've never felt more wretched in my life."

"You'll get used to it. All of you will," Allegra said quietly. She opened and closed her mouth, trying to find the words.

"Remember: there's friction with any beginning, but we all deserve the chance to live a life we love. I have faith that that day will come. For both of us."

When Natalie took her hand and squeezed it then, her eyes had dried. She straightened her spine. She had a glint in her eye, hinting at an inner fire that Eliana would have recognized.

"Speaking of taking the chance to live a life you love, I do need to talk to you."

Chapter 29

From their vantage point on the veranda, the French Riviera glowed, its sinewy light spilling into the blackened Mediterranean. Fragrant air enveloped them. They drank a full-bodied Merlot beneath a moon like a cracked shell in complete silence.

Eventually, Eliana bit her lower lip. "For what it's worth, I'm sorry. I was angry and you were caught in the crossfire. I should've never said what I did to you."

"And I should never have told you how to manage your relationship," Gloria said.

"Well, you were right," Eliana said. "I was miserable without Josh."

Gloria sighed, eyeing the middle distance. "Eliana, I've always envied you with him."

"What?"

"I know what the world thought of your father. A man more respected than loved, certainly," she said quietly. "I was his exception. Where he was cruel to others, he was kind to me. When I was young, I felt exhilarated to know that I could soften such a man. With each passing year, though, I wondered if it was enough to be adored – but only out of sight. In time, I recognized that you'd married your father's opposite. You hadn't ever wanted to become me."

"Oh, Mom! That isn't at all what I—"

"I couldn't understand how you could find fault with your husband when my marriage presented ... more overt challenges. It was unfair of me," Gloria whispered, as she passed her a yellowed, stained sheet of paper. "I don't regret a *thing*. It's important to me that you know that – not a thing. Because our life gave me you. You and Andy."

"What's this?"

Gloria exhaled through her teeth. "Forty years ago, I was a teenage girl living in Bacalar, Mexico, who fell in love with two men. Each man cleared a path to a new life. The familiar man, Julio, came from a good, local family. I knew exactly what my life would be with him. Another man, David, only meant to stay six months while he established a hotel on the lagoon. In the end, he stayed a year, seducing not only me but my family. I loved your father, but I loved the adventure he offered more. When he proposed, he couldn't finish the question because I screamed 'yes' so loudly. In both of our languages. We married in the Parroquia de San Joaquin. Soon after that, we left. Your father never returned to Bacalar with me. When I last visited with you, you were five. It was the last time you would see your grandparents and our big family."

"I don't understand. Why did he keep them from you?"

Gloria shrugged. "Because I never laugh as hard as I do with my sister. Because I was on solid footing in my mother's home, in my own country, and I was forever an immigrant with him. Because he refused to acknowledge the story of my life that had nothing to do with him."

"I'm so sorry," Eliana said, squeezing her hand. "I had no idea."

"He's a better man now, you know. He is softer, warmer, more loving. And now, I can be the one to choose what we will both remember. Look at the card, *mi querida*."

"A recipe for *Empanadas de Chaya*?"

"That is my mother's recipe. It was her wedding gift to me. I have a book of recipes that your father didn't care for me to cook, but together, we will make them all," Gloria said, tearing up while she pulled another treasure from her pocket. "And this is my gift to you: your grandmother's rosary. *Tu abuela*: she loved you so much, Eliana."

Eliana fingered the delicate beads and lifted the rosary, fragrant and fine, to her nose. She breathed deeply, drawing her grandmother close to her. Her breath caught.

Eliana whispered: "Please, let me take you back to—"

"*Sí!*" Gloria shouted, overcome with peals of tearful laughter before Eliana could even finish the question. "Yes!"

Gloria and Eliana had been curled up on the couch, perusing recipes and sharing stories, when a crash rang out from the kitchen. They froze.

"No! I will not. No!"

David's voice echoed. Gloria's face darkened. With pursed lips, Gloria stood.

"Let me. Please?"

Gloria tilted her head to the side. "You're sure? He can be … difficult."

"It's a clear night, Mom. Sit with the stars for a while."

Gloria nodded, smiling halfway. Eliana steeled her shoulders and strode into the kitchen. In the doorway, Eliana stopped. George knelt, picking up pieces of porcelain. Her father sat at the table, gazing out to sea. George caught sight of Eliana and flushed.

"Be careful where you step," George said.

Eliana nodded. "Is everything okay?"

With a weary sigh, George stood. "We're not having the best day today."

"I don't like it," David said, setting his jaw.

"He wouldn't eat dinner," George said. "I offered him the almond cake instead, but—"

He motioned to the floor where the dessert plate had been smashed.

"Can I try?"

George nodded. "I'll go turn down his bed."

Against the sound of George's retreating footsteps, David sighed. Eliana rested her hand on top of her father's. He flinched. Even as her throat tightened, she held still, her hand on his.

"Sometimes, it's not you," Eliana whispered. "Sometimes, it's the cake."

Slowly, she pulled her hand away. As she flitted around the kitchen, opening cabinets and clattering dishes, David never looked at her. After a few minutes, she came back to him.

"Will you come with me? I promise: this one will be better."

When he nodded, she helped her father to his feet. He took her arm. As she guided him out of the kitchen, Eliana planted a tray on her hip. They moved slowly, in step, finding their rhythm. When they reached the veranda, Eliana settled David onto the couch beside her mother, ignoring Gloria's stunned expression. She passed her mother some lemon cake before handing a plate to David. He held up his hand, his brow furrowing.

"I have trouble with the – the spiky thing," he said.

"The fork?" Eliana said. "I can help."

She had expected him to argue, but he opened his mouth. She excavated a small morsel of lemon cake. He swallowed, his eyes closing, before swooning slightly and opening his mouth again. Eliana had another bite ready for him.

"I *like* this one," David said.

"Yes. I thought you might," Eliana said.

As Eliana fed her father, Gloria's eyes welled, her cake untouched.

Beyond the clinking of fork to plate, Eliana could hear waves lap and crickets hum. And just as she was only hours from the fatigued mom who'd fed her daughters lemon cake before bed, she was also still close to the girl who had found a bakery with her father in every city. Their ritual had involved exhaustive research. She would test the chocolate, and he the lemon.

"The Summer Triangle," David whispered, pointing while she set his plate down. "I showed it to a musician once. I forget his name–"

"His name was Kip. Kip Stone."

"He didn't care. But once you see it, you can't not see it."

"I bet he cared more than you think," Eliana whispered, pausing for a beat. "Of its three constellations, Cygnus is my favorite."

"You know it?" David asked.

Eliana nodded while Gloria squinted. "Remind me: Cygnus is the swan?"

"Yes," Eliana said. "It represents beauty."

"Not only beauty," David said hoarsely, his voice fading beneath the incandescent sky. "Swans are fighters. Cygnus is my favorite, too. But not for its beauty. For its fire."

Together, Aaron and Allegra sat under the pergola, busily saturating Allegra's black-and-white photographs with bright paint. They reminded Allegra of silkscreened Warhol's. Allegra couldn't believe these creations had been Aaron's idea, yet there he sat right beside her: his pupils dilating, his tongue poised between his teeth, his mind somewhere far away from her.

After watching him for a time, Allegra sighed.

"So," Allegra began, taking a deep drag of air, "how long have they been bullying you?"

Aaron's hand stilled. A glob of wet chartreuse paint dribbled onto the photograph. He dropped the paintbrush onto a paper towel.

"How did you know?"

"Takes one to know one."

Aaron shot her a look, staring up at her dubiously from underneath a layer of feathery lashes. Catching sight of his expression, Allegra chuckled.

"I didn't always look like this," she said. "When I was your age, I was a head above the tallest boy, very skinny, and super awkward-looking with these wide-set, alien eyes. Fire-engine red hair. Freckles everywhere. I tried too hard to make friends. No one liked me. I ate lunch in the bathroom every day. I like to think of it as a life skill – balancing a tray on your lap in the stall isn't easy, you know."

His eyes narrowed. "Well, screw them. You got the last laugh."

"Maybe. Or maybe I took a job where people would tell me I look pretty all the time because I was so desperate to be accepted. Maybe I was lost for a long time because I still wanted to please people who were just … mean."

"I thought you were going to tell me it gets better. That's what you're supposed to say."

"Okay, then, if that's what I'm *supposed* to say," she said, pausing. "If you don't mind me asking, why do they tease you?"

Aaron sighed. "Someone said I'm doping because I'm pretty good at basketball."

Allegra clucked under her tongue. "That's why you didn't want to go to camp."

"I'm not going to hang out with those guys any more than I have to. And my dad – he's ditched us all summer, so I don't really want to be around him either. I want to stay here. I want to stay away from them. *All* of them."

"Me too. I want to stay here, away from them, all of them – just like you."

They watched Natalie scurry around the yard, with Joe trailing briskly at her heels. They sunk to their knees together in front of a flower bed. They planted zinnias in a neat line, edging out boxwoods with a trail of pink.

"I've discovered one truth along the way: bullies may never change, but you will."

Aaron looked at her then, his wide, brown eyes boring into hers. He was waiting.

"At some point, you'll forget you ever wanted to blend in. You'll realize that what made you different was your strength all along. You'll stop hiding your magic. You'll be willing to be *seen*. Someday, you won't be afraid of them anymore."

"Someday sounds like a long time from now."

"Right now, they're only in the room with us if we let them inside," she said, squeezing his hand. "I promise you: you'll always find your way away from people like them and back to people like us. Better days are coming, Aaron."

"So, you *are* actually saying it gets better?"

Allegra grinned. "I guess I am. I guess that's exactly what I'm saying."

The moon glimmered like a bleached sand dollar over the Mediterranean. While the villa slept, Josh and Eliana slipped into their pool for an evening swim. Eliana had thoughts. There were things to be said, conversations to be had out of earshot of her family or the staff. They'd been in France for nearly a week, and Eliana still hadn't had a chance to talk to her husband.

But then, it might have to wait. With his mouth at the base of her neck and his hand tugging at the strings of her bathing suit, Eliana kept losing her train of thought. He kissed her hungrily. In response, Eliana wrapped her arms around his neck, resting her elbows on his broad shoulders. She traced a line down the wet length of his chest, registering his involuntary shudder, nipping at his earlobe, and then reluctantly pulling away from him.

"You keep interrupting me," she said, rasping each word.

"Were we talking? Because I thought we'd decided to stop talking."

Her thoughts blurred. She shook her head, trying to organize them as his mouth swept the length of her clavicle. "But it's important."

He groaned. "Ellie, I've already made inquiries about moving to the East Coast. I could be relocating my company's corporate headquarters for you. Maybe you should sit with your win."

"Hey, we agreed that you'd be happier there, too. You miss the rain more than me."

"That's true, but I'm giving up the best Baja tacos and street corn of my life."

"Or you're exchanging them for the best bagels and pizza and black-and-white cookies," Eliana murmured, dipping her fingertips beneath the waistband of his swim trunks. "Which brings me to what I really want to talk about."

"New York's inflated real estate market?"

"Mexico."

"Well, that did it," Josh muttered, disentangling himself from her. "The mood is dead."

"I want to talk about your documentary."

Josh winced. "About that. So. Plans have changed unexpectedly. Our production schedule got pushed back. Apparently, no one wants to meet you in Mexico City in late August. Go figure. We're planning to begin interviews in October."

"October? Right after the girls start school?"

"I know. And I know I should have brought it up sooner, but everything has been going so great between us I thought I could stall until—"

"Tomorrow?"

"The day after that."

Eliana smiled. As she looped her arms around his neck, her blue eyes flashed with the sudden, stirring recognition that she hadn't worried about her girls in hours. She had trusted that they were okay. That all was well. Her breath caught. And then, her parted lips curved into a smile.

"Well, I agree that it's much more appealing in autumn."

"You mean, you're not angry about the new timetable?"

"Not at all. In fact, I thought that I might come."

Josh blinked. "To Mexico?"

"You said you were still looking for a translator, right? Well," Eliana continued, no longer looking at him but staring at her hands, "would you consider me for the position?"

"You?" Josh whispered. "Are you kidding?"

Eliana flushed. "I know I'm a little rusty, but I've been speaking Spanish with my mom, and it's coming back quickly. Still, if you'd like me to bone up—"

"I only meant that you're crazy overqualified," Josh said, as he brushed the hair from her face. "My little film would be lucky to have your skill set."

"Are you sure? We've never worked together professionally."

"Only because you've never offered."

"It could change our relationship."

"For the better."

Eliana paused. "I don't want you to say 'yes' simply because I've asked you."

"Fair enough, but what if I want exactly what you want?"

"And what do you want now?" Eliana asked, while she reached behind the arch of her back and began untying the strings knotted there.

Right before he was upon her, before her flimsy material fell away, and before he took her into his arms again, Eliana fell back with her arms outstretched. She was not sinking but was floating, cradled on the surface of warm water stamped with moonlight.

At some point this summer, Eliana had remembered how to float.

Natalie couldn't sit still. As Allegra watched from her perch in the wedge of her new sectional, Natalie reconstructed an arrangement of hydrangeas, fluffed the pillows, and draped a cotton throw over the couch. Beneath her furrowed brow, Allegra sipped coffee and said nothing. The little cottage, bereft of workers, was impossibly quiet. Birdsong filtered through open windows. Natalie's finishing touches, the crisp white trim on the screened-in porch and the pale shell-grey color on her window boxes, still gleamed with wet paint. The bracing humidity wouldn't let her cottage dry yet, but no matter. When Allegra closed her eyes, she could smell the ocean. She felt like the Atlantic held her close, always hovering out of sight, always bigger and more constant than her small, ever-changing struggles.

"Are you sure you don't want to cancel this?" Natalie asked shakily, raking her fingers through her hair. "Because we can opt out of it at any time."

With a gentle smile, Allegra patted the couch beside her. Natalie sat down hard.

"Have I thanked you properly yet?"

Natalie closed her eyes. "All you do is thank me. I'm worried that, in a week's time, you might regret having ever met me in the first place."

"That's impossible," Allegra said, squeezing her hand. "I've lost so many friends. They couldn't stand Etienne and couldn't sit by while I defended his behavior, so they left. I can't blame them. I'm sure it wasn't easy to watch. Still, I didn't realize how lonely I was until you came into my life. Whatever happens today, I'm so grateful for you all. More than you know."

"The feeling is very much mutual," Natalie said, as she squeezed her hand back. "Should we cancel on them and hang out instead? I think I'm going to be sick."

"Natalie, what we're going to do matters. But today is a conversation. It can be fun."

"Fun. Like cliff-jumping. Or skydiving."

"Exactly," Allegra said, grinning. She then reached for a throw pillow, its linen expanse lined with a geometric watercolor pattern of lavender and blue. "By the way, where did you find this? I love this. I've never seen anything like it."

"Oh that," Natalie said, fiddling with the hem of her shirt. "I had it made for you."

Allegra gaped. "You designed this?"

"Design is a big word for pairing some doodles with fabrics. I do it for all my clients."

"Natalie, oh my goodness! Do you know what you're doing? You're creating textiles!"

"I'm being resourceful. When I can't find what I want, I make it."

Allegra raised an eyebrow. "You know what I'm going to say."

"Not a word," Natalie said. "It's just—"

"It's not 'just' anything. It's your passion. And if I have to be brave today, so do you."

All at once, Allegra felt a constriction in her throat. A film of tears blurred her vision. With the back of her wrist, she wiped them away. "We can't hide our magic," she whispered.

When a knock rapped, splintering the quietude like cannon fire, they jolted to their feet.

"What do you want to do?" Natalie whispered, her blue eyes wide and full.

Allegra straightened her spine. "I want to open the door and let them in."

Chapter 30

"I can't believe I'm doing this," Natalie said, as she flicked mascara onto her lashes.

"I can't believe I had to convince you to do this," Allegra muttered. "Who in their right mind turns down free childcare?"

"Well, Damon was ecstatic when I called him, and I can't even remember the last time I asked a man out. It was probably when I asked Harris to join me for Aaron's first ultrasound."

"Yikes."

"Funny. Harris said the same thing at the time."

They laughed. Allegra wore her grin even as she stretched her arms and yawned.

"Because I don't exactly have any new campaigns lined up in my calendar, consider me a dependable childcare option, and remember," Allegra said, wiggling her eyebrows, "no curfew."

"I'll consider lingering with him a little longer, then."

"Hot damn. Natalie, you're a wild woman."

Natalie laughed. "You know, Aaron seems super excited to spend the evening with you. I think you have another fan – unsurprisingly."

Allegra sobered, staring at her hands. She shredded her fingernails.

"I did want to speak with you for a moment."

"Are you upset about what we did today? Because I can—"

"No, of course not," Allegra said, before pausing. "It's about Aaron. He's being bullied."

Natalie went still. "Aaron? Bullied? That's impossible. He's an all-star athlete."

"He's special, which means he's different, so there's a target on his back. Someone made up a rumor that he uses steroids."

"Steroids? He's thirteen!"

"Exactly, it's ridiculous. It's also very much a thirteen-year-old allegation. Trying to be older than you really are. Using big words in a nonsensical way."

"Basketball camp," she breathed.

"It's no wonder he couldn't stomach it."

"How did I not see this?" Natalie asked, her voice quivering. "There've been so many signs. He's been angry and withdrawn. He hates everything he used to love. He never mentions his friends. How could he not have told me?"

"It's not you," Allegra said, as she stood and gave her a forceful hug. "He needed a neutral person to talk to, I think."

"I'm the worst mother in the world," Natalie said, laughing bitterly. "Here I am, taking him to the beach, separating from his dad, dating someone, sending his brother away, and meanwhile—"

"You mean: taking him away from the kids who bullied him? Taking him out of a home where a relationship had turned toxic? Surrounding him with loved ones? Sticking up for him when he didn't want to go to basketball camp, even if you didn't know why yet? Trusting his intuition, even without all the facts? Everything is spin, Nat."

Numbly, Natalie shook her head. "I should cancel my date."

"I have a better idea. Tonight, he and I will post a picture to his Instagram account – let those tough tweens choke on the image of their teammate spending time with a supermodel. You'll go on your date – because you really shouldn't waste a violet fiammata Missoni sweater – and celebrate your hard work. Tonight, we'll all rest. And tomorrow, you'll begin to fix it."

Ten minutes later, Allegra and Aaron took pictures with his basketball. As soon as they found one they liked, Allegra pilfered Aaron's phone. Her fingers fluttered over the screen.

"You don't mind if I caption this, do you?" Allegra said though she'd already walked away. Aaron grinned. Natalie smiled at him, stifling the urge to smooth his curls from his forehead. Just as Natalie opened her mouth to speak, her phone buzzed.

En route to urgent care. I think Everett has an ear infection. Will let you know.

Natalie closed her eyes. She now remembered some extra fussiness and tears – she'd thought Everett had been anxious to leave her. But Natalie now realized that all around there had been signs, infinitesimal details as impotent as muted sirens. She had missed everything.

"Allegra told you, didn't she?"

"She did," Natalie said, and then, after a long pause: "Why didn't you?"

Aaron pressed his lips together. "Because I care what you think more than anyone."

"Aaron, I could never think any less of you."

"It's embarrassing."

"No. It's bullshit is what it is."

Aaron grinned, delighted, as the whites of his eyes shined. Natalie had the familiar sense that he was both so young and so wise, and it was hard for her to choose words that would land.

"I'm sorry I didn't want to go to camp."

"Don't be sorry. You stood up for yourself even when it was hard," Natalie said. "I'm proud of you. And if you couldn't talk to me, I'm proud of you for talking to someone. Your dad and I – we're going to figure this out. This is our burden now. Okay?"

"Okay," Aaron said, his cheeks flushing. His tight shoulders eased before her eyes.

The minute hand ticked to seven o'clock. Somewhere on Lake Drive, Damon was illegally parked, waiting for her. Biting her lip, Natalie smoothed wrinkles from her sweater.

"I was going to meet a friend tonight, but maybe I should stay."

"Nah. You should go. Allegra challenged me to a pizza-eating competition."

Natalie arched a brow. "Did she now?"

"She said she can really pack it away, and we're going to make an Instagram story of it together. You would ... ruin the vibe. Plus, you max out at two slices."

"Well, then, I guess I'm off," she said, planting a kiss on his forehead. She took a breath, gathered her bag, and tried not to look like someone about to sprint around Silver Lake.

"Mom?"

"Yes?" she asked, turning back to him.

"Dad should be here tonight. To call you 'Milady' and hold the door for you."

Her eyes widened. Her voice cracked as she spoke. "Goodnight, Aaron."

" 'Night, Mom."

They'd been making their way south, the sun setting to their right. Clouds like flares shimmered orange and pink, mirrored in neon-tinted patches of marshland and bay. They held hands, not speaking. Every so often, Damon would brush his lips to the back of her wrist, shooting tingles up her spine. She shivered every time, leaning into him.

Damon hadn't told her where they were going, but this time, Natalie had a good idea.

Almost an hour later, they crossed the Verranzo Bridge to Assateague Island. As they ascended it, Natalie's chest filled at the sight of golden light lacquered over Sinepuxent Bay. The amber-toned seagrasses fringing the shoreline. The seagulls foraging, diving in loose arcs into the water. The rippling salt marshes. The stubborn, stooped trees. Upon reaching Assateague, Natalie released the breath she'd been holding and rolled down her window.

It helped that he smelled exactly the same, that the air coating this small barrier island hung heavily with a familiar salt breeze. In minutes, she retraced years. This barrier island had not only shielded the coastline inland; it had been their windswept haven, too. She'd rarely felt safer than when she was here: on this stretch of ever-shifting sands, cocooned inside a fragile tent, with the hard-patter rain and wild wind and swirling sand roaring outside. They'd slept skin to skin, his arms intertwined with hers. Up until that point, Natalie had never slept more soundly than when she was here, with him.

She exhaled. "We're back."

"That we are. How's it feel?"

"Exactly as good as it did back then," she murmured, and she knew – in the fierce way he smiled at her – that she had said the exact right thing.

Just then, Damon spotted a horse due east. He stopped the car. Swinging its tail, the clay-toned horse stood alone in the marshland. Together, they stared in silence at an inky-eyed, regal animal that steadily held their gaze.

"I can't remember why I ever wanted to stay away," she whispered.

"To me, it feels like you never left."

Before she could respond, he started the engine once more and eased the car back onto the road. Natalie didn't look back at the horse, bathed in warm sunlight at the water's edge. Yet, she had the itchy sensation of being watched, of something deep within her having been seen. She reached for Damon's hand quickly, her thundering heart not calming until he took it.

"Here we are," he said.

With a cooler under one arm, Natalie stopped short at their campsite on the beach. She blinked. The tent had already been erected not far from the dunes. Its parted flaps revealed piles of piles of blankets, pillows, and winking lanterns. Two cushioned wooden chairs flanked its entrance. In front of their tent, choppy waves charged the beach, as an insistent wind knocked against the wild grasses. The beach was theirs alone.

"How is the tent already set up?"

Damon lit the fire, breathing into the flame to stoke it higher. "A buddy of mine owns a brewery nearby. He owed me a favor. Also, I remember how we used to set up tents together."

Natalie grinned. "The only time we ever fought. Because you refuse to read directions."

"There's no need if you already know exactly what to do."

"And here I thought that in all these years, you'd finally evolved."

"Nope. Generally, I opt to stay in hotels instead."

Natalie laughed. "If memory serves, you didn't mind the arguing," she began, sinking into the chair beside him, "so long as we spent a long time making up."

His pupils dilated as he stared at her, the air around them thickening with more than the fervent wind. "I'm still not above picking a fight with you for the chance to make it right," he said, as he squeezed her thigh. He paused. "How long can we stay?"

He was one of the few people who would've noticed her darkening eyes. "Until sunrise."

With a wide grin, he opened the cooler. He held out a locally brewed apricot IPA to her, while he chose a more hoppy version for himself. In silence, they clinked cans. Shoulder to shoulder, they watched wave upon rakish wave tumble onto the beach, while the warmth of the sun grafted fiery heat to their skin.

"Does your friend have some sort of a professional glamping business?"

Damon chuckled. "He's never set up a tent this way in his life. This is for you."

"For me?"

"Because he knows who you are," Damon said, staring at the can sweating in his palm.

"You told him your high school sweetheart came back this summer?"

"He knew your name long before this summer, Nat," Damon said. He smiled weakly at her, the waning sunlight streaking his blue eyes with gold. "You were the one who got away. He doesn't trust me to not screw it up – the cocky bastard probably thinks—"

But Natalie had already climbed into his lap, had already planted her lips across his. His large hands roved over her curves. As her tongue dipped into his mouth, she rocked against him. His mouth left hers only sparingly, hurriedly, to mark her elsewhere: the hollow of her throat, the tight skin against her clavicle, the soft mounds of her breasts. She dove into the giddy head-rush of being back on this same beach with this same person.

Then, he stopped. With shaking biceps, he held her away from him.

"We should eat," he said. "My buddy made sandwiches."

She blinked rapidly. "Oh. Sure. Okay."

"I want you, Natalie, but I don't want to rush you."

She smiled. "I kissed you first."

"And I kissed you back. But I've never been able to kiss you before without a curfew."

Her eyes widened. "Oh, my — that's true! I hadn't realized that."

"For the first time, I don't feel like I'm running out of time with you," he said, as he pressed a kiss to the back of her wrist. He wiggled his eyebrows. "Maybe I *have* evolved."

With a laugh, Natalie climbed off of his lap and settled back into her own chair. She clasped her hands together between her thighs, trapping them. She gazed at Damon expectantly.

"I think I'm ready for my sandwich now."

"We really don't have to eat yet. It was just a thing I said. Are you even hungry?"

She looked up at him through lowered lashes. "So hungry."

Their laughter ricocheted throughout the tent. Golden light seeped in between the flaps, raking claret color over their intertwined fingers. Time had fallen away, measured only by the light that unspooled around them. They lay on their sides, eye-to-eye, sharing breath.

He raised her hand to his mouth, kissing her knuckles. "It used to take me ages to pack us a picnic back then. Decisions, decisions."

"You always brought too much food."

"Had to," he muttered, his eyes darkening. "Your fridge was bare most of the time."

She shrugged. "I was raised by artists."

"Wolves, more like," Damon said. "I hated that I couldn't protect you. My favorite daydream for years was knocking out your old man. I wanted to whisk you away from them."

"Damon, you did. Look around: *this* was what you gave me. I escaped with you here."

"It was never enough."

"You did the best you could. We both did."

He swallowed. "You're the bravest person I know, Natalie."

"You always talk to me like we're about to say goodbye."

When his thumb slowly delved beneath the band of her jeans, tracing a faint line across her skin, goosebumps erupted. Blood rushed to her abdomen. She arched against him. Her breath caught to watch him watch her; as, in the candlelight, he watched her body move.

"I can't believe you're here," Damon whispered. "You never reached out to me. I thought you didn't want anything to do with me."

With a ragged sigh, Natalie cupped his face in her hands.

"No. You were the one person who ... I didn't trust myself to come too close."

Damon swept Natalie up in his arms. His mouth found hers hungrily, greedily, hurriedly. His hands slid under her shirt, roaming the length of her back, while she tangled her fingertips in his hair. They shared the same hot breath, their hips already rocking with the same rhythm. Her hands trembled as she unbuttoned his shirt. He tugged at her bra strap, fumbling with the clasp. When she whispered his name, he shivered. He pulled her on top of him.

In a distant dimension – in another world, she felt a faint buzzing. Against the hollow of her throat, his forehead creased. He held tight to her, even as he reached behind him. His free hand felt around the mound of blankets, rifling through pillows.

"What is it?" she asked, raising her head from his.

"My phone, I think. Hold on."

By candlelight, he found the phone. His fingers tensed like he was about to turn it off. But then, all was still.

Natalie lowered her head to rest upon him, smiling against his bare chest. "Tell me something," she began, her eyes shining, "do you believe that there's a person for every person?"

"No. I believe in timing."

She blanched at his tone. He handed her the phone. At the sight of the blue screen, her eyes glazed over. She felt herself falling, though his body still supported hers, her own scaffolding. His grip tightened. Maybe he could feel it, too: this imminent unraveling.

Seven missed calls. Eleven text messages.

"Everett's in the hospital," she breathed.

"I know."

"I have to go."

"Take my car."

"I can't take your car," Natalie said, as she sat up swiftly and peeled her skin from his. Her thoughts spiraled. Ocean waves cracked too loudly; dying sunlight blazed with harsh precision, blinding her. "I won't leave you alone in the middle of an island."

He touched her cheek with his thumb. "Don't you get it yet? There's no place else I'd rather be than here. At some point, our spot became mine."

Biting her lower lip, she bent toward him. Natalie kissed him for as long as her body would let her. And then, breaking into a run, she left him.

Chapter 31

As she trailed the faltering sunset, Natalie ruminated on her past. She retraced the same uninterrupted stretch of Route 50, feeling the same guttural ache of longing that she'd known as a girl – though this time, she wasn't yearning to get away.

This time, she was racing to get to somebody.

The silence in Damon's Jeep itched her. Her fingers danced over the touchscreen, coveting noise. Scanning through radio stations. Rejecting each one. And then, on a crackling radio wave, *he* was with her. Alone in her car, Natalie didn't have to pretend that she didn't know every word. She sang along, her voice layered over his.

> *Windblown, all grown,*
> *Take me home, please.*
>
> *See my color, watch me fade,*
> *Hear my silent serenade,*
> *Every hue that's leeched from me,*
> *Is all that I was meant to be.*
>
> *Take all the light and dark I've seen,*
> *Give me blossoms, make me green,*
> *Take my regret, let me renew,*
> *I've a thousand years of love for you.*

Waves come home in their retreat to sea,
Leave me to mine and let us be,
Windblown, all grown,
Take me home, please.

A handful of hours later, Natalie sprinted into NIH's Clinical Center. She raced down a warren of hallways that all looked the same. Her mind raced. Her feet echoed. She passed the nurses' station and saw Harris: hanging his head, perched in a hard chair.

"Harris!"

At the sound of her voice, he shot to his feet. Harris opened his arms wide, and Natalie raced to embrace him. He clung to her, his fingers balling into fists against her back.

"How is he?" Natalie asked, pulling away first.

"Better. The swelling is down. He doesn't – he doesn't need oxygen anymore."

"I can't believe he's allergic to amoxicillin! You must've been terrified."

"I wasn't with him."

Natalie jerked backward. "What?"

Harris spoke hoarsely. "It's been a long week. I had to work, so Sophia was watching him. She called the ambulance."

"Sophia was with him."

"Yes, and believe me, it will never happen again," he said, his lips twisting. "Sophia puts our worst babysitter to shame. She gave him the medicine and then left him to play alone. Didn't notice the swelling. By the time the EMTs arrived, his lips were blue."

Natalie's hand flew to her mouth. She took a step back from him.

"I'm so sorry, Natalie—"

"Mr. and Mrs. Blackburn, it's good news," the doctor said as he exited Everett's room. "Everett is recovering well. His vitals have stabilized. I'm going to keep him overnight for observation, but if all goes well, I would anticipate discharging him tomorrow."

Standing a foot apart, they exhaled together.

"Thank you, Dr. Voorhies," Harris said.

"Yes, thank you so much," Natalie said. "Can we see him now?"

"Absolutely. Mrs. Blackburn, he's been asking for you," Dr. Voorhies said, before offering a nod and continuing on his rounds.

Natalie turned to Harris, her forehead creasing.

"You heard what the doctor said," Harris said. "Go on. Our son needs his mom."

Natalie gave him a brief smile and rushed into Everett's room. She stilled at the sight of him, so small in his metal bed, an IV pumping fluid into his left arm. His swollen cheeks and lips. His skin blotched with hives. Natalie swallowed away the constriction in her throat. She kicked off her flip-flops and lay down beside him. His eyes flew open.

"Mommy," he whispered. "You're here."

Her eyes filled. With the back of her wrist, she wiped her tears away.

"I'm here. I missed you, Bug."

"I got a bit sick."

She kissed his cheek. "I know. I bet it was pretty scary. You're getting better now."

Everett lurched forward, touching the tip of his nose to her cheek. "I love you, Mommy."

"I love you, too, Bug. So, so much."

"Sing me a song."

Her brow furrowed as his eyelids drooped. Natalie rested her hand on his belly, watching it rise and fall. His heart monitor, all Day-Glo peaks and valleys, found its rhythm. Natalie drew a scratchy blanket over them. She took Everett's hand, brought it to her cheek, and began to whisper-sing:

For my boy,
I wanna build a better world (for you),
For my boy,
Only a kinder, gentler world (will do.)

As though retracing footprints, Eliana raced down the same hospital corridor, her eyes darting over the same bright signs and her body steering toward the same nurses' station. Just as she opened her mouth to speak, she saw Harris. Eliana rushed toward him.

"Harris! How is he?"

"Ellie?" he asked, rising quickly. "Better now. Everett's going to be fine."

"I got Allegra's message on the tarmac at JFK," Eliana said, her voice shaking. She held out her arms to embrace him, only to let them fall. "I took the first flight I could get to Dulles. How terrifying – the idea of Everett unable to breathe – is it too much? That I came?"

"No. It's exactly right that you came. Natalie is with Everett now, but she'll be really comforted to see you here. Especially with – with everything."

Eliana nodded. She stared at Harris as she hadn't in years. She noticed things. She saw the grey hair at his temples, the dark circles under his eyes, and the slight paunch around his midsection. His shoulders slightly stooped. His mouth drooping with a frown.

"I'm not only Natalie's friend," Eliana blurted out, surprising even herself.

"You're not?"

"No. I'm your friend, too. Josh and I – we're your friends, too."

Right then, Harris swallowed hard. A distinct sheen coated his eyes. "Even now?"

"Even now."

"Good to know," he said, smiling crookedly. "Thank you."

Eliana nodded. "Would you tell Natalie I'll wait for her in the hospital chapel?"

"The chapel? When did you start going to church?"

Memories glittered like shards of glass. Eliana conjured a text with smiley face emojis, where Natalie recounted that she was finally able to sleep in on Sunday mornings. In an email, Natalie had mentioned the newfound joy of skipping her church's afternoon small group meetings, of sipping coffee on the porch. Of staying home. Natalie hadn't been raised with religion, as she'd raised herself. Attending church had been a Blackburn inheritance. Natalie would go – because what could be more of an example of stability, of adulthood, than attending church every Sunday? – but she wouldn't go alone. And, at some point, Harris had opted out.

Eliana arched an eyebrow. "When did you stop, Harris?"

"It was easier," he said, folding his arms across his chest. "There weren't enough hours in the week. Not with my job. There's not enough time for anything else with my job. At least not anything that's my idea. Like church or a ballgame or—"

"The boat," she finished.

"That, too. During the pandemic, I came back to my church for a while. Attending virtually was easier, and our whole family missed the connection. But then."

"But then?"

"But then its message and its principles didn't match the man I'd become," he whispered.

Tentatively, she took his hand. She found his fingers rigid and cold.

"I've always prayed for you, though, Eliana," he said, his voice cracking. "For you and for your family. When the girls came prematurely, I prayed for you. And when things were hard afterward, I prayed for you. Even now, in case things are still hard, I get on my knees and say your name. Because you're my friend, too."

Her eyes misted over as she squeezed his cold fingertips, though she said nothing. She walked away from Harris without looking back. All the while, Josh's words were with her:

A story within a story.

"How's he doing?" Harris asked when Natalie tiptoed out of Everett's room.

"He's asleep now."

"Eliana's here."

"Eliana?" Natalie asked, her eyes stretching wide. "Here?"

Harris nodded. "She's waiting for you in the chapel."

"I'm not even surprised," Natalie whispered. "God, how I love that girl."

They stood on opposite sides of the hall, shivering in the cold, sterile air. Not speaking. Not touching. Each waiting for the chance to begin.

"I'm really sorry," Harris said, raising his open palms. "I know I promised you Sophia wouldn't meet the children without your consent. I don't know what I was thinking."

"It's okay.

"It's not. It feels like a second act of betrayal."

"Months ago, I might've agreed with you. But now I think you're being too hard on yourself. Both of us are going to make mistakes in this process. Because we're human, and we're doing the best that we can," she said, pausing for a beat. "I told Aaron about the separation."

"What?" Harris asked, his eyebrows knitting together.

"He asked me outright, and I looked in his big, brown eyes, and I couldn't lie to him. So, I lied to you by not telling you sooner. I'm so sorry. I know we wanted to talk to them together."

His lips puckered, but his words were soft: "I understand."

"You do?" Natalie asked as she released the breath she'd been holding.

"I do. I probably would've done the same thing. Maybe we were naïve to think we could control the timetable or steer their understanding. At least, no matter what, I know your heart is with our boys," he whispered, his voice falling away. "Your ... your cucumbers."

"My what?"

Harris swallowed. "You've always cut their cucumbers into those half-moon shapes. You've always made them eat their vegetables. You've always been worried that the boys would choke or fall or fail. This would've never happened on your watch."

"I've certainly made my own mistakes with them. I just owned up to one of them."

His mouth dropped open. "You're defending Sophia?"

"Not exactly. But I think our focus should be our children now. We're both moving on, and it's only natural that there will be some friction as we adapt to—"

Harris jerked. "Moving on? Are you moving on with someone?"

"Well, it's still really new, but—"

"Who is he?" Harris demanded. "Is it Jack Hadley? It's Jack, isn't it?"

"Who on earth is Jack Hadley?"

"Aaron's former basketball coach. I saw the way he looked at you."

"No. What? It's – he's no one you know."

Harris's breath caught. His fingers tightened into fists, swinging at his sides.

"All I meant to say is that our life won't wait for us. If you're in a relationship with someone, then I want to have a good relationship with her. I want peace. I want our kids to be happy. I mean, these horrible kids at Aaron's school are bullying him—"

"Aaron? Kids are bullying Aaron?"

"Yes, his basketball teammates! Can you believe it?"

"That's why he didn't want to go to camp," Harris said. "Christ. I'm a jerk."

"You're *not* a jerk," Natalie said, touching his shoulder. "You're a good dad, Harris. A good man."

"How can you – of all people – say that to me?"

"Because I chose you, and ... I still love you now for what I loved you for then."

"You still ... You still ..."

Natalie rested her hand on top of his, molding her fingertips to his like an empty shell shaping sand. "Thirteen years ago, you asked me to marry you, and I wanted to elope."

"You did?" he asked raggedly, his breath coming in heavy and rushed.

"I did because I didn't want to wait to be with you. And that's how I feel now: I'm ready for the rest of my life. It's time for us to begin again. All of us."

Her eyes were bright with tears, but she squeezed his hand and tried to smile. Natalie walked away then, shuffling with sunken shoulders toward the elevators, before turning back.

"Did you ever listen to my dad's music?"

"What? No."

"Why not?"

"Because he was neglectful and cruel. He failed you."

"Everyone calls him a genius. His music mattered so much to so many. It still does."

Harris eyed her dead-on, unwavering, looking at her as he hadn't in years. "Why should I care about the rest of the world when he failed the most important person in mine?"

"Hey, you," Natalie murmured, as she collapsed into the chair beside Eliana. Beneath hooded eyelids, Natalie noticed Eliana fingering a rosary. Her forehead creased, but Natalie said nothing.

They were alone in the unadorned chapel. Surrounded by its minimalist wooden panels and dim lighting, Natalie could feel her pulse slow. All of a sudden, everything hurt. She began to rub a cramp in her neck while trying to ignore the pain blinking within her tense jaw.

"How is he?" Eliana asked.

Natalie could still feel sand between her toes. Only a handful of hours ago, she'd been camping on Assateague with Damon. Her face had been turned to the sun, his arms had been around her, and all the while, her boy hadn't been able to breathe.

"He's okay," Natalie croaked. "Everyone says he's going to be fine."

"Then we have to trust them. I've learned that these doctors know what they're doing."

"I know that you despise it here, which is why it means so much to me that you came."

"Of course I came," Eliana said. "For me, we became a family, a real family, when air travel resumed and you canceled everything to be with us on the other side of the country."

"I didn't even see them in the NICU, and they were the littlest four-month-olds I'd ever seen, but still so perfect. Every tiny part still there; everything in miniature."

"In the beginning, when I held them, I worried I'd break them," Eliana whispered, before pausing. "Do you remember what my father said to me?"

"You wouldn't tell me. And because you tell me everything, I knew it was bad."

And then Eliana started shaking. Tears swelled from the corner of her eyes. "Thirty minutes after they were born, after they'd been rushed away, Josh handed me the phone. My dad's voice boomed so loudly that the nurses could hear him. He said I shouldn't let myself get close to them. That I would lose them. That I should go beg for my job back. That I was a fool to follow Josh anywhere. That I'd given up everything worthwhile in my life for nothing."

Natalie closed her eyes.

Beside her, Eliana swallowed. "He said that when I left the hospital empty handed, I shouldn't call him for any kind of handout."

"Oh, Eliana. That's so terrible. I had no idea."

"But when I cut him off—"

"When we *all* cut him off—"

"I didn't know that I was the only one who would remember."

Natalie opened her mouth to speak, before snapping it shut. She looked away, staring at the cross pinned to the front of the room until it blurred into an amorphous, circular shadow that had no end. Even as her pupils dilated intensely, two opal pinpricks undulating with involuntary retraction and expansion, Natalie clutched Eliana's hand in hers. She would not let go.

"He was so angry with me," Eliana began in a small voice, "but his rage might've been a symptom of his accelerating dementia. I never even tried to separate the meanness from the man. It was easier to let him go. In the end, maybe he wasn't a bad person so much as a broken one. What do you think?"

"I think I know what you mean," Natalie said, sighing. "I've thought for so long that my parents were the most selfish people, and they absolutely were at times. But they were addicts, too. I should've been removed from their home. They should've received help."

"Does it bother you? That they'll never know?"

With her eyes now closed, Natalie furrowed her brow. Her head throbbed. Thoughts fuzzed into reflexes, the sparest sensations. "That they'll never know what?"

"The moment we began to forgive them."

Part Four

August

Since ancient times, mariners have relied on the stars to chart their course in open waters. Celestial navigation allowed sailors to mark their position, even out of sight of land. Before modern GPS tools, the United States Air Force referred to the Summer Triangle as the Navigator's Triangle and its airmen used the stellar landmark to find their way.

But the triangle is a notoriously tricky guidepost. In northern skies, the Summer Triangle is most prominent during the summer season. The asterism is less widely known than the North Star and less reliable than circumpolar constellations. It is as unpredictable as the humans it might shepherd. But maybe the weakness is ours. Maybe, we make meaning of stars where there is none.

Sometimes, the darkness refuses to yield any light. It is then that we must make our own.

Chapter 32

"You said you wanted to get a few things?" Eliana prompted.

By the time they turned into the bluestone driveway, it was past two in the morning. Natalie pressed her nose to the car window, taking in the winking dormers, the ivory columns, and the tall oak tree anchoring the front lawn.

Eliana yawned. "Should we go inside? I'm exhausted."

"No."

"What do you mean 'no'? It's the middle of the night. We're sitting in your driveway. We probably have to run the dishwasher or something—"

"For so long, this house was my favorite place in the whole world."

"Do you know what my favorite thing about it is? The bedding in your guest room."

"But I don't live here anymore."

Eliana blinked. "I don't understand – this house is your little fiefdom. It's certainly more yours than anyone else's. It's who you are!"

"It has nothing to do with who I *am*. It only represents who I wanted to *be*."

"Okay. Understood. But it's cold," Eliana pleaded. "And my feet hurt, and I want to take off my bra and brush my teeth and go to sleep."

"It's not my home, Ellie. Not anymore."

"But what about Everett?"

"I do need to get back to Everett. I'm going to pack up our things and bring Aaron back here on Saturday. It might not be home anymore, but it's all we have left. I'll meet with an agent to sell it as soon as possible," she said, exhaling a heavy sigh. "I feel like I failed this place."

"Your tastes might've changed, but your house looks perfect. It always has."

"It's not enough. I thought if I could make the outside beautiful, my insides would eventually get there, too. I thought if I never talked about what happened, the ugliness of the past wouldn't touch me anymore. So, I never said a word to Harris about any of it."

"You mean, the abuse?"

Natalie nodded. "He thinks my parents were bohemians. He knows my dad was cruel to me, but not the details. He knows they owned two homes, but doesn't understand that my dad controlled the finances. He knows I was tutored, but doesn't know how many times the school pestered them with questions. That I almost didn't graduate on time. I have a story for every scar. I've painted a picture for him that never existed. He was so loyal to me, but he had no idea as to what he was defending me from. How can I blame him for wanting to leave a lie?"

After a long pause, Eliana took her friend's hand and squeezed it hard. "I suspected you'd kept silent. But bear in mind, they raised you not to tell anyone. Like everything else, it's not your fault. And it's in the telling – that's how you finally let them go."

"I can't stay here anymore," Natalie whispered. "Not for one more night than I have to."

Tears pooled in Eliana's eyes. "Let's not stay, then. Let's go home."

"Home," Natalie said the word, and her lips puckered. "What's that?"

"It's where you're finally able to tell the truth. Don't worry; it will find you."

As soon as they entered the beach house, Aaron rushed into the foyer to greet them. Wild-haired and bleary-eyed, he burst into Natalie's open arms. She could tell by his blotchy cheeks that he'd been crying, and she buried her face into his soft hair.

"I can't believe Everett's in the hospital," Aaron whispered.

"He's going to be okay," she whispered, dropping a kiss onto his forehead. "I promise. It was only a reaction to his medicine. He's fine now, and he knows how much you love him."

Within her arms, Natalie felt Aaron's shoulders ease. They followed Eliana into the great room. There, they found Allegra draped over the couch, sound asleep with her fiery hair splayed over a pillow. They tiptoed back into the foyer.

"She has the right idea," Eliana whispered. "I think I'm going to take a nap before Josh arrives with the girls."

"Me too," Aaron said, already disappearing up the stairs. They listened as his leaden footsteps halted on the landing. His voice wavered. "Love you, Mom."

"Love you, too," Natalie whispered. She and Eliana stood in silence then, soothed by the familiar collapse of ocean waves outside an open window.

"So, are you going to return Damon's car now?"

In their hours in the car together, Eliana hadn't slept at all. Their conversation had taken the ambling trajectory of their late-night, wine-soaked, collegiate talks. Eliana planned to move back East. Natalie planned to move, somewhere – anywhere. Eliana couldn't wait to begin her new job, while Natalie sought out a beginning that hadn't yet taken shape. They reminisced about mothers and fathers, about the fear of inhabiting those same flaws, about the fear of forgetting what had made them good. They talked about Damon. And in talking about Damon, in the loaded spaces between, they talked about Harris, too. But they never once said his name.

Natalie nodded. "He's waiting for me."

Damon had texted her that he was on the boardwalk. He would meet her there before opening the gallery. He wrote that he walked by the water every morning. As Natalie read the text, still sitting in his parked car and not yet wanting to leave the insulated space where his evergreen scent hung heavily, she realized how little she knew him.

Minutes later, Natalie found Damon sitting on a bench by the dunes. He offered her coffee from The Point. "It's a latte," he said. "Took a guess. I realized I don't know how you take your coffee. If you even like coffee."

"I *love* coffee. Any coffee. Thank you," Natalie said as she exchanged the coffee for his keys. "How'd you get home?"

"My buddy who set up the site came and got me. He loved that you loved it all. Almost seemed a little arrogant. Next thing I know, he'll open an Airbnb."

"I'm relieved that you weren't stuck there," Natalie said, exhaling a sigh.

"I could never be stuck there. I actually go there alone to get unstuck."

"So you tell me."

Damon took a breath. "I'm so happy your son is well."

"Me too. We've never had a scare with him. Aaron was the one who caught every ear infection, every virus, but Everett has always been so easy. We've taken him for granted."

"I can't imagine you taking anyone for granted."

"I have with you."

"Don't say it."

Natalie faltered where she stood, swaying slightly in the wind.

"I promised myself that I'd be kind to you this time."

With a hard swallow, he nodded. Damon took her by the hand and led her toward the ocean. The sea appeared smooth, torn open only when a seagull cracked its silver-toned surface. They walked in lockstep, marking the sand with footprints that would not last.

"I'm taking Aaron home on Saturday."

Damon nodded. "So, you'll go home, and then what? Where will you be?"

Natalie hesitated for mere seconds, long enough for Damon's face to fall. "Not here."

A muscle in his jaw worked. "You won't even consider it? The town is quaint. The schools are good. Once you've lived by the ocean, you won't accept a life anywhere else. And there's something else."

"What's that?"

"Me."

Natalie paused. "Damon, being here with you this summer has been like stepping out of time. It has let me forget and remember and heal. It's been a dream. And like every good dream, I convinced myself it was real. But it wasn't real, and it *is* time for me to wake up now."

"So, I helped you get back on your feet. Now that you're stronger, you're over it."

"You know that's not what I meant. Your life is here, and mine—"

"Your life could be here, too! Look at what you did to Allegra's house — real estate is everything to the local economy! You can't tell me you can't make a life here."

"I wasn't building my portfolio with Allegra's house. It was a form of closure for me."

"Closure," he repeated. "I've always just been a summer fling for you, haven't I?"

Her mouth hung. "I wasn't using you. I've given you my heart twice now—"

"Maybe. Come August though, you sure as hell take it back—"

"Would you move for *me*, Damon?"

His full lips, still lined with yesterday's stubble, fell apart. He looked away from her, gazing over her head to the ocean. She knew what he was seeing. The place where he walked every morning, where he surfed every weekend, where he worked on his boat, where he waited out hurricanes, where he sold his art and lingered with friends and visited with his parents. Damon had always come back. After every milestone, every evacuation, every obligation that had ever taken him away, Damon had always found a way to come home for good.

"It's okay, you know," she whispered, nudging him in the side and nodding toward the ocean, "that you love her more than me."

He kissed the crown of her head. "I *do* love you, Natalie. I always will."

At once, her chest heaved. Natalie could feel sobs rising within, gnashing dark waters buttressed against a dam. She would not cry. When she finally spoke, her voice was hoarse. "Promise me that you'll stop waiting for me. I don't like thinking of you alone."

With a tight nod, he exhaled. "If you'll promise me that you won't settle to feel safe."

Hand in hand, they sat on a bluff of sand. She rested her head on his shoulder. The calm, shimmering water, its obedience belying its capacity for havoc and destruction and degradation, taunted her. It would be so easy to follow him home. To live here. To know this wind-raked peace. To wake up beside him. To be a family. It would be so easy to follow another man to the place where he wanted to build his dream. She'd done it once. She could do it again.

Damon spoke in a whisper, barely audible above the waves' roar: "I don't understand why this can't work. My feelings for you are so clear. It should all be so simple."

"With someone else, it will be," Natalie said. "For me, too, I hope."

The buzzing of her phone roused her. In the darkness, Natalie groaned. Even before her eyelids cracked apart, she knew the day of the week. Gone was this rare, languorous summer, where the days had each bled into each other. It was Saturday. It would be a day of sorting, packing, and mourning the fast-approaching moment when she and Aaron would leave. Her chest ached with the cruel reckoning of it: that Natalie must leave this place that she loved so deeply, but where she could not live.

Her phone buzzed. She saw the time first: 6:37 AM. It took a minute for her eyes to adjust to see the glowing text. Natalie then straight up and clapped a hand across her gaping mouth.

The text was from Birdie Wellington.

I hope it's not too early to reach out, but I felt waiting another minute would be a moment too late. I just finished reading the exquisite piece on your latest project. I have never been so impressed by a design partner, nor so embarrassed by my own impulsiveness. I would be remiss if I did not explain that the demise of our professional relationship had nothing to do with you and everything to do with me not wanting to answer uncomfortable questions. You see, I met a man. A much younger man. My sons assumed that he only wanted me for my wealth. I defended him only to realize that they were right. In any case, I was wrong to let you go as I did. I hope that you will accept my apology. I never hired another designer, and I would love for you to finish what you started. You inspire me to go on, to endure my loss with dignity. May we all be as brave as you are. Well done, Natalie. With this and with everything else.

There was a ringing in her ears. Alone in her bed, Natalie swayed. She fell back into a pillow. Her heart hammered in her chest. With trembling fingertips, Natalie scrolled back through past text messages. Diana Weatherly had texted her at 6:00 AM.

We're published! The piece went live just now on Brickhaven's *homepage and social media platforms and was emailed to our subscribers. I feel privileged that you made yourself so vulnerable with me and with our readers. I hope you like the end result of our talks. Thank you, friend. Let's make good on that lunch date. XX.*

With her stomach churning and her heart in her throat, Natalie clicked on the link. Instantly, a photograph of Allegra's cottage flashed. At the sight of it, Natalie gasped. And then, as the scent of magnolia blossoms enveloped her, she began to read.

A Coastal Escape
By: Diana Weatherby

Here at **Brickhaven**, *we focus on how to best make our homes embody ourselves. We construct, hoping to birth a home befitting our needs. We gut. We flip. We rehabilitate, hoping to breathe new life (our life) into decay. The design process is always aspirational, as a home renovation should reflect not only who we are, but also who we hope to become.*

This is the story of a little house, a 1950s bungalow in Rehoboth Beach. It is also the story of the two women who have each made their mark upon it before they someday bequeath it to someone else.

Natalie Blackburn has enjoyed a professional relationship with our publication for years. She is well-known for her unique capacity to become invisible. Rather than imprint a signature style into her clients' homes, she tailors each house to individuals who reside inside it. "I won't live there," Blackburn says. "A home that isn't mine shouldn't look like me."

Yet long before Blackburn began her business designing clients' homes, this little cottage shaped her. "It was my childhood summer home," she explains. "Most summer homes are intended as an escape, but I've spent most of my life escaping this place."

Blackburn, the daughter of the late Adriftwood lead singer Kip Stone and the late artist Annabel Huxley, suffered verbal and physical abuse within these walls. Blackburn lived in a constant state of hyper-vigilance, the chaos exacerbated by her parents' drug and alcohol abuse. As many children do, Blackburn suffered in silence. Ultimately, Blackburn was drawn to interior design out of her own longing for a stable home. Blackburn now says that "a home is the most important thing. It's the anchor. Without it, we're all so lost."

When Blackburn departed the cottage, she left for good. She never intended to return, attempting instead to bury her trauma and move on with her life.

It was at this point in our interview that celebrated model Allegra (née Jane Riley) cut through the heaviness of these dark memories by reminding Blackburn of how they met. Both women laughed at the recollection. Blackburn had finally worked up the courage to return to the little cottage, only to be shot down on the spot by Allegra. "Because I thought she was a particularly aggressive paparazzi – even though she'd brought her kids," Allegra says.

Allegra's caution is understandable, considering the extent to which her personal life has been chronicled by the tabloid media. We have followed her whirlwind courtship with a European count, her extravagant marriage, and her sudden divorce. Allegra reports that, in this case, fact has been far more demoralizing than fiction.

As Allegra endeavored to set the record straight for the first time, she became emotional in detailing the continued psychological abuse by her ex-husband. "He's always threatening me," Allegra says. "He throws things at me. He's hired photographers to capture damaging images. He's destroyed my reputation. He doesn't want me dating, having friends, or even working."

However, Etienne's most aggressive action to date has been "kidnapping my children, snatching them without my consent, and taking them to Luxembourg," Allegra reports. Allegra has never publicly defended herself for fear of losing her children completely. However, a new love and a new home have given her new courage. Allegra has applied through The Hague Convention to have her children returned. Such legal actions move notoriously slowly, but Allegra appears energized with a sentiment she had once forgotten: hope.

Ironically, where the little cottage was once a prison, it is now a sanctuary.

Upon realizing the turmoil that Allegra and her children had endured, Blackburn took on the project to renovate her childhood home pro bono. Her initial inclination was "to gut the whole thing," Blackburn says with laughter. "Soup to nuts, I wanted a clean start." However, when budgetary constraints altered her initial plans, Blackburn soon realized that Allegra loved the historic character of the house. "The breakfast areas, the large fireplace, and the screened-in porch have always been a comfort to me. I love its nooks and crannies," Allegra says.

Slowly, in seeing the little cottage through new eyes, Blackburn began to love it, too.

While Allegra preserved the cottage's structural integrity, she extended the outdoor living space by transforming the screened-in porch into an insulated sunroom and constructing a pergola with the patio. Blackburn's design touches reflect Allegra's eclectic taste. Hand-painted chinoiserie wallpaper coats the powder room; Turkish tiles color the kitchen; Scottish slate floors punctuate the first level. Such choices all herald Allegra's rich life experience.

But when Blackburn said that she likes her homes "to surprise," in this case, she meant literally. Because Allegra is a talented photographer, Blackburn converted her mother's former attic studio into a dark room. Blackburn revealed her surprise during our interview. Reader, Allegra wept at this unexpected gift. When she had gathered herself, Allegra spoke with awe: "It means more to me than I can say. This isn't just a space for me to work – it's the beginning of a new life. I feel so empowered here."

Both women report that this singular home renovation has changed their perspectives. And in keeping with this season of transformation, Allegra and Blackburn hope to empower other survivors to escape untenable situations and rebuild their lives. In September, Allegra will showcase her work in conjunction with an unprecedented exhibit of never-before-seen Annabel Huxley art at the Backlit Gallery in Rehoboth. A portion of the proceeds will go to domestic abuse shelters in the Delmarva region.

Allegra is adamant that the little beach cottage does not belong to her alone. She insists that Blackburn will always be welcome, even going so far as to keep Blackburn's childhood growth chart intact. With eyes that have graced countless magazine pictorials, Allegra now looks to the future: "I think of the house now as a beacon. It's a torch I'll keep burning until I can pass it on to someone else." For Blackburn, too, the project has been an act of stewardship: "It's a visual reminder that we can evolve. The house will outlast us, but the love within will remain."

Because sometimes, in building our home, we build a legacy.

Chapter 33

When Natalie walked into the great room at 7 AM, she blinked to find everyone wide awake. Lola and Silvia flanked Aaron on the couch, watching a movie. Josh perused *The Washington Post* at the island. She could see Eliana reading a book on the deck.

"Looks like I slept in," Natalie said.

"Lola woke me up," Aaron muttered, while Lola snorted with laughter.

"Still jet-lagged," Josh offered.

"Mommy making pancakes," Silvia said.

"But we got to wait for *you*," Lola said, glowering.

Natalie smiled halfway. "I'll go talk to your mom, then."

As she opened the sliding door, the ringing in her ears intensified. She padded outside, folding her arms across her chest.

"I guess Lola lit a fire under us both to get those pancakes started, huh?" Eliana asked.

"It's out," Natalie breathed.

"The article? Congratulations! Wait. Are you okay? You look pale."

"I'm fine. I'm going for a run."

Eliana arched a brow, eyeing Natalie's bare feet and loungewear. "Okay."

"Don't wait on the pancakes for me. I – I need a minute."

"Understood," Eliana said quietly. "For what it's worth, I'm proud of you."

With a curt nod, Natalie trotted down the stairs.

Biting her lower lip, Eliana watched Natalie's retreating form. Damp air swaddled the water's edge in a dense fog. A milky sky blanketed the ocean. As Eliana watched her friend, a pale silhouette in her tunic sweater and leggings, she saw the same slight girl staring out to sea.

Eliana took a deep breath and reached for her phone.

"Hello?" Harris asked, that one word saturated with alarm.

"Did I wake you?"

"No. Is something wrong?"

"Our girl is having a big day today, and you should know about it," Eliana said, before pausing to better hear the unexpected background noise. "Wait. What are you doing?"

In the milky light, Allegra and Andy sat in his idling car on Main Street. A steamy latte reddened her palm, but Allegra made no move to drink it. From the corner of her eye, she watched him read on his phone. Allegra looked away from him, sighed loudly, and forced herself to people-watch. Her eyes trailed a young family, pausing with them when they knelt to offer a pacifier to their toddler; and then, following a man who walked briskly away toward the boardwalk; and then, inching behind an elderly woman eating a pastry; and then—

"It's stunning."

Her breath hitched. "You really think so? I'm sure I'll be hearing from Etienne shortly, but I wanted to be strong. And my new attorney – thank you for Amy, by the way – gave me the green light to open up. I've never given an interview like this. It was exhilarating. And if we can help even one person rise above the fear of leaving, maybe this pain will have been worth it—"

"I love you."

Her jaw went slack. "What?"

"I love you, Allegra, née Jane Riley."

She said nothing, staying silent until more seconds collected into a minute.

"Andy. We haven't known each other for very long, and—"

He took her face in his hands. "And I've been looking for you my whole life, Allegra. I just didn't know your name. Either of them. Whenever I don't think I can love you any more than I do, there's a new day."

"A new day," she breathed.

The edges of his eyes crinkled as he bent his head to kiss her. She felt the now familiar euphoria of being wrapped up in his arms, his mouth working over hers, his warm hands imprinting upon her skin. She pulled away, breathless. That bit had become familiar, too.

"Believe me yet?" Andy asked, wiggling his eyebrows.

"I do, Andy," she whispered. "But make your case, anyway. One. More. Time."

Josh was descending the stairs when he caught sight of the car pulling into the driveway. He walked to the window and pursed his lips. Outside, Harris parked the car.

"Pancakes are ready!" Eliana called out as she walked into the foyer. "There's a fresh pot of coffee ready too and—"

Josh nodded toward the window. "Was Nat expecting him?"

"Not exactly."

"She doesn't like to be surprised."

"It wasn't my idea. I called him, and he was already on his way."

"*You* called *him*?" he asked, but she had already touched his arm, quieting him.

"Yes, and I'm not sure yet if I'm happy he's here," she murmured.

"Maybe we don't have to be happy to see him. Maybe we just have to let him in."

"You're sure you don't want any pancakes, Dad?" Aaron asked, his mouth full. He had wolfed down a stack of pancakes standing next to Harris, their shoulders touching.

Harris shook his head. "I'm all set with coffee for now. Just happy to be with my boys," he said, his voice cracking.

"Maybe when you're done, we could play some basketball. It's still my favorite sport, you know," Aaron said, gazing at Harris from the corner of his eye. "I'm sorry for what I said."

"And I'm sorry for not paying more attention. For not being here when you needed me."

Josh cleared his throat. "Aaron, let the man drink his coffee. He's running on fumes. What time did you leave?"

"Everett woke up at four and wanted his mom, so I decided to bring him to her."

"You didn't want to wait until after breakfast?" Josh asked.

"I've waited too long as it is," Harris said evenly, meeting his eye.

"Bagels! Coffee! Come and get it!"

"My brother and his need to make an entrance," Eliana muttered.

After rounding the corner, Andy came to an immediate halt. His eyes narrowed.

"What's *he* doing here?" Andy asked.

Allegra's eyes darted between Andy and Harris. When she recognized a charge in the air, she took the girls by the hands. "Kiddos, there are donuts in the car! Who wants to race me for them? Winner gets to eat two!"

Immediately, all four kids sprinted out the front door. The grown-ups listened, waiting, until the door snapped shut.

"How many breakfast items can we possibly consume? Am I right?" Josh asked, laughing too loudly. No one spoke.

"You selfish, sad, cliché of a bastard," Andy seethed.

Harris rolled his eyes. "You're so excited to insult me that you can't pick just one, huh?"

Andy stepped toward him. Harris set his coffee down.

"That girl is like my sister," Andy said, enunciating every word.

"That *girl* is my *wife*," Harris retorted, bunching his fists together.

"Exactly."

In pieces of seconds, time now as fractured as confetti, Andy's closed fist connected with Harris's right eye. Harris yelped before crashing backward to the floor.

"Andy!" Eliana screamed, rushing to Harris's side. "What is the *matter* with you?"

"Please," Andy said, as he breathlessly shook out his hand. "That prick has had it coming for years. There's a line of people waiting to thank me. Holy hell, that hurt, though."

"Hold on, Harris!" Josh yelled. Burrowing into the freezer, Josh cursed under his breath. "We're not prepared for this. No one keeps frozen vegetables on vacation."

"Andy, is your thumb broken? It looks limp," Eliana said.

"An ice pack would be nice," Andy muttered.

Harris smirked. "Wouldn't surprise me at all if you broke your hand throwing your first punch."

"Who said it was my first punch?" Andy asked.

"Please, we both know it was. Look at you writhing in pain over there."

"Says the guy on the goddamned floor," Andy said. "Regardless, we all know it wasn't your first time on the receiving end. You with your very pretty, very punchable face."

"You really think I'm pretty?" Harris asked, raising his good eyebrow. "Nope. Can't say that it's ever come up."

"Really?" Josh asked as he ducked to check Harris's reddening eye.

"You sound surprised," Harris said flatly.

"You *are* a lobbyist," Josh said, his hands splayed.

"You're all missing the point!" Eliana shouted. "Andy, you have no right to hit him – regardless of what he did! Harris came here on his own to talk to Natalie. We should be supporting him, not castigating him. They're always going to be in each other's lives and, God willing, so will we. You're acting like Dad right now. The ultimate final arbiter. Except for one thing: Dad never hit anyone."

"Are you ready for us?" Allegra called.

"Not a chance! Can you stall?" Eliana responded.

"Sure thing!" Allegra yelled back.

As soon as the door closed, Eliana continued, "And Harris, you're in no position to taunt anyone. You hurt someone we love deeply, and we've spent the summer holding your family together while you weren't here. We're all still reeling from your bad choices," she said, and then she looked pointedly at both men. "If you're both old enough to run for president, you're old enough to know better than this."

Harris waved away the ice pack that Josh held out to him. "I'm going to find my wife."

In leaving them, Harris tried to slam the sliding door, but it bounced back open with momentum. He cursed loudly and, with painstaking control, closed the door behind him.

Andy sighed. "Maybe I did go too far," he allowed, before palming the discarded ice pack and holding it against his hand.

Josh and Eliana locked eyes.

"What do you think?" Josh asked.

Eliana stared out the kitchen window. The fog functioned as erasure, disappearing the climactic point where the ocean ascended to land. Eliana couldn't tell if a storm was circling close or if the worst was already over. But she had the eerie sense of having been here before.

"I think that he came."

Battered by the wind, Natalie stood alone, shivering just beyond the water's reach. Her bare feet sank into sand like pudding. Her arms coiled tightly around her chest. It was the place that she used to run to as a teenager: as far away from home as she could get, with the ocean's lip delineating the limits of her freedom. It hadn't been an escape, so much as a reminder of the contours of her prison.

Natalie closed her eyes. She couldn't believe she was still here, anchored to this same sliver of sand that would never fully belong to land or sea. This place marked the transition point. The place where the ocean fired its rage, where it grew greedy for more. She wriggled her feet in the cold sand, sinking deeper with each movement.

"'Verbal and physical abuse'?!"

Her neck snapped as she shot a look over her shoulder. Her mouth dropped open.

"'A constant state of hyper-vigilance'?!"

Harris reached her, his pristine boat shoes swallowed by rippling waves. She raised her hand to touch his face, his swollen wound a muted scream to her. But he stood beyond an arm's breadth away; they were so separated. She dropped her arm to her side.

"What happened to your face?"

"Andy happened. It's fine – we all know I deserved it," Harris said, and then he shook his head. "How could you not have told me?"

"You read the article."

"Yes, I read the article. My God, Natalie. How could you not have told me?"

"Because I didn't tell anyone."

"Do the rest of them know?" he asked, waving his arm back toward the house.

"Only Eliana, though I didn't say much. We rarely talked about it. I assumed that she'd told Josh and Andy, but I didn't confirm any of it until, well, until today."

He pushed a fist through his hair. "Those white marks on the small of your neck?"

"Cigarette burns."

"The hard knot at the back of your elbow?"

She bit her lower lip. "Thrown down the stairs."

"The scar under your chin?" he asked, his voice trembling.

"Yes, those were all him, but let's not do this. Please."

"I can't believe I didn't know."

Her eyes shrunk to slits. "Are you really going to act like *I* betrayed *you*?"

"No. But still," Harris said. "It always felt like you were standing behind a veil. Like there was some layer of skin I couldn't touch. I never felt *let in*. There was some shadowy, threatening thing. And now, after all these years together, it has a face. *He* has a face."

Natalie suddenly thought of Aaron. He hadn't told her his truth on his own, but when she had asked, he had told her everything. He had let her in. Remembering, her face softened.

"I didn't tell you," she began, her whisper faint and halting, "because I cared what you thought more than anyone."

"Did you honestly believe I would think less of you?" Harris asked incredulously.

"I – I thought it would taint things. Make everything unclean. I wanted to be normal."

"Normal," Harris whispered, staring beyond her head at the ocean. She watched his eyes dart, skimming over whitecaps and alighting on frothing, tumbling waves. "You know, I always thought I was so square next to your old man."

"What?"

"I knew he'd been a distant, mean father. I knew he wasn't around, but I thought that's all it was. When random fans would ask you about him, when journalists would call, you always said no. While I respected that, I always thought that your life with him was way more exciting than ours. I thought you didn't want to make me feel insecure by remembering."

"Harris, listen to me: what I love most of all is that you are *nothing* like him."

"What you love ..." he whispered. "I suppose I can believe that now."

She raised her face to the sky, jutting her chin. "Everyone looked at him as a god. To me, it felt like the whole world would take his side. And because his music lives on forever, he always seems to be there. So, I ignored him to feel free."

"I understand, Nat. I just wish I'd known. I would've done everything differently. I've made such a mess of things, haven't I?" Harris asked a question wrapped in a sigh, pinching the bridge of his nose. "You should know that I ended it with Sophia."

Her eyes widened, a slight, bird-wing flickering of her eyelid, and then nothing. She pressed her lips together, siphoning off all the muddled sounds she couldn't form into words.

"And there's something else I need to tell you."

Natalie blinked fast against the relentless wind. "Okay."

"I never wanted the pandemic to end."

"What?"

"Obviously, it was horrific – an immeasurable loss of life and economic insecurity and political upheaval and food scarcity—"

"And I almost lost my business!"

"I know, *I know*, but I played basketball with Aaron after every single day. I built LEGO villages with Everett. I loved every colleague's kid that interrupted every interminable Zoom call. And you were as beautiful as I've ever seen you: with no make-up and your curly hair. Painting those abstract watercolors for hours. It was *heaven* to me. Money was tight, and I was scared for our health, but I wanted to exist right there, as we were, forever. With my tribe."

"I don't understand. You loved us so much that you left us?"

Harris sighed. "I couldn't do the hard thing. I couldn't open up the way you did in that article. I told myself I was forcing a change with the affair, but I was hiding out."

"So, what would you have told me if you had been honest?"

"I would've said I was terrified," Harris said, exhaling. "I would've said I didn't ever want to go back to normal – to a job I hated, to a house we couldn't afford without my job. I hated missing dinner, missing too many moments with the kids. I would've told you that I loved you, but that I was miserable. I wish I'd told you."

"Me too," she whispered.

Harris cleared his throat. "I hurt you, and I used her. I was treading water. Numbing the pain with her. Whatever it was with her was so broken that it had an addictive quality. I hated it even as I returned to it. I realize I'm not making any sense."

"Actually, that part makes perfect sense to me," she murmured. "I do know addicts."

He shot a glance at her, his eyes sable and bloodshot. Something within her unspooled at the sight of them. She dug her heels deeper into the sand, rocking away from him.

"Natalie," he said, drawing out her name in a sigh. "I am *so* sorry. It was the mistake of my life. I would give anything to go back in time."

"But then I might never have known how you really feel," Natalie whispered. "Is that why you came here – to finally tell me?"

"I came because you're here. I'd follow you anywhere—"

"Mommy!" Everett shouted, his voice echoing within the fog. In lockstep, they both turned toward the house. Everett raced toward them; his arms outstretched. At the sight of his nubby-toothed grin, Natalie and Harris smiled.

Behind him, everyone stood on the deck. Josh hugged Aaron

to his hip. Allegra stood with her head resting against Andy's chest. Eliana held both of her girls to her, watching them.

As always, their audience remained right there. With them.

Upon reaching his parents, Everett grabbed their hands. He took them with him. Everett then crashed into the water, reveling in the ocean's dark underbelly, studded with foaming bubbles. He shrieked with laughter. It was then that sunlight pierced through the threadbare cloud cover, goading them all with come-hither patches of bright, blue sky.

Natalie could hardly believe it: her boy had finally gotten wet. He soon led Harris and Natalie farther out until they were knee-deep in the ocean alongside him. Everett writhed against the constraints of their hands, wanting to hold them close even as he wanted to break free. Wanting to stay. Wanting to float away. Wanting to be on his own. Wanting their union.

And suddenly it was all so simple. It was all so clear.

Epilogue: Christmas

"Summer Stars"
Lyrics and Melody by Kip Stone

I look for stars that left for southern skies,
I itch for long days and for short goodbyes,
To sing my baby one last lullaby,
And to get out on the road.

I see Orion shining from afar,
Polaris and the promise of a Christmas star,
Waiting on the solstice night, so long and dark,
And I'll cast down my heavy load.

I had a family, but I chose a tribe,
Could've dreamed, but I chose to survive,
Now I'm drowning while I'm still alive,
I cling to my paper abode.

Regrets, how they twinkle when night casts its pall,
Promises, now merely words that I just can't recall,
Could've had it all; now see me fly and fall —

Ignore the North Star; find three points of light,
Might lose your way, but how they glow so bright,

May the summer season cast your wings to flight,
And come autumn, reap what you have sown,
Never home, not 'til you're all alone.

As the song's last haunting chords faded to dead air, Aaron whistled. The car circled Silver Lake, and Natalie turned off the music.

"I don't understand, Mom. He wanted to leave you?"

Natalie sighed. "He would start touring again after the holidays, but he loved the summer festival circuit best. He visited us a lot at the cottage in the summer, though."

"Not sure about this one. I like his other songs better. Kinda seems like a jerk."

Beside her, Harris took her hand. He eased the car to a stop. As he stroked her fingertips, Natalie pressed her nose to the window and watched the falling snow.

"It's a warning to the rest of us," Harris said, kissing her knuckles. "It's about wanting to be a different kind of person. Wanting to be a better man."

Natalie squeezed his hand. Harris killed the engine and opened the backdoor to attend to a sleeping Everett. Natalie moved slowly. Even as she shrunk deeper into her coat, ducking away from the wind's raw assault, Natalie grinned at the sight of snow laying on the sand. She had never known the beach in winter. With a loose smile, Natalie stared at the roaring, unending blackness where she knew the ocean to be.

"Hello, old friend," Natalie whispered.

"You ready, Milady?" Harris asked, having roused Everett.

"Since August."

With that, Natalie shot past them all, racing up the steps to the house for the chance to ring the doorbell. A spotted beagle nipped at her heels. Behind them, she could hear Aaron and Everett's protests. When Eliana opened the door, the dog tore into the house.

"Oh, my goodness, a puppy!" Eliana squealed. "I didn't

think you would actually do it!"

"He failed his obedience class, isn't housebroken at all, and we call him Cuddles—"

"But he doesn't cuddle. He nips," Everett finished.

"Worst dog in the world," Aaron muttered, smiling.

"Well, you know how much I love a bad decision," Eliana said, wiggling her eyebrows, before bending low to meet Everett's eye. "I'm so sorry we missed your birthday, Everett. There are presents inside."

"Presents?" Aaron asked. "As in plural?"

"Depends on if you've completed that sketch I commissioned for the new house?"

Aaron flushed. "Almost finished."

"Well then, check the kitchen table. The girls are waiting for you two."

As they raced inside, high-pitched laughter followed their pounding footsteps. Natalie smiled. "Looks like they're all set to pick up right where they left off."

"They're not the only ones," Eliana said. She then offered a smile beyond Natalie to the man filling the open doorway. "Harris, it's good to see you. Happy to see that you've healed."

"Thanks. Have you loaded up on frozen veggies since last time?"

"The freezer is packed."

"Are you going to invite me in?"

"Depends. Are you going to behave?" Eliana asked.

Harris grinned. "Not a chance."

"Well, at least you're in good company," Eliana said, stepping to the side. "Josh has a bourbon on ice waiting for you. It's a peace offering. Don't waste it."

When he eased past her, Harris squeezed Eliana's shoulder. He leaned in, whispering *sotto voce* behind his gloved hand. "I'm going to earn back my hug from you yet."

"We'll see about that," Eliana said, nudging him.

"You two," Natalie murmured as she chuckled and pulled

the door closed. "Let me look at you! It's been forever."

"It's funny how a season can feel like a lifetime."

"I almost flew to Mexico City when you told me," Natalie whispered, embracing her tightly. "I thought it would be too early to tell, but, lady, I can *tell*. You're glowing."

"Only because I finally stopped vomiting."

"That bad, huh?"

"Seems to be my trademark," Eliana said, sighing. She linked arms with Natalie then, and together they walked toward the rising voices, the music, the laughter. Before they walked into the great room, Eliana stopped and lowered her voice. "Did I tell you how I found out?"

"The mole sauce you thought was bad? The pregnancy test?"

Eliana shook her head. "I had a dream. I was pushing the baby in a stroller through Central Park, trailing after the girls, yelling at them to slow down. But I was yelling at them in *Spanish*! It's the only language I know but had never dreamt in."

"Who would've thought that would be the part that would make you happiest?"

"There's more: my *abuela* was walking with me. And when I fixed his blanket, I called him *nene*, and he smiled at us. She and I both held her rosary."

"That's so beautiful and – *Him*?"

Eliana nodded, grinning. "Confirmed by a blood test last week."

"Him," Natalie whispered as she embraced Eliana again.

"Him," Eliana said. "And while he's a complete surprise, I feel like we've been expecting him. I feel like we're not alone in this, and all will be well."

"Yes, all will be well. Just think: next summer, he'll be here, too. Part of our tribe."

Under the watchful eye of Lola, Aaron leafed through a book of Mexican folk art. Silvia and Everett danced his marionettes, all while noshing on tortillas and guacamole. In the kitchen, Harris took another sip of bourbon and visibly relaxed as the amber warmth spilled within him. He tossed a Brie tartlet into his mouth.

"Good idea. Make sure you load up on appetizers because my brother is running late," Eliana grumbled.

"Doesn't matter," Josh said, pressing a kiss to her cheek. "The tamales that Eliana's prepped all day will be well worth the wait."

Eliana smiled. "My *abuela*'s recipe."

"I love that you're finally getting the chance to know her," Natalie said, her eyes shining. "Please help us remember to call Andres by his real name."

"Especially me. I've been trying like hell to get back into his good graces," Harris said.

"Andy is his real name, too," Eliana said. "He just wants to be open about who actually is, rather than who my father intended him to be. So, he updated his LinkedIn. As one does."

Natalie shook her head. "All these years, and I never thought to ask more questions."

"You and me both," Josh said, meeting her eye with a wink. "But we can't know what people won't share."

"Touché," Natalie murmured, winking right back.

"Word on the street is that you're making an appearance at an Adriftwood concert?"

Natalie reddened. "They're trotting me out like a prize pony, but I've decided not to be in denial anymore. For better or worse, my dad gave my life a soundtrack. His music was the best part of him. And you were right, it's my loss to ignore his gift."

"*You* were the best part of him," Eliana said. "We're so proud of you for trying so hard to heal."

As Lola walked by, Harris scooped her up in his arms, tickling her until she cackled. When he released her, she leaped out of his reach. "She's too quick for me," Harris said, laughing.

"You seem happier," Josh said, smiling. "Looks like the new gig is agreeing with you."

"Let's just say that the Chesapeake Bay is the best client I've ever had," Harris said. "It never disagrees with my strategy. It presents inimitably well."

Josh shook his head. "When Eliana said that you'd jumped ship for a non-profit and the whole family would be moving to the other side of the bridge, I took to my bed. Needed my smelling salts."

"This from the man who finally bucked his Peter Pan syndrome," Harris said. "When Nat said you were making a movie in Mexico, I assumed that a superhero needed to rescue the world from an evil meteorite—"

"Well, that's not even believable. Not sure that I would try to *personify* space matter—"

"Yet, here you are, out of Neverland," Harris's voice boomed, his arms gesticulating widely. "And for your documentary debut, you're venerating some of your favorite filmmakers. You remind me of who you used to be. You've come home, my man."

"He's not the only one," Natalie said, grinning.

"Yes, and we're proud of you both," Harris said as he poured himself more bourbon. "Just shocked that you two actually pulled the trigger. Coming back east. Buying a second place at the beach."

"We're only surprised because you've been so ... itinerant," Natalie added.

Josh shrugged, his mouth full of salsa and tortillas. "It's where we belong."

"We were ready to plant some roots," Eliana added.

Natalie smiled. "And how did you know this was the place to come home to?"

"Because our people are here," Eliana said, while Lola and Silvia, shrieking with laughter, tumbled from their pyramid position on top of Aaron's back. Everett whistled with the toy train encircling the tree. Cuddles bounded around the twinkling locomotive, growling and wagging his tail. Watching them, Eliana's eyes misted over.

Josh nodded, before offering helpfully: "She means you guys. You got that, right?"

In the dining room, Natalie finished pouring ice water into crystal glasses. Everett positioned homemade place cards at each place setting. Across the table, Eliana lit candles and poked at a table-scape filled with winterberry. Her stomach growled aloud.

Natalie pouted sympathetically at her. "I'm sure they'll be here soon."

As if on cue, the front door opened with a bang. They heard Andy's unmistakable baritone-chuckling, his feet squeaking as he slid on the wet floor. They heard the lilt of the girls' voices, their quick footsteps scampering to greet him.

"We're here!" Andy called out, his voice echoing. "We know we're late for this Christmas Eve-eve event, but we come bearing dessert! Make way, minions."

As Eliana locked her hands to her hips, Natalie followed her into the front hall.

"You were supposed to be here two hours ago, and it's slick out there, and you know your pregnant sister is famished—"

With a sharp gasp, Eliana stopped short. Natalie gaped. In the front hall, Delphine and Jules were exchanging fast hugs with Aaron and the little ones. Amidst the raucous noise, they sought out Allegra, their brows raised. Beside a glowing, flocked tree, Allegra shrugged.

"What have you got there?" Josh asked while he meandered into the room. He paused, his brow furrowing. "Looks like we need to add more place settings."

"Hi there," Harris said, as he knelt and extended a hand to Delphine. "I'm Harris, Aaron and Everett's daddy. It's nice to meet you."

Delphine blushed. "Hello. I'm called Delphine. This is my brother, Jules."

Harris nodded to Jules. "You'll have to excuse our hosts. They're hangry. Is there a French word for hangry?"

"Yes. It's 'cigarette,'" Eliana muttered.

With a grin pinned to her face, Allegra circled the towering Christmas tree to stand with Eliana and Natalie. She spoke from behind her hand: "Sorry we're late. It took a certain someone a while to choose a dress. I think Delphine may have her first crush."

"Aw," Natalie said. They looked over at Aaron. He showed Jules his new basketball while Delphine bent close to hear them. "My lucky, oblivious boy."

"Red velvet Smith Island cake for dessert," Andy said.

With a low whistle, Josh clapped Andy on the shoulder. "You're forgiven for taking your sweet time," he said before disappearing into the kitchen with the bag.

With a sheepish grin, Andy handed Harris a bottle of Lagavulin. "Merry Christmas, Harris. Vintage Scotch. Extra Peaty."

"Thanks for this, Andy – Andres," Harris said.

"I'm still Andy for short, but I appreciate the effort. We're good," Andy said. "Your eye – you look better."

Harris offered a wry smile. "You think I'm still pretty?"

Andy grinned. "You're still something, all right."

"Oh, for God's sake, apologize to him, Andy," Eliana demanded.

"But," Andy began, his bewildered eyes stretched wide, "that's what the Scotch is for."

"Apology accepted," Harris said. "Looks like the earth's tilted further on its axis and you've settled down, Andy?"

Andy made a face. "I'm set to sit for the Delaware bar this winter."

"No kidding," Harris said, raising his brow. "Tell you what: after you pass, I'll pour you some of my fancy Scotch, but then you have to give the bottle back."

"I can't believe you're leaving the city," Natalie murmured, striding forward to embrace him. "I'm so proud of you."

"Well, after her success with her photography exhibit this fall, I have no choice but to come to Allegra," Andy said with a wink. "She's my retirement plan."

Allegra frowned. "I'm a newbie small business owner. You might want to diversify."

"I'm so happy for you both," Eliana said, embracing Andy tightly. "And for me – finally surrounded by sisters, rather than this dud."

"Ellie Jelly, can you believe it? You and me: settling down close enough to his retirement home to force a relationship," Andy said as he nudged her. "Dad would hate it."

"I know," she whispered, her eyes shining. "Isn't it the best?"

After plating her tamales, Eliana joined her friends in the dining room, surveying the long table replete with hot, fragrant platters.

"I think that's everything," she said.

"Well, if we're finally ready, we should round up the troops," Natalie said.

Allegra cleared her throat. "Should we take a moment before eating?"

"I don't really think – oh! Yes. Natalie, let's go up to my closet for a minute."

Natalie blinked. "Your closet? Now?"

"Only for a minute," Eliana said, as she grasped Natalie by the arm.

Moving quickly, they climbed one of the stairwells, trailing its berry-studded garland up the stairs. Out of earshot of the others, Natalie caught Allegra's eye.

"How are the kids here? I thought Etienne had called dibs on Christmas."

Allegra shrugged, smiling. "After our article came out, his family came down hard on him. To them, *any* press is bad press. Véronique said he seemed panicked. A week ago, Etienne called out of the blue and offered me Christmas."

"That's amazing! But you're still pursuing The Hague action?" Natalie asked.

"Absolutely," Allegra said. "My concerns haven't changed, but I wouldn't mind a better dialogue in the interim. Also, I love the idea that I've made him squirm."

"Sounds like he's twitching," Eliana said, wiggling her eyebrows.

Natalie smiled. "You must be over the moon—"

With a flick of the wrist, Eliana opened the door to her closet. There, anchoring its wall, was a painting that Natalie hadn't realized she'd put to memory.

"Assateague," she breathed.

Eliana and Allegra exchanged a loaded glance.

"Nat, we're sorry to surprise you with this tonight," Eliana said. "With you all staying with us, though, I didn't want you to wander in here and be ... surprised."

"How is this here?" Natalie asked, her voice hoarse and distant to her own ears.

"Damon sent it to my house this week," Allegra said. "I never met him because – well, remember how he had his friend from art school handle the exhibit?"

Natalie's cheeks reddened. How could she forget accepting kind words on her mother's behalf and answering press questions and posing for pictures with Allegra, all the while scanning the room for one man who never came? Harris, who by then knew the most crucial details about her summer with Damon, had held her hand with a closed fist. But his strong grip had been unnecessary, as Damon had seemingly finally decided to let her go.

Allegra continued. "The note congratulated us on the exhibit and said the painting was for you. It's too big for my little house, so—"

"We found a place for it here," Eliana finished. She paused. "Have you spoken to him?"

"No. We both agreed to move on."

Allegra sighed. "We weren't sure what to do. We didn't want to disrupt your life."

"We know that you made the best choice for yourself and for your family," Eliana said firmly, resting her hand on the small of Natalie's back.

"I made the only choice I had. I was so overcome with nostalgia that I forgot the reason we didn't work years ago: I wanted to build a life elsewhere, while Damon wanted to stay. Harris is the one man who would follow me home."

"Oh, Natalie," Eliana whispered, her voice falling away.

Natalie cleared her throat. "When we were in Tennessee, we spent a day with the boys scouting bald eagles. They're the most amazing creatures. When they mate, they trust-fall together out of the sky. Clinging to each other. Hurtling towards the earth. They pull apart right at the last second, coming as close as they can to annihilation together. After that, they're one. I guess it took us almost losing everything to realize we had to save it."

At once, they both wrapped their arms around her. They held her close, drawing out the moment as long as it would last, letting it breathe. In time, Eliana kissed her cheek.

"We'll start dinner while it's warm," she whispered. "Come down when you're ready."

"Take as long as you need," Allegra said softly.

With her arms locked against her chest, Natalie's breath hitched as the door closed. Her eyes blurred at the 40x50-inch behemoth, a riot of color and texture. Her mother would've loved to splatter paint on a canvas this size, but her father thought they took up too much space. He'd kept her small that way, even as his own silken voice bellowed, penetrating every room.

Her upper lip curled, remembering. Her eyes closed, trying again to forgive.

She opened her eyes once more. It was summer, Natalie could see that now. Golden color saturated the russet-toned marshland, gilding dunes spiked with grasses. Splotches of pink and lavender recalled the scrappy island flowers. Early-hour sunset tones streaked the waves, tinting everything in rose-gold lashes of color. In the fast twitches of the painter's palette knife, she could hear her father's music. In the painter's whimsical, circular strokes, in its sky replete with gradient color, she could see her mother's hand. They would have loved the painting, just as Natalie loved it now.

And then, there was him. Maybe, there would always be him.

Natalie had only ever been to Assateague with him, had only ever known its landscape in the long, hot days of summer. When she closed her eyes now, she could smell his skin. She could remember his mouth, his touch, his heat. She swayed where she stood, overcome with vertigo from pondering how close she'd come to making a different choice. Her world would be a foreign country – with its own language, its own private customs – had she chosen him. She almost couldn't imagine it. Maybe her life would always be a series of close calls, of choices upon choices tumbling like waves, each upon the other, a vast ocean of almost.

But then, the seasons had changed.

As if to convince herself of this, Natalie stepped away from the painting, left the closet, and crossed the master bedroom. She unlocked the doors to the balcony, opening them wide. Frigid air slapped at her skin, grazing her skin in tiny, serrated cuts. It hurt to breathe while the cold wind whirled and whistled around her. Clumps of snow gathered in the dunes, as countless crystalline snowflakes disappeared into the sand. Distant tide pools shone like mirrors, frozen to ice. The ocean roared and howled, bucking like a feral animal. Natalie shivered. The beach was as barren, as whittled to the bone, as she'd ever seen it. Yet she saw herself breathing easily, exhaling rhythmic white clouds in the frigid air.

For the first time in her life, Natalie didn't feel split in two. She didn't need to run to the horizon line. There was no one to escape. There was nothing left to flee. She wasn't dissociating any longer, but was solidly *right here, right now*. She could feel herself finally taking up this space where her feet were planted. She was staying put, here in this home that didn't belong to her, here with these people whom she'd made her family.

Ice-cold wind raked over her face. The swollen moon hung heavily, illuminating a path to the vast, black water. As Natalie pulled a deep inhale of wintry air, she stilled. She tilted her head toward music rising from a distant room like a fire's potent, primal smoke:

> *Yellow dress, may I have this dance?*
> *Take my hand, let me take just one more chance,*
> *Your toes riding on mine,*
> *Music sent from the divine,*
> *Would you stay a while, in my arms?*

Her heart hammering, Natalie took long strides out of the darkness. She moved toward the warmth, back toward the twinkling lights, the rich laughter, and his voice.

> *Yellow dress, let me be the one to lead,*
> *Let me in, let me sweep you off your feet,*

With sweaty palms, Natalie lifted her tartan skirt and descended the winding staircase.

I love to see you twirl,
Can't see beyond my girl,

At the landing, Natalie stopped short. She could hear the clatter of cutlery and winsome chatter, while Adriftwood's melody swelled through the speakers and guided his voice toward the bridge, but she barely noticed the cacophony. Her eyes instead fixed on Harris, standing at the foot of the stairs. He had been waiting for her. Harris smiled, held out a hand to her, and mouthed the next line of her father's song:

Won't you stay a while, in my arms?

Her feet moved slowly, taking time in their descent. Her eyes locked on his. She took a breath right as her father inhaled, the song's soft percussion matching her own heartbeat. As the acoustic guitar stitched chords together, binding her to a union that transcended lost time, Natalie reached the last step. Her open hand outstretched.

Acknowledgments

Thank you to everyone at Atmosphere Press. I'm particularly grateful to Kyle McCord for your openness to answering all of my (many) questions, and Alex Kale for shepherding me through the publication process. Ronaldo Alves and Felipe Betim designed the most exquisite cover to house my story. I'm also extremely thankful to Megan Turner for her keen editorial insights and immense kindness. In addition, I'm grateful to BE Allatt and Chris Beale for proofreading *Summer Triangle* with such care. Thank you as well to Cameron Finch for the invaluable marketing advice. I couldn't be more appreciative of my publication journey with the Atmosphere team.

While I'm so proud and humbled to have completed my debut novel, it's heartbreaking to have published it two summers too late to show my grandmother. Patricia Peck, who was never without a book in hand, would have been delighted with any novel set on the Delmarva peninsula. And maybe, most especially, with mine. Gee – thank you for the beach house and for all the love you poured into it. None of us has ever left it behind.

Thank you to my parents, Robyn and Sam Spragins. Thank you for filling every house with teetering stacks of books and for giving us the space to lose ourselves inside them. Thank you for demonstrating that, while building a life, I should also be building a library. Most of all, thank you for inspiring us to realize our dreams.

Through some stroke of magic, I find myself forever latched to the best pair of siblings in the world. To Tim and Katherine Spragins, thank you for your unconditional love and support. I hope I manage to show up for you with as much enthusiasm as you do for me. I love you lots. Thank you as well to Stacie for being such a wellspring of encouragement, advice, and kindness.

Thank you to my favorite foursome: Owen, Luke, Reid, and Colin. I am forever grateful to be your mom. I'm so inspired by the way you make time for your passions, your creativity, and the people you love. I'm thrilled that one of you recently said, "Maybe I'll write a book someday, too." I love that you know you can. I can't wait to see the places your hearts take you.

Thank you, Jordan, for everything. You've been my greatest champion through this process. I'm not sure that this book would have happened without your unwavering encouragement. You and our family bring me more peace than you'll ever know. I did my best to give each of these characters a happily-ever-after as true and real as the one I call home.

About Atmosphere Press

Founded in 2015, Atmosphere Press was built on the principles of Honesty, Transparency, Professionalism, Kindness, and Making Your Book Awesome. As an ethical and author-friendly hybrid press, we stay true to that founding mission today.

If you're a reader, enter our giveaway for a free book here:

SCAN TO ENTER
BOOK GIVEAWAY

If you're a writer, submit your manuscript for consideration here:

SCAN TO SUBMIT
MANUSCRIPT

And always feel free to visit Atmosphere Press and our authors online at atmospherepress.com. See you there soon!

About the Author

Photo Credit: Colin Webster

ELIZABETH WEBSTER is a freelance writer and a licensed attorney. Her work has been featured in *Critical Read*, *The Startup*, and *An Injustice!*, among others. She lives in Pennsylvania with her husband and four sons. *Summer Triangle* is her debut novel.

For more information about *Summer Triangle* and Elizabeth's upcoming work, please visit her website at www.elizabethwebster.com.